Industrial Management Series

Managers in the Making

Managers in the Making

Careers, Development and Control in Corporate Britain and Japan

John Storey, Paul Edwards and Keith Sisson

SAGE Publications
London • Thousand Oaks • New Delhi

First published 1997

 SAGE Publications Ltd
6 Bonhill Street
London EC2A 4PU

SAGE Publications Inc.
2455 Teller Road
Thousand Oaks, California 91320

SAGE Publications India Pvt Ltd
32, M-Block Market
Greater Kailash – I
New Delhi 110 048

British Library Cataloguing in Publication data

A catalogue record for this book is available from the British Library

ISBN 0 7619 5541 0
ISBN 0 7619 5542 9 (pbk)

Library of Congress catalog record available

Typeset by Mayhew Typesetting, Rhayader, Powys
Printed in Great Britain by Biddles Ltd, Guildford, Surrey

Contents

Biographical Notes

John Storey is Professor of Human Resource Management at The Open University Business School. He is editor of the *Human Resource Management Journal*.

Paul Edwards is Professor of Industrial Relations and Deputy Director of the Industrial Relations Research Unit, Warwick Business School, University of Warwick. He is the editor of *Work, Employment and Society*.

Keith Sisson is Professor of Industrial Relations, Warwick Business School, and Director of the Industrial Relations Research Unit, University of Warwick. He is the editor of *Personnel Management* (first edition 1989, second edition 1994).

Preface

The analysis presented in this book results from a detailed and systematic comparative study of British and Japanese managers and the way they are 'made'. The study was funded by the Economic and Social Research Council (ESRC) over a three-year period. The fieldwork was conducted in Britain and Japan.

The study was one of the lead projects in the ESRC's Competitiveness of British Industry Initiative. This initiative was launched in order to encourage a coordinated assault on the underlying sources of competitive success in economic enterprises. A team of scholars (at that time all located at the University of Warwick) was awarded a grant to undertake comparative case studies in Britain and Japan. The aim was to understand, describe, and evaluate the dynamics at play in the way managers were made in these countries.

The Warwick team included Keith Sisson, Paul Edwards, John Storey, Ian Gow and Lola Okazaki-Ward. The last two subsequently relocated to the University of Stirling. Ian Gow was a member of the group which produced the 'Handy report' published in 1987 under the title *The Making of Managers* (Handy, 1987). His long-standing and in-depth knowledge of Japan gave a sound foundation for the study reported here. Lola Okazaki-Ward was born in Japan and had previous experience working for a Japanese company in Europe. Her facility with the Japanese language enabled in-depth interviews to be conducted with all levels of management in Japan. It also allowed other methods of data collection including, for example, the translation of company documentation into English. Both Ian Gow and Lola Okazaki-Ward made invaluable contributions to the success of the ESRC research project.

We also acknowledge the help given by the many managers and other officials in both Britain and Japan. In Britain, managers at Lucas, National Westminster Bank, British Telecom and Tesco were generous with their time and helpful with accounts of their experiences. In Japan, managers at Sumitomo, Mitsui Trust and Banking, NTT and Jusco were genial and cooperative. They submitted themselves to a style of questioning which went well beyond the norm in Western studies of Japan. Our special thanks also go to Dr Miyai, President of the Japan Productivity Centre; to the Japan Management Association; to Professor Koichi Ito of Chiba University; and to Mr Yasuo Tanaka, Managing Director and Main Board Member of Sumitomo Electrical Industries.

With the combined efforts of the five members of the research team, and the generous help of the many practitioners who contributed enthusiastically, it became possible to construct a detailed picture of managers and management development in the two countries.

John Storey
Paul Edwards
Keith Sisson

March 1997

1

Introduction: Managers and their Making

If they signal anything, the mountains of books on the subject of managers and management would seem to suggest that managers and management are deemed rather significant in the struggle for corporate and indeed national success. Guidance about the way in which managers should behave in order to secure this success constitutes the largest proportion of these books. Such books take a prescriptive approach: that is, they educe 'lessons', offer checklists, outline procedures and elaborate models. In the mid 1990s, running parallel with the outpouring of optimistic and upbeat material on 'the learning organization' a more sombre tone was struck. Concern has been expressed about downsizing, managerial redundancy and even the 'end of careers'. Managers have been advised to alter their mental sets fundamentally. Onto this terrain of uncertainty have ridden new prophets. They have advised managers to forget the 'old' psychological contract which traded loyalty for security of employment and to think primarily about adaptability, 'employability' and the negotiation of 'new deals' (in the UK literature see, for example, Handy, 1994; Herriott and Pemberton, 1995). In the United States, Heckscher (1995) echoes much of this sort of message: he diagnoses the end of the corporatist ethic while Quinn (1992) has heralded a new era where managing intellect rather than physical assets is the issue.

It has become almost a commonplace that, given that technology and finance are increasingly internationally mobile and that innovations can be copied rapidly, it is the unique use of human resources which is especially critical to long-term organizational success. This is the central message of the 'resource-based view of the firm' (Grant, 1991; Peteraf, 1993). According to this analysis it is the coordination of the internal competencies of the firm which is fundamental. This suggests a central role for management. Such a premise echoes arguments which have been advanced before. Consider the following quotations from one of the classic books on Japanese management:

> If anything, the extent of Japanese superiority over the US in industrial competitiveness is underestimated. Japan is doing more than a little right. And our hypothesis is that a big part of this 'something' has only a little to do with such techniques as its quality circles and lifetime employment. We will argue that a major reason for the superiority of the Japanese is their management skill.

> Management is the problem and more effective management is pivotal in improving our lot. (Pascale and Athos, 1981: 21, 26)

This being so, the important quest is to clarify how management skill is honed, that is, how managers are made. This study was intended not as an account of formal management development and training systems in isolation but as a *deeper and wider analysis of the totality of processes through which managers are made.*

This inevitably raises the issue of the organizational context in which development activity takes place, and in particular how far national systems shape the process. Unlike many books on management, which seek the essence of some supposed national secret, we wanted to compare actual practice closely. At the same time, we wanted the study to retain sufficient fine-grained detail to permit close examination of practices and subjective meanings at the level of the individual manager. In order to allow access to these different levels of analysis we decided to adopt a two-country comparative study and so allow attention to societal factors without losing sight of the kind of detail which would only be achieved through case study research.

There is a strong line of argument in international comparative research (see Bean, 1994: 10–15) that comparisons should be made between countries which can illustrate analytical issues. That is, the purpose of inquiry is not merely to reveal differences between two or more cases but to understand the reasons for those differences. Our analysis is set within a framework devised by Ronald Dore (1989a; 1989c). This posits a continuum with *organizational orientation* at one end and *market orientation* at the other.[1] Japan is often placed along with Germany at the former pole, while Britain and the United States share features which place them under the market-oriented approach.

We studied Japan and Britain, but not because we expected to find lessons that could be simply 'lifted' from the former and replanted in Britain or any other country. In so far as Japanese management development has been seen as more systematic than that in Britain, we certainly hoped to find a challenging set of comparisons. More important was the fact that in both countries management development is very largely the responsibility of the company. The typical large Japanese firm recruits its managers from the leading universities and then trains them to suit its own needs. There is less of a role for the state than is the case in, say, France or Germany. A further rationale was the *prima facie* similarity between frequently recommended practice in Britain and seemingly actual developmental activity in large Japanese companies: such firms are widely thought to use planned systems which incorporate the formal and informal methods of development identified, for example, by Mumford (1987b) as highly pertinent to Britain and other Western countries. We seek to go a stage further by examining not so much current Japanese management practice (which after all changes and adapts continuously) but its well-springs. This will involve us in a close examination of the production of managerial capability. This in turn might be viewed as a mix of intellectual capital plus the social arrangements for its effective use. Among other things we will be exploring the way managers are recruited, maintained, controlled and developed. This will involve us also in making enquiries about careers, the relative roles of corporate planners and individuals in shaping careers and development, and, crucially, the views held by managers themselves about this range of processes and structures.

Despite the massive Western interest in Japan during the recent past (for example, Abegglen and Stalk, 1985; Clark and Fujimoto, 1991; Dore, 1973; 1989a; 1989b), there is rather less information available to help answer our key questions than might be expected. The reasons for this lie in the approach taken by many of our predecessors to capture the 'essence' of the Japanese way – see, for example, the studies by Ouchi (1981) and Whitehill (1991). First, they characterize the system of Japanese firms as a whole, neglecting variation between sectors. Second, they are often driven by a concern to find out how the Japanese do things 'better' than the West, thereby playing down tensions in the system. Third, while they characterize the system in general terms, describing such things as seniority and consensus decision-making, what is rare is an assessment of *how these things work in practice*, and, in particular, how those managers who are subjected to these techniques actually respond. There are, it is true, numerous attitude surveys comparing Japanese and Western workers. However, these often study workers as a whole, rather than managers in particular, and they, too, tend to characterize 'the Japanese' instead of exploring attitudes in their organizational contexts. What are the actual conditions and attitudes of these managers? How, for example, do they respond to lifetime employment and to the tightly planned career paths that tend to accompany it? Do they see themselves as pawns on a chess-board? In contemporary parlance, what is the nature of the 'psychological contract' in Japan at managerial level and what, if anything, makes it distinctive?

Several studies, notably those by Whittaker (1990) and Sako (1992), have, however, used Japan–Britain comparisons in the more analytical tradition in terms of organization and market orientation. In particular, they conduct case studies of comparable organizations in the two countries. The approach has not, however, been applied to the making of managers. We also develop it in some distinctive ways, explained below, notably by blending information on structures and systems with that on managers' own views. Within the latter, moreover, we combine quantitative survey data with qualitative interviews.

We have mentioned a neglect of variation between sectors. This was largely true also of the important comparative study of managers in Japan and Britain (plus some other countries) published in the report *The Making of Managers* (Handy, 1987). We have built on this work by moving beyond models of entire systems to understand variations between firms. Related to this is the desire to understand how management development actually takes place. This may sound odd, for surely the essence of the Japanese system (annual recruitment from elite universities, lifetime employment, structured career paths, and so on) is well known. But just how the components of the system fit together, and indeed how they can meaningfully be called a 'system', have been subject to remarkably little scrutiny. One of our goals was to analyse in some detail the structures of management development and how they cohere.

Fascination with Japan, it might be argued, has faded somewhat in the 1990s. There is growing recognition that earlier studies focusing on Japanese success were one-sided and simplistic. But the attempt to reach a more balanced view does not of course invalidate the attempt to make a bilateral comparison. Even Berggren (1995: 88), who is among those who rightly qualify the earlier belief in Japanese invincibility, stresses that Japan will still 'maintain a formidable competitive strength in many sectors where it has achieved high world shares'. There are still important lessons to be learned. One of the points underlined by Berggren is sectoral variation, in particular the fact that some sectors in Japan are not internationally competitive whereas others remain as world leaders. We are well placed to consider this issue.

There are two broad views on the future of the Japanese system. The first underlines competitive slow-down, the decay of lifetime employment, and the evidence of dissatisfaction with long hours and the demand for total loyalty. The second acknowledges these challenges but argues that they have yet fundamentally to alter the system. We tend towards the latter. The Japanese economy continues to be very powerful. As we demonstrate from a detailed analysis of the management development system, this system not only had its own strengths stemming from its interconnected nature but also had clear links with competitive outcomes; not surprisingly, firms are reluctant to abandon it. We also demonstrate that the system is able to handle change. For example, we compare a British and a Japanese organization undergoing privatization, and show that the latter was able to maintain more of its pre-existing management development apparatus. In relation to Japan, then, we can place our specific results in the wider context of debates about the future of the system. Our evidence shows, in detail, the strengths of the system and its ability to respond to change, yet we also identify some growing challenges.

This point brings us back to the issue of national structures and sectoral variation. While underlining the latter, we do not wish to imply that the importance of the national context can be reduced to vanishing point. On the contrary, using various statistical techniques, we measure the degree of influence which the national context exercises. It is still relevant to talk of a Japanese system, and a significant contribution of this study is to reveal which aspects of firms' development systems were generic and which were firm-specific. This is an underlying issue in current comparative studies of management and business, and we see our results as having lasting value in addressing it.

A final reason for the relevance of the comparison turns on the British side. We analyse in detail events around 1990. In many ways, subsequent developments have heightened the relevance of our conclusions. The period was distinctive. After the shock of mass unemployment during the early 1980s, there was a widespread feeling that the economy was now leaner but fitter and that painful structural adjustment had succeeded. Firms were in a position to think about investment, including investment in their managers. We analyse the problems that some leading firms were finding, in particular the decay of their older assumptions about predictable careers and their search for new ways of handling uncertainty. Since that time, the uncertainties have intensified with the experience of a new recession in the early 1990s coupled with an even sharper focus on the marketplace. In sectors such as banking, retrenchment and job loss have been commonplace. In short, the period of our study was a particularly favourable one for serious attention to management development, and we found significant tensions which have become even more salient subsequently. (A profile of management development in Britain in 1996 can be found in Thomson et al., 1997.) Putting the point in comparative terms, our study of Britain at the turn of the decade was an opportune time and context to make the comparison with Japan: we were able to see the market-oriented versus the organizational approaches in sharp contrast.

In the final chapter, we draw out explicit lessons about the British case. These lessons stem in part from the Japanese evidence, but also from the internal dynamics of the British situation. In short, the research evidence has strong continued relevance to debates about the nature of management development and its prospects.

Aims of this Book

An elaboration of the core aims of the study can be made by posing them as a list of key questions. In *practical* terms, these questions can be stated thus:

1 What methods and systems of recruitment and selection are used to 'find' managers? Are these broadly similar in the two countries or are there some identifiable, systematic, differences?
2 What kinds of targets or goals are set for managers: for example, how clear and precise are they – and how stretching?
3 How are managers evaluated? Is performance measured against specific targets?
4 How tightly, or loosely, are managers controlled? Do they have extensive discretion or not?
5 What training do managers receive?
6 What forms of 'development' (including, for example, one-on-one mentoring) are experienced and with what results?
7 What are the main forms of reward?

8   How is the management development function organized? What struc-
    tures are in place to prepare people for management positions and what
    mechanisms, if any, exist to facilitate continual development?
9   Arising from all of the above, what lessons can be drawn for improved
    effective practice?

The study, however, goes beyond immediate practical issues; contributions
are also made to important *theoretical debates*. The central questions here
include the relative significance of national cultural, sectoral, and organizational variables. This addresses also the wider questions about the operation of managerial systems, about managerial orientations and attitudes,
and about the extent to which lessons can be drawn from different
organizational models (see also, for example, Barsoux and Lawrence, 1990;
Hickson and Pugh, 1995; Lawrence, 1996; Roomkin, 1989). Japan and
Britain are apposite contrasts here, as exemplars of Dore's 'organizational'
and 'market' approaches to society. There are also parallels between Britain
and America in the way these two countries share many attributes and
ideas about management (see Lawrence, 1996). These kinds of comparisons
also of course have applications in many other countries. We seek to make
a distinctive contribution by moving beyond national-level stereotypes to
explore variations between sectors. Work on small firms, for example,
shows striking similarities between such firms across national boundaries
(see Kondo, 1990; Ram, 1994). As Whittaker (1990) found in a comparative study of 18 firms in Britain and Japan, the two smallest Japanese
firms were very similar in their organizational features to the British firms.
We limited ourselves to large firms but carried out comparisons between
four very different sectors. We are thus able to examine how far there are
differences in managerial careers between all sectors in the two countries,
how far a difference is in fact a sectoral effect and perhaps not one of
difference between countries, and whether in some circumstances 'country'
and 'sector' effects interact with each other.

Research Methods

In order to tackle the above set of practical and theoretical issues this book
draws upon a rich source of new data. The data were derived from three
years of study in British and Japanese companies (1988–91). Follow-up
contact was made in 1995. This was a period of significant change.
Corporate restructuring was occurring on a large scale. Managerial layoffs
were increasing and companies were thinking deeply about the underlying
models of management development which they had been using. We picked
up the beginnings of the uncertainties about careers and training which
have continued to the present day. The central part of the study was
intensive fieldwork in matched-pair companies. Eight companies were
studied in four sectors as shown in Table 1.1.

Table 1.1   *The matched case companies*

Sector	Britain	Japan
Engineering	Lucas	Sumitomo Electric
Banks	NatWest Bank	Mitsui
Retail	Tesco	Jusco
Communications	British Telecom	NTT

The matched pairings were made in order to allow a certain degree of like-for-like comparisons. But why these particular sectors and these particular cases? We selected these sectors in order to allow representation of a range of contextual circumstances. Thus, first of all we wanted a setting which would reflect a fiercely competitive international industry. To meet this criterion we chose electrical engineering where products and components are sourced and sold extensively across national boundaries. This was also a sector in which the Japanese had been especially successful in capturing world markets. Second, one outstanding feature of Japan is the so-called lifetime employment system and the reliance on internal labour markets. And yet some British employing organizations had also long been associated with similar practices. For example, until relatively recently employment in banking had displayed many of the same features: indeed it used to be virtually impossible to move between employers in this sector during a career. Hence in order to make comparisons while controlling for the effects of *de facto* lifetime employment we included two banks in the study. Labour market conditions were, conversely, quite different in the retailing of food through supermarket chains. Here, the managerial labour market was characterized by frequent changes of employer. We chose the sector for this reason and also partly because retailing is one of the few industries in which British firms could claim to be world leaders in terms of efficiency and profitability. Hence, this sector was selected to allow comparisons which could not be written off to 'British industrial weakness' or 'Japanese success'. Finally, we chose two former public sector ('privatized') utilities to take account of the effect of tradition in public sector employment which, in the British case, included the legacy of an internal labour market every bit as distinctive as that in the bank, and to see what difference privatization was making in the two countries.

In all cases we studied Japanese firms 'on their own ground' – that is, in Japan itself – and no attempt was made to include European 'transplants' where management development processes operate under different rules of engagement.

As for the invitation to specific firms within the chosen sectors, two main approaches were possible. We could, on the one hand, have focused on 'typical' (that is, 'average') cases. But this would have been a problem – not only in terms of determining typicality but more importantly in that any differences might be explained away in terms of the overall relative success of the Japanese economy. Instead, we wanted as strong a comparison as possible with Japan and so took a second route. We started therefore by identifying the British companies which we wished to study and then sought out Japanese counterparts. Thus the British firms, while perhaps not strictly 'industry leaders', were well regarded and had been at least relatively active in terms of management development. It could be safely assumed that any comparable 'failings' across the British sample taken as a totality and the Japanese sample taken as a totality would, if anything, be magnified if the full population of firms in the UK were to be considered.

The firms in each pair were closely comparable. The two electrical engineering firms produced a range of very similar products and used similar technologies. The retailers were multiple chain stores with an emphasis on superstore grocery retailing. The two utilities sold the same service and had both enjoyed a long-standing monopoly until they were both privatized in the 1980s. The banking pair were, however, different in that the Japanese bank was much smaller than NatWest. It did, however, have a branch network and, in so far as banking activities are relatively uniform, the comparison seemed valid enough. It should also be noted that, in most instances, the case we selected as our preferred first 'site' of study accepted our invitation for them to be included. But the negotiations to fill this last slot were sufficiently prolonged in the Japanese bank of first choice as to cause us to take up the opportunity to study the one reported here.

In each case a three-stage approach was adopted. First, the senior 'architects' of management development systems were interviewed about the design, objectives and links with company strategy of the company management development systems and about the wider methods for the management of the management stock.

Second, samples of managers at various levels who were the 'objects' of the development systems were asked to complete detailed self-completion questionnaires. In total, 239 managers completed questionnaires. The results were treated to a range of statistical tests as reported in subsequent chapters and as described in Appendix A. The questionnaire itself is reproduced in Appendix B.

Third, these managers were then subjected to in-depth interviews which took the data gathering beyond what could be captured using questionnaire techniques and instruments. By this stage, the interviewees had already completed their written questionnaires and so, with completed instrument to hand, we were able to spend quality time exploring each individual's expectations and experiences. In addition, we also seized the opportunity to check through the completed written questionnaire and to follow through on any unusual responses. The interview scripts were shared among all members of the research team for further analysis. In total, the resulting study, reported here in full for the first time, constitutes an unusually systematic and in-depth analysis of a set of managerial issues which have been the subject of speculation over a long period.

The Scope of the Study and its Relationship with Previous Literature

Given the objective of undertaking an analysis of the totality of processes through which managers are made, this inevitably raises the issue of the organizational context in which development activity takes place. Are Japanese methods part of a wider means of generating employee commitment, and how far are such means peculiar to Japan, or is Japan one exemplar of an approach which could, in principle, be applied in other countries? We need to review some of the debate on these questions in order to establish the significance of our own research. Do our findings about forms of training or methods of motivation in Britain and Japan illustrate wider contrasts in the two countries' approaches to personnel management or do they qualify (or even question) accepted contrasts? And do the observed differences tell us that Japanese systems can be emulated in Britain or that there are structural constraints making such transfer difficult?

The clearest point of departure for our study is, as we have noted, the work of Ronald Dore. In his early contrast between manufacturing firms in Britain and Japan (Dore, 1973), he argued against the then popular view that Japanese practice was deeply rooted in the country's traditions. Instead, many aspects of it could be attributed to a 'late start' in industrialization, which meant that firms were not constrained by a legacy of history. Japanese firms had been able to 'jump ahead' of their Western counterparts, and there was a tendency for firms to converge on a new form of organization. Dore has subsequently elaborated the idea of evolution. For example, Dore (1989a) identifies two ideal types. The first, the 'organization oriented', approximates the Japanese case; while the second, a 'market orientation', is more like the British case. The key elements of the contrast are summarized in Table 1.2.

Dore argues that the organization-oriented firm is superior to the market-oriented type in several respects. In particular, its emphasis on market share and long-term growth encourages it to focus on developing new products and processes and on adding value through its own resources. The parallel with the more recent 'resource-based' view of the firm, with its emphasis on the internal resources of the organization, particularly the human ones, as the key to competitive advantage, is evident (Barney, 1991; Hall, 1992; Mahoney and Pandian, 1992). There are echoes too in the literature on 'knowledge management' (Nonaka and Takeuchi, 1995). Organization-oriented firms are expected to capture business from the more short-termist, less 'strategic' market-oriented types.

There is one key point to underline about this issue. Much of the recent work on 'Japanization', particularly its more popular and populist variants (see especially Womack et al., 1990), argues that there is one best way to produce, called 'lean production', and that it can be adopted anywhere in the world. Critics (Lyddon, 1996; Williams et al., 1992) have rightly pointed out that the contrast with mass production is overdrawn and at

Table 1.2 *The organization and market ideal types*

Market-oriented	Organization-oriented
Characteristics	
High labour turnover	Low turnover; permanent workers differentiated from temporary workers
Wages based on going market rate	No going rate, stress on age, seniority and merit
Entry to firm at all levels	Fixed lower entry points
Motivation based on individual interest, with allocation of responsibility to individuals and with strong interpersonal competition	Shared interest in firm's prosperity; responsibility given to groups; rarity of demotion promotes loyalty; interpersonal competition restricted
Bases and facilitating conditions	
Firm as property of share-holders, with a strong market in company acquisitions	Firm as community of people, with no hostile takeovers
Managers relate to workers at arm's length	Managers are senior members of the community, with strong trust relations
Short-term profit the dominant objective	Long-term growth and market share the main goal
Reliance on equity capital, plus a finance-oriented culture	Use of bank capital; financiers focus on growth, not immediate returns; culture is production-oriented

Source: Abbreviated from Dore (1989a: 427–9)

times incoherent, and that the evidence showing superior productive efficiency is in fact sketchy. A further central point is that the success of firms such as Toyota rested on capturing a large share of a growing market at least as much as on internal organization. By the same token, the collapse of the British-owned car industry was due to market-led failure. There has been an over-emphasis on management and internal organization. Dore was much more circumspect, stressing that the organization-oriented approach rests on broad societal conditions and cannot be freely generalized.

For the present study of management, two themes stand out. First, if we can identify distinctively Japanese methods these may well rest on social structures outside the firm, thus raising issues about the transferability of 'best practice'. Second, different social structures may support different approaches. This was indeed the conclusion of the celebrated international study *Making Managers* (Handy et al., 1988): Britain should not ape any particular overseas model but should develop approaches reflecting its own circumstances.

This analysis has several implications for the present study. First, it leads to expectations concerning the ways in which managers in the two countries are motivated and rewarded and their perceptions of their firms. Second, it points to possible variations within countries. Third, it answers the question about learning from Japan by identifying an organizational model which firms elsewhere, it is argued, could and indeed should emulate. We deal with each of these points in turn.

Managerial Systems and Attitudes

The accumulated body of previous studies of British and Japanese management systems has bequeathed to us a cluster of general expectations and stereotypes. For example, in general, one would expect in Britain more individualized payment together with more precisely defined targets, in comparison with the overall situation in Japan. As Campbell et al. (1990: 28) put it, the Japanese system is based on high demands which are deliberately left ambiguous. When seeking broad comparisons about managerial perceptions, previous research suggests that Japanese managers would be more likely to say that they are motivated by the respect of their peers, while in Britain, meeting individual targets would tend to be emphasized.

Some other expectations call for more extensive comment. Consider, for example, Abegglen and Stalk's (1985: 182) simple conclusion. Japan has, they argue, 'a work force that is more dedicated' than those of the West and a management system that 'has gone further than others to minimize conflicting interests'. Leaving aside the obvious point that such a characterization applies only to the large firms, employing only 30 per cent of the workforce, which use lifetime employment and seniority-based pay systems, we need to consider the accuracy of such a one-dimensional appreciation. In stressing dedication and harmony, it states that commitment to the firm will be high and it strongly implies a high level of job satisfaction. Yet commitment can mean two very different things: a moral identification with the firm, reflected, for example, in pride in working for a particular firm, and a more structural condition wherein workers are bound to a firm through economic and other ties without their necessarily experiencing any sense of normative integration within it. What research evidence is there on these issues?

The most comprehensive study is that of Lincoln and Kalleberg (1990). Comparing Japan with the United States, they distributed questionnaires to more than 8,000 employees who worked for 98 manufacturing firms. Along with many other researchers, they reject the idea that job satisfaction is high in Japan. Indeed, it tends to be lower than that in the West. As for commitment, they focus on moral identification, which they sub-divide into two elements: commitment to the idea of work, and loyalty to the particular employing organization. Again, the raw data show, surprisingly, lower levels in Japan on both aspects. On the former, 44 per cent of Japanese agreed that 'I have other activities more important than my work', whereas only 30 per cent of the Americans said this. On the latter, while 54 per cent of Japanese said they were 'willing to work harder than I have to in order to help this company succeed', a much larger proportion of Americans (74 per cent) made this claim. The authors argue, however, that the satisfaction data may mask the true levels of commitment. They show that the two measures are correlated, in both countries. In a key passage, they say that

> the strong association between commitment and satisfaction stems primarily from the latter's influence on the former rather than vice versa: good feelings about one's job and employer breed company identification and loyalty; while commitment, by increasing expectations, may produce a net reduction in satisfaction. If these assumptions are correct, and if differences in job satisfaction between the US and Japan are exaggerated due to cultural and other differences, then the inflated satisfaction gap may be masking real differences in organizational commitment. (1990: 76–7)

They show on the basis of these assumptions that the 'corrected' level of commitment is indeed higher in Japan.

The authors offer no detailed justification for their assumption. One could at least argue that commitment and satisfaction reinforce each other. Nor is it clear why commitment should heighten expectations; indeed, the point of commitment is surely that workers temper expectations because of their deeper loyalties. There are, moreover, quite strong arguments that the evident behavioural commitment of Japanese workers – their long work hours, low absence levels and so on – stems not from psychic commitment but from the structure of the enterprise. Briggs (1991), for example, lists an array of employment practices and argues that these lead workers to be obedient. For example, lifetime employment means that one's interests are dependent on the company's success, while job rotation leads to awareness of the interrelations of the parts of the organization. Kamata's (1983) account of life in a Toyota factory underlines permanent workers' dependence on the company and the insecurity and discipline experienced by temporary workers. According to the Japanese scholar Iwata (1982: 72), lifetime employment and seniority wages can be a cheap means for firms to increase motivation. The earnings differentials involved are very small, with the symbolic status of extra reward being more important than the cash sum; and the fact that sharp gaps do not appear until well into managers' careers keeps many more people involved in the race, whereas in the West winners and losers are identified much earlier. We might add that promotion systems also foster obedience. Success is measured primarily by the speed of one's promotion as compared with that of one's peer group. Though, as Dore says, individualistic striving on the Western model is discouraged, individuals also know that they need to perform better than others if they are to be promoted. As Whitehill (1991: 200) notes, managerial competition in the West revolves around individual striving for immediate success; there is competition in Japan but it comes through teamwork, and recognition in terms of high office may come only at the end of the career.

There is thus substantial evidence that Japanese workers' behavioural commitment is influenced by the structural conditions of their work. Some of Lincoln and Kalleberg's (1990) findings are consistent with this view. For example, one of their important results is that there was less of a difference in attitudes between managers and other employees in Japan than there was between these two groups in America. That is, attributes such as loyalty to the company tended to be more widespread in Japan. The result is important because it suggests that Japanese firms have gone further than Western ones in building up the involvement of lower-level employees. Since this reflects such familiar practices as single status for blue- and white-collar workers, it arguably reflects the material ways in which non-managerial Japanese workers are treated.

Lincoln and Kalleberg also produce several findings which contradict the commonly held image of Japan. One of these concerns the image of the firm as a family, as against the instrumental calculus allegedly characteristic of the West. In fact, the authors found, the idea of the firm as a family was endorsed more strongly in America.

The relevance of each of these sets of findings for our own study is that the connections between organizational structure, managers' attitudes and behavioural commitment have not been firmly established. Certain elements – the prevalence of seniority-based pay and highly structured career planning in Japan – have been more clearly described and, in some respects, our study confirms the earlier work on these points. But managers' views of these things have not been explored in detail. Much of the questioning has been about such general issues as the 'image' of the firm and overall 'job satisfaction'. It seems to have been rarer to ask managers about the more immediate and concrete aspects of their work such as systems of career planning, training, pay and performance appraisal. In looking at such matters, we complement other studies. Finally, we can explore the connections within the data. Existing research has not conclusively demonstrated the reasons for the behavioural commitment of Japanese workers, and our study adds a distinct view on this debate. Throughout the study, we compare our detailed findings on such issues as career planning with the body of existing knowledge.

Inter-Organizational Variation

What of the second issue, the variation within countries? Dore (1987) stresses that an organization orientation is not peculiar to Japan. He cites such obvious cases as the British civil service, in which *de facto* lifetime employment was exchanged for loyalty. We selected our particular sample of case study firms in order to permit some test of this view. As noted in the discussion above about the choice of firms, banks are a good example of a sector where lifetime employment used to be the expectation. How far does an organizational model apply in Britain? It is also true, of course, that an organizational orientation is far from universal in Japan. Dore argues that it is becoming more common, as employment practices that used to be confined to the very large firms filter down to smaller enterprises. We were not in a position to test this theory since we focused on large enterprises in both countries. Nonetheless, the fact that we chose firms from very different sectors allows us to explore how far sectoral influences shape any overall national approach. As noted above, many studies offer a model of 'the Japanese system'. Following the logic of Dore's analysis, which identifies characteristics of organizations which may or may not apply instead of assuming that there is something essentially Japanese or British about a particular combination of factors, we try to examine different ways in which managerial labour markets and employment practices operate.

Organizational Evolution and Learning from Japan

This leads to the third issue, the question of trends. Is there in fact a general move across the industrial world as a whole towards an 'organizational model'? Lincoln and Kalleberg (1990: 247) concur with Dore that there is. They show that, in the USA as well as Japan, their measures of commitment are associated with some key aspects of the organization model such as its system of decision-making. Whitehill (1991: 287), by contrast, argues that features such as lifetime employment are sustained by an array of societal supports and that there is 'no reason to expect [it] to survive in American soil'.

There are certainly grounds for questioning a natural progression towards any one organizational form. Consider the lessons of the past. The large multi-divisional firm based on professional management emerged in the United States towards the end of the last century. An analyst at the time might have been justified in arguing that it was the emergent form. Yet industrial capitalism in the other leading countries, Britain and Germany, developed in significantly different ways (Chandler, 1990), while Japan has added another variant. There is of course similarity, but this does not imply convergence to one model.

Looking at current developments, a move towards one type of firm also seems questionable. There may well be a globalization of the world economy, but different types of organizational form may be appropriate in different conditions. In an influential work, Porter (1985) has argued that firms in certain sectors gain competitive advantage from occupying a home base in one particular country rather than another. Italian firms are influential in ceramics, Germans in cars and so on. Processes of competition in a capitalist economy are likely to produce a variety of types of firm. Those with an organizational orientation may well have certain advantages, but it does not follow that they will squeeze out all others.

Dore's account in fact contains two elements with rather different implications. The first is the model of the organizationally oriented firm, which is seen as the product of Japan's late industrialization and as a culture-free form. The second concerns the conditions for such a model to exist. As Table 1.2 reveals, Dore has identified several of these. Much turns on how influential they are felt to be. A plausible argument can be constructed that they are powerful forces. Thus, it is often argued that Britain is an extreme case of market orientation: the dominance of the finance function, the centrality of the threat of takeover, and the equation of a firm's interests with those of its shareholders are all factors widely seen as promoting a short-term perspective and discouraging a long-term view of the management of human resources (Cosh et al., 1990; Edwards et al., 1992). In such an environment, organizationally oriented firm's might find it hard to survive. This is not to suggest that they could never exist. American firms such as IBM and the Mars Group have deployed aspects of such an approach, as of course have some of the Japanese firms such as Toshiba and Nissan. But certain key elements of the 'Japanese model', notably lifetime employment, have been absent. And the presence of such firms does not deny the general point: under certain conditions, some aspects of an organization orientation are feasible in Britain, but the environment tends to constrain it within special cases.

In the case of the firms that we studied, two of them, NatWest and BT, had strong traditions approximating to the organizational model. They had highly formal career structures, tended to recruit at low levels and to use internal labour markets as the source of senior managers, and offered very high levels of job security. A theme throughout this study is the extent to which this approach was breaking down. In NatWest the driving force was competition in the financial services market, while in BT it was the growth of commercial pressures which culminated in privatization. There were thus pressures moving these firms away from, and not towards, an organizational orientation.

Dore focuses on structural conditions leading towards one or other ideal type. But factors going under the heading of 'culture' should not be forgotten. At one time it was necessary for Dore and others to argue against simple culturist views of Japan which explained the country's large firms in terms of deeply rooted Japanese beliefs in the importance of the group and consensus. But there is also a danger in dismissing historical and social forces. Dore acknowledges this in referring in the sub-title and preface of one of his books to a 'Confucian' perspective (Dore, 1987). This implies that there is a distinct approach to management which cannot be reduced to a set of structural conditions such as reliance on bank capital or a production orientation. Firms and their employees are located in economic and social relationships outside the workplace. Thus part of the Japanese employee's willingness to submit to the lifelong demands of the corporation reflects a fear of loss of status which would arise from loss of position.

The limitations of invoking culture or history to explain troublesome findings are of course evident. There are, however, numerous studies which give history its proper place. Sisson (1987), for example, demonstrated the development of managerial policies on collective bargaining in the major industrialized economies. These reflected the choices made at key junctures. They were influenced but not determined by structural conditions, and they helped to shape later developments. For present purposes, in any event, we do not need to offer a detailed argument about culture. It is simply a matter of suggesting that the rejection of heavily culturist accounts of Japan may have created the impression that everything about its management development systems sprang from the twentieth-century *zaibatsu*. The weight placed on teamwork and the group and the extent to which managers are expected to immerse themselves in their firms and to work long hours can hardly be reduced to the structure of the organization. Norms, understandings, and assumptions help to give structures meaning.

We therefore approached comparison between the UK and Japan in the light of questions about an evolutionary model. This has implications for the sorts of lessons which might be learned from the comparison. The more societally specific Japanese methods are, the more difficult it is for firms elsewhere to copy them directly. Lessons can certainly be drawn, but they are not those of trying to evolve along a pre-set path. As we have already pointed out (Storey, 1990; Storey et al., 1991), a key element of Japanese practice is not this or that technique but the integration of a variety of approaches to such issues as recruitment, career planning, and reward systems. One method in isolation (say, for example, frequent performance appraisal) may not have any effect in a British company. Indeed, it could well be counter-productive if it clashed with other methods or created uncertainty in the minds of managers subjected to it. The main argument of the earlier comparative study, *Making Managers* (Handy et al., 1988), was not that there was a Japanese, or for that matter an American or a German, model which Britain should follow. It was, rather, that Britain needed to develop its own methods to reflect its own circumstances. Lessons could be learnt from abroad: but these were more a matter of understanding how systems were integrated than of copying one particular set of techniques. This is not to say, however, that specific techniques cannot be emulated providing they are adapted to home circumstances and appropriately embedded.

A second element of the comparison concerns the conditions for certain practices to exist. We studied a range of Japanese firms – not to extract the essence of an organizational orientation, but to consider just what sustained Japanese practice in general and how this approach could vary in different circumstances. Looked at from the British point of view, this means examining to what extent an organizational orientation existed and what factors shaped the balance between organizational and market approaches. These two approaches are, as Dore stresses, ideal types, and it is relevant to consider where real firms lie on the various dimensions that have been identified.

Third, by studying the subjects of management development we hoped to obtain a view of practice. Counterpoising practice and formal organizational policy has two elements. On the one hand, it is possible to see how far claims by planners about, say, a new training system are confirmed by practising managers. This approach, of comparing rhetoric and reality, is the conventional justification for in-depth study. It often implies using the reality as an implied critique of the rhetoric. But it is also possible to see whether there are more positive implications of the views of lower-level managers. For example, a common view is that there was during the 1980s a growth of individualism in Britain; the expectation is that managers would have adopted strongly entrepreneurial values and would thus be even less open to organizationally oriented policies than 10 years previously. As it happens, the initial premise would seem to be wrong: there is no evidence of the widespread adoption of individualistic values, even among the higher social classes (Marshall et al., 1988). Our findings also point to a well-established wish among our British managers for a corporate environment in which teamwork is stressed. This parallels Lincoln and Kalleberg's (1990: 129) findings that a 'company orientation' was more marked in America than in Japan. We can thus indicate the extent to which conditions on the ground correspond with current policy.

In short, the purpose of the analysis was not to place our companies within an evolutionary schema. It was to compare approaches, to explore the links between policy and practice, and to examine the conditions promoting one approach rather than another. The lessons may be less simple than those implicit in an evolutionary model, for they call for firms to consider the integration of their operations and how they can question environmental constraints. It would be wrong, both analytically and in terms of policy, to neglect such constraints: it would imply that change could be brought about merely through the will of senior managers. Once constraints are recognized, it becomes clear that simply willing the ends is not enough and that the structure of the external environment also has to be addressed. Such lessons may not be the easiest ones, but they are likely to be the ones most worthy of learning.

Conclusions: Themes from the Eight Companies

If we take our eight companies on a country by country basis, then, not surprisingly, they exemplify some established contrasts between the two countries. These include the importance of internal labour markets and planned career progression in Japan. But beyond such points, each company illustrates more specific themes. Sumitomo stands as an example of the 'typical' large manufacturing firm in Japan, with highly structured management development systems which have undergone relatively little change. Lucas shows how a British firm with a traditionally good reputation for training had found it harder to insulate itself from a turbulent market, which in any event, because of the decline of the British car industry, was more threatening than that faced by Sumitomo. Lucas had begun to respond, and we were able to assess how far continuing market uncertainties and internal reorganizations were undermining management development systems.

The superstores illustrate variations on national stereotypes. Jusco stood out from the standard Japanese model in placing weight on merit and in recruiting from the external labour market. Tesco had consciously distanced itself from the British model of short-termism by seeking market share and high-value-added activities, and in the process making the development of its managers a central theme. There is space for choice within national constraints. The choices made by Tesco reflected the nature of retail markets in the 1980s, notably the demand for superstores and the presence of a customer base supporting high-value-added products: choice is never made entirely freely. But the firm was able to take the opportunities available and to sustain a considerable push in the management development field. The two telecommunications companies illustrate the pressures on firms with less favourable market circumstances. At NTT privatization pressures were fairly muted, and it was possible to sustain established development activities, though the move to the new processes described above contrasts with the more stable world of Sumitomo. The 'Japanese model' is not unchanging. At BT, by contrast, the forces of change were greater. In addition, we would argue, the internal structure of the company was more open to the winds of change. There was a willingness, indeed an eagerness, to make radical changes to overall organization and to management development systems. The result was a sense of uncertainty which was in some ways more extreme than that at Lucas.

Finally, Mitsui, like Sumitomo, exemplifies relatively stable Japanese systems but with the interest that as a service sector firm it complements the usual focus on manufacturing. NatWest, like BT, is an example of how, under new competitive forces, British firms have been pushed away from an organizational model and towards a market-led one. The difference is that there seemed, as we will see in later chapters, to be more of an acceptance that new approaches were consistent with the business environment, whereas in BT any systematic new approach had yet to emerge. NatWest shows some of the positive as well as the negative aspects of a market-led approach.

So much for systems. But what of the managers who were subject to them? Did British managers feel dissatisfied about the comparative absence of career planning in their firms, or did they welcome the freedom to carve out their own opportunities, or was it (as we will in fact argue) a balance of the two? Were Japanese managers contented with their lot or did they feel that they were merely pawns on the chessboard? We will show that there were some of the latter concerns and that the Japanese were not particularly satisfied. We thus proceed to blend an account of the systems with analysis of the experiences of those subject to them.

Approach and Plan of the Book

As described above, we have three forms of information upon which to draw: (1) detail on firms' histories and policies and practices in management development and career planning derived from interviews with the 'architects' of the systems; (2) qualitative information derived from interviews with managers who were the 'targets' of these systems; (3) quantitative data from our questionnaire survey. In the following chapters we do not set all these data out in a rigid format; instead we use the most relevant information for the task at hand. For example, in some chapters we provide accounts of developments in individual companies. In others, it is more relevant to make formal contrasts between all eight cases. For the latter style of analysis we have used the technique of loglinear analysis which is explained briefly in Appendix A.

The themes which have been briefly sketched in this introductory chapter are examined in detail in the following chapters. Chapter 2 describes the contexts of work organizations in Britain and Japan. It gives the necessary information about the key socio-economic attributes of the two societies. In Chapter 3 the eight case companies are profiled and the main contours of their management development systems are described in broad terms. In Chapter 4 the first substantial findings from the study are presented. They are used in order to compare entry into, and through, managerial labour markets and careers. Career planning, career mobility and the subjects' experience of these are closely examined. Chapter 5 describes and assesses the differences in education and training experienced by these managers. Chapter 6 assesses other developmental processes such as mentoring and personal development plans; it also examines the management development functions found in the case organizations. Chapter 7 is devoted to the analysis of managerial target setting, evaluation methods and rewards. The concluding chapter pulls the various strands together and makes an overall evaluation.

Note

1 The corporate/paternalist pole of Heckscher's (1995) first type can be seen as reflecting the former, and his 'new' professional type can be located at the other. Likewise, we also see the models sketched by Handy and Herriott as locatable on Dore's dimension.

2
Contexts: Britain and Japan

The purpose of this chapter is to set the national scene and establish the context before presenting and interpreting our new data. Accordingly, in this chapter we profile the economic, educational and training systems of the two societies. The varying roles of government are compared and recent trends in the two economies and in their training and development provision are assessed. In essence, therefore, in this chapter we seek a succinct review of the current state of knowledge about Japanese industry and Japanese management. The comparative UK situation particularly with regard to the changing management development 'system' is outlined; and this is brought all together in a summary way in order to provide a launch-pad for the analysis of our new research data in subsequent chapters.

This chapter is structured into five sections. In the first a bilateral comparison is made of the two economies; the second section examines the claimed sources of Japan's economic success; the third section reviews in broad terms the nature of Japanese management; and the final two sections consider the educational, training and management development systems in the two countries. Readers in the United States and elsewhere are likely to find it as useful to study the briefings on the British scene as those on the Japanese. British readers who are already *au fait* with the national educational and training developments in the UK may wish to focus mainly on the Japanese sections of this chapter.

The Two Economies Compared

Japan, with a population of 124 million people, is more than twice as populated as the UK (57.9 million). Its total land area is just one and a half times that of the UK and it contains relatively few natural resources. While Japan contains over 1,000 islands, 95 per cent of its area is made up of the four main ones of Honshu, Hokkaido, Kyushu and Shikoku. The fascination (perhaps even obsession) with Japan over the last couple of decades has of course largely resulted from its phenomenal economic growth in the post-war period. The country moved rapidly from devastation and isolation to assume a position as an economic world leader. From 1950 to 1973 (the first oil supply crisis) the country recorded an average growth rate of 10 per cent per annum. The total gross domestic product (GDP) of Japan by 1992 was $3,346 billion – over three times that of the UK ($1,008 billion)

Table 2.1   *Japanese trade balance, 1980–7 ($ bn)*

	1980	1981	1982	1983	1984	1985	1986	1987
Exports	129.8	152.0	138.8	146.9	170.1	175.6	209.1	229.2
Imports	140.5	143.3	131.9	126.4	136.5	129.5	126.4	149.5
Surplus	−10.7	8.7	6.9	20.5	33.6	46.1	82.7	79.7

Source: Bank of Japan, *Comparative Economic and Financial Statistics*, Tokyo, 1987, 1988

(OECD, 1995). The GDP per capita in 1991 was $27,005 for Japan compared with $17,492 for the UK (OECD, 1995). The average annual rise in GDP 1987–91 was 4.8 per cent for Japan and 2 per cent for the UK. In the light of such exceptional performance it was understandable that Japan became regarded as a model economy and was held up as an object lesson in modern management.

Japan not only came to compete with the superpowers but even earned the title *Japan as Number One* (Vogel, 1979). The decade that ensued upon Ezra Vogel's famous book seemed to confirm his judgement. In the 1980s, Japanese industry captured world-leading market position in a progressive number of sectors: steel, shipbuilding, consumer electronics, automobiles, machine tools, semiconductors, copiers and laser printers. In illustrating their now famous treatise about 'strategy as stretch' and the patient building and exploitation of 'core competencies', Hamel and Prahalad heavily cite Japanese companies such as Honda, Canon, Sony and Hitachi as prime examples of upstarts who surpassed mighty Western rivals despite 'far fewer visible resources' (1994: 127).

Japan recovered from the 'second oil shock' of 1980 to build a large surplus in the trade balance by 1983 of $20.5 billion. This surplus continued to increase year on year until 1987 (see Table 2.1).

The Japanese economy has demonstrated remarkable resilience. Despite a rising yen (between 1985 and 1990 the currency appreciated 100 per cent against the American dollar) the trade surplus continued to increase. By 1990 there was still a $80 billion trading surplus with the rest of the world.

Using other measures also, the Japanese economy compares favourably. The unemployment rate in the early 1990s has fluctuated around 2 to 3 per cent while the UK rate has been around 9 to 10 per cent (*The Economist*, 1 October 1994: 162). General living standards are also comparable. Productivity increases have been higher in Japan. For example, over 1975–85 (using 1975 = 100) the indexed increase was 217.3 for Japan and 132.4 for Britain (Itoh, 1990).

Japanese achievements, especially in the 1980s when their comparative success became acutely evident (indeed painfully so, as American and other Western industrial giants went into decline, layoff, plant closure and bankruptcy), resulted in a deluge of books and reports on the Japanese miracle. Western business leaders queued up for study tours of Japan to uncover the secrets of Japanese economic success.

Even in recent years the genre of tracing the roots of that superiority has continued unabated. In a widely respected book, Clark and Fujimoto (1991) analysed product development performance, engineering productivity, lead times and quality conformance in the car industries of Europe, America and Japan. The Japanese auto companies were judged top performers in these industries. Similarly, in the even more famous study by Womack et al. (1990) *The Machine that Changed the World*, the Toyota system (relabelled 'lean production') was held up as not only 'the best' but so superior that it heralded the future of industrial production (in cars and other products) for the rest of the world's producers.

Not surprisingly, given this measure of awe, there has been some backlash. In a work reflecting Vogel's earlier title, Berggren (1995) has analysed *Japan as No. 2* – a title incidentally also used in *Newsweek* (Samuelson, 1993). Berggren traces American resurgence in a number of industries and notes the halt of growth in Japan in the 1990s with an actual decline in GDP of 0.5 per cent in 1993. Japan has certainly struggled with recession in the 1990s. The growth in labour productivity has also ceased and there has been negative growth on this measure between 1990 and 1994 (*Monthly Labour Statistics and Research Bulletin*, September 1993). The American business magazines have picked up the same story: *Business Week* for 13 December 1993 carried the front-cover report 'Japan – How Bad?', while on the same date the *Newsweek* cover story was 'Japan: The System that Crashed'.

Recent economic indicators (as reported in *The Economist*, 1 October 1994: 162) reveal an annual GDP percentage change of 3.8 for the UK and just 0.1 for Japan. Industrial production in the UK rose 4.8 per cent compared with a fall of 0.5 per cent in Japan during 1993. Such figures can, however, fluctuate: industrial production in Japan during the three months to October 1994 showed a rise of 10.7 per cent compared with the previous three months. The year on year GDP figures, however, remained broadly the same with 4.2 per cent for Britain and 0.1 per cent for Japan (*The Economist*, 3 December 1994: 162).

Evidently, Japan is not invincible. Its economy is subject to set-backs just like everybody else's. But, as the data already presented clearly indicate, there has been for four decades a remarkable story of industrial success which more than merits close examination. Recent set-backs serve as a useful reminder to approach such an analysis in a critical rather than an adulatory way. Our dataset, which is presented and evaluated in subsequent chapters, reveals the weaknesses as well as the strengths of the Japanese management system.

Japanese Society and the Sources of Japanese Economic Success

Beyond the most basic of facts, many of the characteristics of Japanese society are problematical and contested. In the following brief summary we have drawn upon an extensive literature and upon the research team's own collective experience. The generally accepted picture goes something along the following lines (we reproduce it here as a working backcloth to the study though each of the elements remains open for reassessment). Attempts to trace the sources of Japanese economic success are often virtually indistinguishable from the general descriptive accounts of Japanese society. Four sets of features are usually seen as key.

First, there are distinctive cultural features. Japanese culture is imbued with a strong work ethic. Indicative of this is the statistic that Japanese managers usually only take about 60 per cent of their paid leave entitlement. The extent of late night working well beyond contracted hours points in the same direction. Conformity is another cultural feature: dress codes are sober and closely adhered to, behaviour is uniform and constrained. There is a strong sense of 'duty' and an anxiety to avoid shame. Ruth Benedict (1946) noted the importance of feelings of 'obligation'. These cultural attributes are closely related to the emphasis on 'groupism' and the suppressed degree of individualism. Certain Confucian values are seen to permeate Japanese society: fidelity to family; loyalty to superiors; paternalism with a demanding edge; the importance of education and self-development.

Second, despite a long and rich history the characteristic features of Japanese management are judged by expert Japan watchers to be of a 'distinctively post Second World War vintage' (Whitehill, 1991: 5). There are, of course, aspects of modern culture which reflect historical patterns. For example, from feudal times the country was singular in its one-race, one-language character, and the strong sense of national identity has deep roots. Even today registered aliens only amount to some 1 per cent of the population. Class divisions are rigid and there is a strong sense of 'place' in society (Yoshino, 1968).

Third, there has been a close working relationship between government and industry. The Ministry of Trade (MITI) which was established in 1949 has been particularly noted for its active interventions on behalf of Japanese industry. Through MITI the government has operated an effective strategic industrial policy. The national drive to catch up with Western industrial economies has earned it the title of 'Japan Inc.'. The Japanese economy benefited greatly from the General Agreement on Tariffs and Trade (GATT). Japan adopted a national policy to be a leading trading nation. This sense of purpose has been supported by two other factors – one cultural and the other structural. The cultural phenomenon concerns the commitment to learning from others. The structural feature concerns the role of the *zaibatsu*. In the pre-war period these were powerful family-owned combines which linked a wide range of economic activity and interests. Famous examples included Mitsui and Mitsubishi. The *zaibatsu* were important in various ways – not least because they were economic modernizers. The Mitsui Group maintained connections between some 2,000 companies. These were separate but cooperating enterprises. The *zaibatsu* had no legal standing as such. While the *zaibatsu* post-war have been formally disbanded there are new groupings known as *keiretsu* based around large companies such as Honda and Sony. Each group has some 40 or 50 firms in loose association (Whitehill, 1991: 96). In addition there are hierarchies of affiliated companies associated with the big corporations. These can number 200–300 companies. The complex networks of subsidiaries and contractors can sometimes constitute virtual pyramids of related companies with linkages traceable in terms of personnel and even financial control (Sasaki, 1990). The financing of business is also therefore different in Japan compared with Britain. The system of corporate ownership and control with corporations acting as principal shareholders and maintaining a long-term interest in the business has been termed 'alliance capitalism' (Gerlach, 1992).

Fourth, among the attempted explanations for Japanese economic success the 'late developer' thesis has been especially influential. This suggests that the rate of growth has been swift because the country has been able to avoid the mistakes of the industrializing pioneers and been able to borrow the more successful practices. As it moves from pursuer to pioneer, it has been suggested, the rate of progress will inevitably decrease.

Despite all these positive features Japan is of course not without its problems. The position of women in society is far from equal. Despite the Equal Opportunity Law of 1988 the proportion of managerial and senior employees who are female is very small. In addition there are many workers both male and female who are in much more precarious positions than that normally described under the lifetime employment system. 'Part-time' workers often work long hours and lack social insurance benefits. Temporary and contract workers (*rinjiko*) experience low wages and insecurity.

Even among the core, male, workforce all is not entirely well. Many work very hard and for long hours: overwork, stress and the ill-effects which ensue from these are significant problems. Questions are asked about the motivation of younger workers and their preparedness to tolerate conditions similar to those experienced by their parents. There is also an ageing workforce – and this is occurring at a faster rate than in Britain. The Japanese Ministry of Health and Welfare estimate that by 2020, 25.5 per cent of the total Japanese workforce will be aged 65 or over compared with 18.2 per cent in the UK (Atoh, 1995).

Housing is inferior to general Western standards. In 1985, 32 per cent of housing units were still without flushing toilets. Houses are mainly small and cramped. The cities are highly congested. Nor has the political scene been quite so stable as it is usually portrayed. There has been a series of financial scandals (most notably the Recruit Company scandal of 1989) which have impacted badly upon the Liberal Democratic Party.

But despite the undoubted problems, the extent of Japan's economic success when compared with all other nations remains a truly remarkable phenomenon.

There have been, no doubt, multiple sources of that success. The one we want to examine in some detail in this book is the managerial factor. This will include a range of features: how managers are 'found' and 'made'; how they are managed; and how the managers themselves react to their experiences. But before introducing each of these we need to describe, in broad terms, the nature of Japanese management and the general pattern of training and development for managers in the two countries.

Japanese Management

For more than a decade business analysts, academic researchers and other commentators from many countries have entertained a profound interest in teasing out the key elements of the Japanese 'model' of management (Clark, 1979; Oliver and Wilkinson, 1992; Ouchi, 1981; Whitehill, 1991; Yoshino, 1968). There have emerged differing schools of thought including, for example, those analyses which focus on the 'hard' production system features of Japanese methods (Schonberger, 1982; 1986; Womack et al., 1990) and those which focus on the 'softer' cultural elements (Abegglen and Stalk, 1985; Ouchi, 1981; Wickens, 1987). Drawing upon these and other sources the general Western depiction of 'the Japanese management model' would typically include:

1 lifetime employment
2 internal labour markets
3 seniority-based compensation and promotion
4 'groupism', consensus decision-making and the use of quality circles
5 just-in-time production
6 enterprise unions.

Other features include relatively compressed wage differentials; the effective use made of suggestion schemes; and the learning which takes place not only about a technical field but about the employing organization as a whole. Such a composite listing clearly throws together a complex mix of manufacturing, systems, personnel and economic practices. It does, however, raise interesting questions such as which of the elements are more 'central' and the extent to which these features are mutually interdependent. As a package, these elements do seem to augur well for long-term success. They equally seem favourable from the point of view of human resource development.

In the main, the literature and commentary upon the Japanese management system adopts a positive, even laudatory tone. Critical voices have, however, occasionally been interjected. The conventional depiction neglects the vast small-firm sector in Japan and the pattern of subcontracting. The discrimination against women is ignored. Work intensification and rigorous managerial control are in fact key features (Fucini and Fucini, 1990;

Garrahan and Stewart, 1992; Kenney and Florida, 1988; Turnbull, 1986).
The work experience in Japan is stressful and possibly unsustainable
(Watanabe, 1988). Thus, rather than a model to be emulated, it is possibly
one to be avoided.

In this book we do not attempt to adjudicate on these wide-ranging
debates. Our aim is much more modest. The scope of our enquiry is
restricted to the leading large and economically successful corporations.
Our target group is composed entirely of managers. What we do offer is a
dispassionate and critical evaluation of this crucial population: their
responses to their own work situations, the demands placed upon them and
their own evaluations of management work in Japan. The underlying
rationale for this choice of focus is that the main features of the Japanese
production system have already been extensively studied. The idea that
Japanese *management* has played a crucial part in whatever economic
success has been achieved is also well established. In these circumstances, it
seems logical to focus attention upon the way in which this management
stock is built and upon the methods used to maintain, control, motivate
and enhance that stock. This particular focus is also especially appropriate
for comparative study given the amount of resources devoted to the
problem of 'management development' in Britain in recent times.

Management Training and Development in Japan

Education and Training

When reviewing managerial training and development it is necessary
to consider the educational base upon which the 'trainees' are building. It
is already known, for example, that the majority of managers in the
large Japanese enterprises are university graduates (Gow, 1988: 23).
Nowadays employees with only a senior high school diploma rarely progress
beyond the lower management tiers. The educational system in Japan is
generally judged to be thorough and effective (Department of Education
and Science, 1991; Felstead, 1994; Horsley and Buckley, 1990; Masatoshi,
1994; Stephens, 1991). Compulsory state education starts at age 6. Pupils
progress through six years of elementary school, three years of junior high or
middle school until 15, and then three years of high school. All post-15
education is privately funded. At each stage the demands are high and
competition is fierce. Approximately 95 per cent of pupils stay at school
until at least 18. Then approximately 36 per cent proceed to a four-year
university or two-year college course.

In general terms, the contrasts between Britain and Japan are marked. It
would seem that the Japanese education system has many crucial attributes
which the British system is often seen to lack: teachers enjoy high status,
the pupils are highly motivated, and parents are highly 'supportive'. They
are willing to spend money on extra private tuition for their children in
evening and weekend crammer schools. This translates in practice into

attendance at crammer schools (*juku*) for as many as six days a week, followed by as much as two hours of homework – resulting in a working day for some children which may not finish until midnight or later. Approximately 50 per cent of junior high school pupils attend these extra classes. Such a cultural practice is not entirely restricted to Japan: there are similar examples today in other Asian countries including Singapore and Hong Kong. The basic school year in the UK is 200 days; in Japan it is 240 days. Schools open for half a day on Saturdays.

Japanese children have followed a 'national curriculum' for a much longer time than the British and this includes a formal list of approved textbooks. There is a strong emphasis upon basic skills. In all, schooling is normally judged to be thorough and to achieve among the highest standards of all advanced industrial countries. The private sector is, however, growing; nearly 30 per cent of senior high school students now attend private school. The erstwhile equality of opportunity is decreasing.

Japan has 460 universities (if two-year colleges are included), of which 331 are private (Gow, 1988: 24). The public universities, although charging lower fees, are often ranked higher in terms of prestige. The business elite has traditionally been drawn from a select number of top-ranked universities. After the fierce competition for entry into the universities, the experience within the college years is seen as far less demanding. Fees are mainly privately funded.

In Japan's attempt to catch up with the West in the Meiji period (1867– 1912), education was always seen as a vital component. The model was that of nineteenth-century France: a central, state-determined curriculum. By the end of the Meiji period in 1912 there was virtually 100 per cent literacy (Horsley and Buckley, 1990). The Americans subsequently reformed the education system during the occupation years. Locally elected education boards were introduced, for example. But there has been some reversal. Even as early as 1956 the government moved back to the previous arrangement of centrally appointed boards.

An American Department of Education report in 1987 credited the educational system with many of the achievements of Japanese society, observing:

> it has been demonstrably successful in providing modern Japan with a powerfully competitive economy, a broadly literate population, a stable democratic government, a civilization in which there is relatively little crime or violence, and a functional society wherein the basic technological infrastructure is sound and reliable. (cited in Horsley and Buckley, 1990: 216)

The key features of Japanese policy on education are stated in the Japanese Constitution: 'All people shall have the right to receive an equal education corresponding to their ability. People shall be obligated to have the boys and girls under their protection receive ordinary education as provided by law. Compulsory education shall be free' (Article 25). The specifics are further set out in the 1947 Fundamental Laws of Education: equal opportunity, nine years minimum compulsory education, coeducation, and no religious education in schools.

Central control of education covers school hours, the number of hours devoted to each subject, class sizes, pupil–teacher ratios, teacher salaries, teacher training and the provision of textbooks. Selection is mainly reserved for entry into the upper secondary schools (the 15–18 age group). All upper secondary/high schools have selective entry exams and the resulting sorting and sifting tends to finely grade the general ability level of the total school population at this age. The hierarchy is much clearer than in Britain.

Throughout the school years the emphasis is on rote learning. The central driver is acquisition of knowledge. Pupils are tested on their ability to memorize facts and concepts. Very little regard is given to discussion or questioning. Competition for entry to the top universities is fierce. A national university test was introduced in 1990 and in addition the better universities administer their own tests. The universities also draw upon school reports and interviews. The pecking order is well known and established.

In addition to the above structure of schools and universities there are vocational educational and training colleges. These cater for technical and professional education – mainly in engineering, business and medical care. Miscellaneous schools offer courses in cooking, book-keeping, typing and computer skills. The vocational education and training (VET) system is the responsibility of the Ministry of Labour. The Ministry encourages industry to establish human resource development plans and administer VET grants. It also engages in vocational education courses in publicly maintained training institutes. Correspondence courses and evening classes offer alternative paths to a certificate of upper secondary education for young workers who want to continue with some secondary-level studies while they work. Most vocational training, however, is provided in industry. The links between the 'lifetime employment' system and in-company education and training are strong (Shimada, 1980):

1   There is a preference for recruiting at career entry level.
2   Recruitment decisions are long term and systematic.
3   Long-term training and development are seen as crucial.
4   Externally accredited educational certificates become less important.
5   Occupational identities are weak, organizational identities are strong.
6   The personnel function is regarded as important.

Training is therefore very important in Japanese firms. As Table 2.2 shows, 69 per cent of all undertakings provided their workforce with off-the-job education and training in 1991. The proportion was even higher in the larger firms: 96 per cent of enterprises with more than 1,000 employees provided this type of training, as did 95 per cent of those with between 500 and 999 employees.

In addition, large numbers of workers are engaged in self-development activities. A Ministry of Labour survey published in 1992 found almost two-thirds of all workers engaged in some form of self-development during

Table 2.2 *Off-the-job education and training in Japan by industry and by size of undertaking, 1991 (% of undertakings)*

	Provided training	Did not provide training	Data not available
All undertakings	69.0	27.2	3.8
By industry, all undertakings			
Manufacturing:	67.3	30.9	1.8
garment and textile	42.7	54.1	3.1
chemicals, oil related	71.6	24.9	3.5
steel and non-ferrous metals	70.6	28.8	0.7
machinery	75.5	23.9	0.6
others	62.8	30.9	6.3
Construction	65.9	30.1	4.0
Transport and communication	67.8	26.5	5.7
Wholesale, retail, catering	72.2	25.7	2.1
Finance, insurance, real estate	87.1	10.7	2.1
Services	65.3	27.8	6.8
By size of undertaking, all industries			
Employing:			
over 1,000	96.2	1.7	2.1
500–999	95.0	3.7	1.3
300–499	88.0	9.0	3.1
100–299	80.5	15.4	4.2
30–99	63.2	33.0	3.8

Source: Japanese Ministry of Labour Report of Survey on Education and Training in the Private Sector, 1992; adapted from Centre for Labour Market Studies, *The Japanese VET System*, 1995, University of Leicester, p. 33.

1991. Managerial staff reported 73 per cent participation rates in self-development (see Table 2.3). In firms with over 1,000 employees, 75 per cent of all employees undertook self-development in 1991. Moreover, 77 per cent of all employers offered some support for these activities by giving time off work, offering financial help and providing in-house seminars (Ministry of Labour, 1992). Supplementary to all of this is a high level of provision for on-the-job training (OJT). Firms themselves report that on-the-job training is considered more important than off-the-job training (off-JT) (Ishikawa, 1992: 23).

The significance and reliability of figures on the expenditure allocated to training by firms is notoriously problematical. However, as an indicator it is worth noting that the Ministry of Labour (1992) survey showed that firms with 5,000 employees or more were spending on average Y31,620 (£190) per employee per annum.

Overall, the VET system in Japan is seen as noteworthy in that it accords education and training a very high profile in government circles and in society at large. It is possible that weaknesses stem from a concentration on narrow, firm-specific, skills.

Table 2.3   *Working people undertaking self-development[1] in Japan by sex, occupational category, age and length of service, 1991 (%)*

	Undertook self-development	Did not undertake self-development	Data not available
All respondents	63.4	34.5	2.1
By sex			
Male	68.4	29.6	1.9
Female	47.9	50.3	1.9
By occupational category[2]			
A	53.5	44.5	2.0
B	75.7	22.6	1.7
C	57.6	40.8	1.6
D	62.0	35.4	2.7
E	73.0	24.5	2.5
By age			
Under 25	51.7	46.8	1.4
25–34	66.0	32.6	1.4
35–39	65.2	32.6	2.2
40–44	63.6	33.3	3.1
45–54	67.8	30.4	1.8
Over 55	64.5	30.8	4.7
By length of service			
Below 1 year	59.2	39.8	1.0
1–3 years	64.7	34.0	1.3
3–10 years	64.0	33.8	2.2
Over 10 years	63.4	34.2	2.4

[1] 'Self-development' means voluntary activities of the workers intended to develop or improve occupational capabilities and includes attendance at in-house or external courses/seminars, enrolling in correspondence courses, self-study by TV or radio etc.

[2] Symbols A to E represent the following occupational categories: A, craftsmen and production process workers, construction workers, and transportation and communication workers; B, professional and technical workers; C, clerical workers; D, sales, marketing and services workers; E, managerial staff.

Source: Japanese Ministry of Labour Report of Survey on Education and Training in the Private Sector, 1992; adapted from Centre for Labour Market Studies, *The Japanese VET System*, 1995, University of Leicester, p. 35.

Development

Management development in Japan is a process largely conducted within companies, upon graduates, and sustained over a considerable number of years (Notzli, 1982; Warner, 1992). There is still very little activity in the Master of Business Administration (MBA) market and even the degree of external management training is small in comparison with the UK. Some courses and overseas visits are, however, organized by such bodies as the Japan Productivity Centre and the Japan Management Association (see Whitehill, 1991: 168).

The large corporations invest a great deal in the careful and systematic selection of the best graduates. The top companies concentrate their efforts upon the brightest at the elite universities such as Tokyo, Kyoto and Keio (Gow, 1988). Particularly in the technical and engineering faculties the companies maintain close links with the professors who in turn assist in pre-selection of potential recruits. Once recruited, graduates undergo intensive induction training. This includes a far stronger emphasis upon the transmission of company values, mission and culture than in the UK. There are some mid-career recruits from the open market but these are the exceptions. This practice tends to be restricted to certain technical specifications such as software engineering.

Management development in Japan therefore is reported to occur largely through on-the-job training, planned job placements and rotation, mentoring, correspondence courses and in-company tests (Gow, 1988; Notzli, 1982). Where international opportunities exist, overseas postings of usually between three and five years are also used as developmental opportunities.

While these basic features have been noted in the literature there are whole areas where little, if anything at all, is known about the actual operation of these elements. What is the nature and content of the in-company training which is provided? How, in reality, does mentoring operate? Similarly, how is on-the-job training actually managed? How is career planning done and how do the frequent job moves fit in? Not least, how do real-life Japanese managers at all levels respond to each of the above? These are the kinds of gaps in knowledge which the rest of this book will seek to fill in. But first we need to take a summary view of what is known about the general state of play in management development in Britain.

Management Development in Britain

Activity in the field of 'management development' has been particularly heightened in the past few years. Numerous initiatives have been launched at every level of the British personnel system: the idea of the 'learning organization' has been thrust to the fore; the dichotomy between 'manager' and 'leader' has been extensively explored; various models of 'informal learning' have been subjected to close analysis. But many questions have remained. What are the skills, competencies, capabilities or realms of expertise required of managers? Are there ways to achieve these which can be regarded as more effective than other ways? What are the principal current techniques in management development and what evidence is there of effective use?

Conceptualizations about what management development *is* are obviously closely intertwined with what it is deemed to be *for*. As many senior managers can be increasingly heard to say, it is not an end in itself. There is an interesting tension in the provision of developmental opportunities. On the one hand economic utility is frequently demanded of it: it must be shown to 'meet the needs of the business', declare managers from within and without the function. To this end there has been an increasing interest in attempts to evaluate the outcome of 'investments' in management development activity. Yet on the other hand one finds much talk of the inherent value of developmental opportunities and even open declarations of the willingness to take its beneficial outcomes on trust.

Apart from the question of measurable impact there is yet another equally fundamental issue which runs throughout the theory and practice of management development in Britain. This issue turns on the question of whether there is a known body of knowledge and set of generic skills which management professionals must have, much in the manner, say, of a qualified accountant, lawyer, doctor or skilled tradesman. If extensive and possibly expensive steps are to be taken to 'develop' managers, what is the shape of the accomplished end state to which we are aspiring? The whole controversial 'competencies' debate hinges on this issue. Much of the defence of the idea of codifying and itemizing generic managerial competencies at each main level of management is based on the assumption that certain demonstrated areas of expertise must be attained and recorded if progress is to be made manifestly observable. There are many laudable aspects to this endeavour and in the face of much criticism it is worth noting the merits and value of it. But the inherent problems associated with a fixed list of competencies in the sphere of *management work* is the extent to which the needed role behaviours are subject to such tremendous *variation*. The source of variability may lie in the divergent business strategies (Schuler and Jackson, 1987) and it may lie in the periodic change in priorities concerning what is required of managers and workers as paradigms of 'good practice' change over time (Storey, 1992). For example, for a number of years in the banking and building society industries, reliability, attention to detail and sound leading capabilities were the priority behaviours which were rewarded.

Hirsch and Bevan (1988), in a study for the Institute for Manpower Studies (IMS) pointed to the problems which organizations had in being able to express what they are looking for in managers. What do organizations want their managers to be able to do? What skills do they expect their managers to have? Drawing upon over 100 documents (recruitment and appraisal documents, for example) from 40 companies, and following up with interviews in a selection of these companies, Hirsch and Bevan found that the 'skill lists' (or competencies) were broadly similar. Skills in communication, leadership, judgement, initiative and organizing were listed by most companies. These have all the hallmarks of most typical generic competency lists.

It has also become increasingly common to treat management development simply as a *device* to engineer organizational change – in particular, 'culture change' (Marsh, 1986). Thus Lippitt (1982), for example, talks of management development as 'the key to organizational renewal'. This link between culture change and management development has been particularly noticeable in the finance sector. Banks, building societies and insurance companies have all been subjected to broadly similar treatment. Smith (1987) suggests that building society managers are traditionally unlikely to be innovators or risk-takers. Yet under the new competitive conditions these attributes are now necessary for organizational survival. The key to accomplishing this transformation is seen to be in management development interventions. Similar attempts to use management development as a tool to engineer wide-ranging culture change are reported from Allied Dunbar in insurance (Skemp, 1987) and from other sectors such as railways (Thackway, 1987), health care (Annandale, 1986) and telecommunications (Smith et al., 1986).

A related theme is the objective of using management development as *a tool* in pursuit of quality, cost reduction and 'profitability through excellence' (Alexander, 1987; Nagler, 1987; Wagel, 1987). Companies increasingly declare that their training activities are to be seen as explicitly linked with establishing 'company values' such as 'existing for the customer'. Following the famed British Airways example, chief executives are now routinely drawn into training programmes to symbolically signal 'top management commitment' to the message being conveyed.

The use of management training and development not only to upgrade skills but also to *structure attitudes* is now firmly established. Management development may also be used as a means to forge a common identity following a takeover or merger. Fulmer (1986) describes how it was used by Bendix Corporation to reduce resistance to a merger and to build a 'positive, blended corporate culture'.

If, then, these are among the wide-ranging and ambitious objectives of 'management development', how has the phenomenon itself been defined in the British context?

A much quoted definition conceives of it as 'an attempt to improve managerial effectiveness through a planned and deliberate learning process' (cited by Mumford, 1987a: 29). But interestingly Mumford (1989) now avers that, despite an erstwhile attachment to this definition, his recent empirical research and consulting activity lead him to conclude that it is defective. His main objection now is that it over-emphasizes the importance of deliberate planning in the process of management learning. Formal definitions typically place considerable emphasis upon planning and conscious intent as elemental features of the phenomenon. For example, Ashton et al. have defined management development as 'a conscious and systematic decision–action process to control the development of managerial resources in the organization for the achievement of organizational goals and strategies' (1975: 5).

The fact that these sorts of definitions are now out of favour serves to highlight the fashions and trends within the field of management development. As Pedler et al. (1991) remind us, managerial training and development have evolved through a number of recognizable phases. Immediately following the Second World War the perceived urgency of upgrading skills in order to meet productivity targets led to an emphasis upon systematic training. The limitations of this planned, formalistic approach, they suggest, led to the emergence of organizational development (OD) as an antidote to bureaucracy. Another 'reaction' was the coming into favour of self-development methods and action learning.

These latter approaches have in turn been subjected to criticism. They are now sometimes perceived as all very well for 'personal growth' but as less functional for moving forward the organizational needs. This same point can be found embedded in the popular and useful distinction between 'manager development' and 'management development'. The former can include all manner of educational and training experiences which enhance the individual, while the latter denotes an upgrading which is seen to impact more directly upon the functional capability of the managerial stock as a whole in a manner relevant to business needs.

According to Pedler et al. (1991), the individual-centred approaches such as self-development which were popular in the later 1970s and early 1980s in turn triggered their own reaction. Not only did they come to be perceived as somewhat indulgent, but they were unduly restricted to a fortunate few and were 'sometimes used as an excuse to provide no development opportunities at all' (1991: 15). The current state of play which emerged from this reaction is seen as 'the learning organization'. This is defined as 'an organization that facilitates the learning of all its members and continuously transforms itself' (1991: 1). Pedler at al. go on to claim:

> We have seen, then, that the Learning Company is here, in the time–space era of the early 1990s in the UK. This is because the ideas of organization, training and development and of quality management, have evolved to that point. It is no coincidence that an increasing number of organizations are faced with the true bureaucratic crisis phase in their developments such that the Learning Company is needed. (1991: 16)

But there lies the rub. It may be 'needed', but is it 'here'?

The tension between two fundamental and divergent 'models' of management development can be seen today and throughout its formative history. The first model sees appropriate management development as being provided in a formal top-down and highly structured manner. The emphasis is placed therefore upon formal training programmes. Associated with this approach are corporate training colleges, a corporate training department staffed with qualified trainers, a well-publicized programme of 'core' and optional training courses, and an integrated system of appraisal which identifies both training needs and candidates for the training programmes. The opposite, 'informal' model is decentralized and places the emphasis upon self-development.

It is not possible, in the abstract, to claim that one or the other is more effectual in all circumstances. It can, however, be observed that the profile of management development activity is more pronounced when a more formalized posture is adopted. This prominence should not be confused with impact or efficacy. Burgoyne (1988) identified six main levels or stages in organizational management development. At the first stage there is no systematic development in any sense of the term. Whatever development of talent may happen to occur does so in a totally unplanned way. At the second stage there are isolated fragmentary activities perhaps in sporadic response to identified acute problems. At the third stage a range of development activities do occur and are to a degree coordinated and integrated with each other. At stage four the integrated approach is taken further in that management development is treated strategically and plays its part in implementing corporate policies – for example, through human resource planning to meet the preordained corporate strategy objectives. At stage five the practice becomes even more sophisticated in that management development in turn makes an input into corporate strategy formulation. The final stage is really an embellishment of the fifth, in that management development processes enhance the nature and the quality of corporate policy formulation and they are also used to implement these enhanced policies. Other reports which have also used a staged model of different approaches to management development include Barham (1988).

Popular Techniques and Approaches in the British Context

As noted above there are clear signs that fads and fashion play a vital role in influencing the selection of particular techniques and approaches by organizations. There are innumerable ways in which managers and potential managers might be trained, educated and developed. It would be impossible and not particularly helpful to attempt to describe them all here. What is useful to note, however, is that the variety of methods can be classified as follows:

1 formal, directed, structured methods such as centrally provided training programmes which all managers must progress through in order to rise up the ranks
2 self-development through informal, unstructured learning
3 self-development which is guided and supported by various organizationally provided mechanisms.

Using these three categories it is possible to illustrate the features associated with each by focusing on examples. Thus, the prime example of the first approach is the provision of structured training. The informal, unstructured approach can be illustrated through self-development. The third, 'middle way' of guided self-development can be illustrated by reviewing the method known as 'mentoring'.

Sending managers away on courses represents a relatively simple and yet high-profile way for management development to be seen to be happening. The efficacy and appropriateness of such activity are dependent upon a range of factors. Many a training and development department has degenerated into a state where its function is merely to administer training course programmes. Course details are circulated and the department simply handles the paperwork by matching nominees and volunteers to the available places. At worst there is no real investigation of whether the courses offered are really the ones which are most needed by the business, or of who would benefit most from the courses. The handling of follow-through and impact is likely to be a further area of weakness in such cases. In these circumstances training may be seen as being offered as a *substitute* for effective management development.

The problems often associated with management training are fairly well known. Managers, especially at senior levels, may be reluctant to accept the idea that they have weaknesses which require rectification through training. Managers may maintain they are simply always too busy to spend the time away on a course. Training content and process may themselves come under attack. Courses may be described as irrelevant, too 'academic', insufficiently practical. They may not be appropriately tailored or targeted to the particular audience. If they *are* provided in-house then they may conversely be attacked as too simplistic and too insular. Finally, there is the seemingly perennial problem of transferring learning back into the work situation. Even if end-of-course measures do reveal considerable learning there is no guarantee that this will be carried over into subsequent work behaviour. In the absence of such behaviour change, questions are inevitably raised about the value of this investment of time and money.

These problems highlight certain key points in the management training and development debate. It is as well to acknowledge that in some circumstances these sorts of complaints may be fully justified. Not all training courses are valuable. The training lobby may imply that training *per se* is 'a good thing' but time spent on an inappropriate course can be a simple waste. The problem is that having acknowledged these instances there is divergence of judgement about the appropriate nature and place of training. One position, currently very popular, is that training should be demonstrably related to 'business needs' and that its outcome should be measurable in specific realms of business improvement.

One thing seems clear – the amount of training offered to managers and the priority accorded to it has increased significantly since the Constable and McCormick (1987) and Handy (1987) reports. This was the finding from the largest and most systematic survey of its kind conducted by Thomson et al. (1997) of the Open University on behalf of the Department for Education and Employment and the Institute of Management. Drawing on a statistically representative sample of large and medium sized employers ($n = 501$), plus a sample of small and medium sized enterprises ($n = 403$), this research revealed that the average amount of formal training in the large companies was 5.8 days per manager per annum, and 4.6 days in the small and medium sized companies.

With appropriate planning training can constitute an integral and critical element of a management development programme.

Given the varied nature of managerial work and the wide range of individual strengths and weaknesses which every individual manager brings to it, there are, however, some advocates of the view that formal training approaches are simply inappropriate. Moreover, in reaction to disappointment about the overall impact of formal training courses – and perhaps as a way to avoid their costs – the enthusiasm for 'self-development' grew apace. Dunnell (1987) proselytized a self-development scheme at the insurance company Guardian Royal Exchange under the title 'Management Development on a Tight Budget'. Others have preferred to emphasize the motivational effects of individuals devising their own development plans, taking responsibility for their own development and in effect 'owning' the problem. A popular idea has been the notion of 'learning contracts' (Boak and Stephenson, 1987; Garfield, 1987) whereby company and individual act in partnership on the development question. Burgoyne and Germaine (1984) see 'mutual benefits' in linking self-development and career planning, while Nixon and Allen (1986) emphasize the need to create a conducive organizational climate if self-development is to have any chance of taking off in practice.

The plethora of books and articles on the subject of self-development (Burgoyne et al., 1978; Pedler, 1986; Pedler et al., 1986, 1988) suggests that as a matter of chronological fact Mumford (1979) was incorrect in describing self-development as a 'flavour of the month'.

There are, however, some cautionary notes struck among the general enthusiasm for the concept. Pedler (1986) himself observes that many managers may not be really capable of self-development and that, where packages of measures are provided, those who need them least are most likely to make use of them. There are also attendant dangers of isolation if self-development becomes too heavily relied upon. Consequently, Pedler suggests some form of group support to underpin self-development.

The main mechanisms of self-development might be regarded as comprising initial activity in 'self-awareness', for example, through assessment or development centres; followed by familiarization with career development options, including a realistic view of possible career paths; followed by the preparation of an individual development plan (IDP). An IDP should ideally incorporate: the preferences of the individual, objective assessments of his or her capabilities, and a realistic view of opportunities within the organization. The unfolding of events may involve ongoing lobbying (by subordinate and boss) relating to emerging opportunities and amended action plans to develop skills in preparation for desired options.

This third category of approaches to development includes methods which are designed to combine the merits of informed self-development with more formal organizational support mechanisms. One of the foremost champions of this third way has been Alan Mumford (1989).

It is claimed that research supports the thesis that mentoring, along with achievement motivation, is highly predictive of ultimate success for both fast-track and steady-track managers. There are many articles which argue that 'recycling' the experience of older senior managers must be cost effective (Tack, 1986). Other reports suggest that older managers who are left out of corporate training schemes may be found useful alternative roles as mentors (Skapinker, 1987). But this contradicts Clutterbuck's (1987) advice which is only to use as mentors those managers who are currently highly active and who are at the height of their credibility, standing and influence. These people are more likely to be in their 40s and early 50s rather than in their 60s.

A range of varied approaches to developing managers can be put under the heading of action learning (AL). Their common theme is the view that 'management' is a cluster of practices which can best be upgraded and honed by direct exposure to problem-solving situations. Much of the credit for bringing recognition to the concept of action learning is given to Reg Revans (1971; 1983). He pioneered an approach which engaged managers in 'programmes' wherein they were assigned problem-solving situations, often in organizations other than their own, and for which they were given various types of support. For example, the participating managers would meet regularly with each other in a self-help group and with a facilitator. The analysis of issues was thus problem-directed and closely aligned to felt need.

This 'learning by doing' is clearly adaptable to many situations and it can take many forms. One key mode adopted by Revans himself was to initiate an exchange programme which involved collaboration between a consortium of companies and universities. The participants spent a period of months in their receiving organizations interspersed with university-based periods to discuss and analyse the problems they had encountered and their other experiences. The package was designed to 'constantly challenge each manager to review and reinterpret his previous experience' (Revans, 1983: 163).

Currently, action learning is marketed in a range of forms. It is possible for the in-company trainer to purchase off-the-shelf packages containing guidebook, videos, case notes and learning instruments. Workshops are also offered to familiarize clients with these materials. Another form of AL is that of 'outdoor learning'. The underlying principle here is that managers will benefit speedily by the character-forming experiences which can be engineered by pitting them against the elements in the great outdoors. Through experiential learning opportunities it is postulated that the advantages of such fundamental managerial tools as planning, organizing, effective communication, teamwork, appropriate leadership and so on will be embraced and realized.

Management Charter Initiative and Competencies

Following a string of influential reports in the mid to late 1980s (Constable and McCormick, 1987; Handy, 1987; Mangham and Silver, 1986) an atmosphere of acute concern about the state of management development and the quality of British managers was engendered. The reports revealed the poor state of training, education and development for Britain's managerial workforce. There were approximately 3 million people in managerial jobs with about one-third of these being in senior and middle managerial posts. On average, it was found, these 3 million received only about the equivalent of one day's formal training per year. The majority received no training. Worse still, of the 100,000 persons entering managerial roles each year, the majority had received no formal management education or training.

The Handy report puts this record in international context. Although some organizations were doing a lot for the development of their managers and were doing it well, the main conclusion was that overall the main competitor countries do more and do it better. A key feature of 'doing it better' was that while other countries followed varied and discrepant models they were relatively consistent in their application of these models. Thus, for example, the Americans placed considerable emphasis upon the provision of formal business education in colleges and universities. The output of MBAs for example was some millions per annum. In contrast the Japanese output of MBAs was close to zero, but in place of the business education approach the Japanese had a successful formula of recruiting potential managerial talent in the form of high-quality well-educated graduates from the elite universities followed by a highly systematic approach to in-company development. In contrast, Britain followed neither the 'external' nor the 'internal' model but toyed ineffectively with elements of both. The overall message was that Britain should not import wholesale any particular foreign system but should attend to the provision of some coherent and logical approach which fitted its home circumstances. As it was, the general state of affairs for management development in Britain was summarized as 'too little, too late, for too few'.

Both the Handy and the Constable and McCormick reports made a number of recommendations. The Handy report suggested that leading companies should commit themselves to a 'development charter' of good practice. This would include, for example, a benchmark standard of five days off-the-job training per annum for all managers. Other recommendations related to the provision of education. The most far-reaching of these was Constable and McCormick's call for the establishment of an apprenticeship or 'articles of management' approach in the form of a new national Diploma in Business Administration and an expansion in MBA programmes. They suggested a target output of 10,000 MBA graduates per annum by the late 1990s. The Thomson et al. (1997) report reveals that, in the main, these training and MBA targets have been met.

It was also recommended that access to both of these courses should be made more easily available to working managers through the wider provision of part-time, modular courses. The hallmark of these would be flexibility. Their character would be shaped by a careful melding of academic and work-based activity.

In many respects the Mangham and Silver (1986) report, which was a major survey of the nature and extent of management training, anticipated the findings of Constable and McCormick. Over half of British companies were discovered to be making no training provision for their managers, and even the larger companies with over 1,000 employees figured in this group: one-fifth of these were simply failing to train. Even among those that did train the extent of provision was in the main found to be small. The median expenditure per annum was only £600 per manager; senior managers were apportioned even less. There were other interesting findings emerging from this report. Difficulty was encountered in establishing a statistical link between the incidence of training and company performance. Perhaps one reason for this was that few respondents were able to articulate the competencies which were required of senior, middle and junior managers.

A report by Mumford (1987b) drew on a survey of 140 directors from 45 organizations. The main finding was that although some companies could point to considerable systematic management development (and some could even claim a direct linkage with subsequent performance by the recipients) others had no schemes in place. Mumford also tracked those instances where provision had been made but had been perceived to fail. His assessment was that failure occurred where schemes were insufficiently related to the real concerns of these senior managers, were insufficiently related to other planning processes in the companies and offered too little perceived return to the individual. Most directors interviewed appeared to judge that the formal processes of management development had not been very influential. Most claimed to have learned more effectively from an admix of accidental and unstructured experiences. Mumford goes on to advocate what he terms an 'integrated' approach to management development. Under this model he recommends that the kind of learning by experience which occurs without planning and without clear objectives being set could be much enhanced if it was underpinned by certain rather more formal interventions. For instance, he refers to the need for the setting out of developmental objectives; the 'owning' of development by the individual managers themselves; the making it happen within the context of everyday managerial problem-solving activities; and the need to undertake conscious reviews of what has been learned. In short he recommends a judicious blend of planned learning and learning by doing. This learning from the accomplishment of ongoing tasks lends itself to self-development guided by a coach or mentor.

Clearly, the reports, and the Mumford report in particular, are not without messages for individual organizations. In the main, however, they are largely concerned with questions of national policy. They imply a need for concerted action at the supra-organizational level. This has traditionally been an area in which British provision has been characteristically weak. Following the publication of this unprecedented cluster of reports the challenge to take action was, in part at least, taken up on this occasion. The most immediate response was the establishment of the Management Charter Initiative (MCI). This was launched in 1988 by a consortium comprising the Confederation of British Industry (CBI), the British Institute of Management, and the Foundation for Management Education. The new consortium body was named the National Forum for Management Education and Development.

The MCI is an employer-led initiative which is backed by the Department of Education and Employment and the Department of Trade and Industry. It is the designated lead industry body for the development of standards in management. Its precise relationship with the training and enterprise councils (TECs) remains, however, somewhat unclear and problematical.

The MCI started out with three major items on its agenda: (1) the founding of a mass movement of organizations prepared publicly to commit themselves to a code of good practice to promote the development and application of high standards in modern management (the Management Charter Movement); (2) the construction of a set of management qualifications designed to provide recognizable steps of accreditation for professional managers (the Chartered Manager); (3) the formation of a Chartered Institute of Management with a Royal Charter to advance the 'profession' of management (the Chartered Institute).

This became a highly controversial agenda. There was considerable internecine strife among the membership of the original Council for Management Education and Development, and other interested parties outside the MCI such as the Association for Management Education and Development (AMED) contested the aspiration of codification and standardization. The whole future of the MCI at certain points in the late 1980s looked to be in some doubt. However, the MCI has survived, though progress on the threefold agenda has been variable.

The first thrust, towards the signing up of major employers to form a critical mass of champions of management development, has been the easiest part to achieve. By July 1991 more than 900 employers representing 25 per cent of the UK workforce had joined MCI. These major employers, including companies such as ICI, Marks and Spencer, Sainsbury's, IBM and the major clearing banks, have thus publicly committed themselves to a 10-point code of good practice and paid a subscription fee.

Despite the rapid progress in numerical terms on this first leg of the MCI agenda there is some scepticism about the significance of organizational membership. There is a certain suspicion that some companies have signed up mainly for public relations purposes. A particularly important facet of this is the projection of a training and development image to the graduate market.

The second leg of the MCI agenda has been concerned with the definition of national standards of managerial competence and the establishment of a nationally recognized hierarchy of management qualifications. In 1990 MCI published a comprehensive set of guidelines for the 'certificate level' aimed at all providers of training for first-level managers. Also published were draft guidelines for the 'diploma level' which is deemed appropriate for middle-level managers. MCI endorses management training arrangements which meet its declared quality standards and in other ways conform to its promulgations. These arrangements relate to training and assessment procedures and validation processes. MCI endorses qualifications and training providers. Qualification awarding bodies and professional institutes have to demonstrate that their arrangements meet MCI requirements. MCI will then help these bodies gain endorsement from the Council for National Vocational Qualifications.

At each of these levels key competencies are being investigated, refined and codified. The emphasis is upon demonstrated capability to do rather than the possession of knowledge or the amount of time spent on courses. In other words, the MCI likes to stress its interest in 'outputs' rather than 'inputs'. The desire to construct definitive lists of generic managerial competencies has stirred great controversy. Nearly a dozen consultancy and research contracts were sponsored by the Training Agency and the Council for National Academic Awards to refine these competency lists. The published lists for the certificate in management level can be purchased directly from MCI.

Part of the initiative is the accreditation of prior learning (APL) launched in 1990. APL allows candidates to receive formal recognition and credit for 'competencies' already built up through work experience. This allows for individuals to be accredited for demonstrated capabilities or competencies regardless of how these were gained. MCI has now piloted a methodology for APL. Pilot centres have been established, ranging from colleges and other training providers to MCI networks and employers, to engage in the assessment of individual managers' prior learning. MCI will act as coordinating and overseeing body for this national string of centres and trained assessors. The centres offer a competency accreditation service directly to employers. The concept is that managers must 'reflect on their own experience, analyse the units of competence they have gained against national standards, and develop a portfolio of evidence to demonstrate that competence' (*Employment Gazette*, 1991: 403). APL and competency crediting have won government backing and £11 million has been allocated over three years to TECs in order to implement the process nationally.

The third leg of MCI, the formation of a professional Chartered Institute, was the one which ran into the fiercest opposition. Established professional groups such as the (then) Institute of Personnel Management (IPM) and the Institute of Industrial Managers were particularly alarmed. It would appear that this idea has now been quietly dropped.

A key development for the MCI was the establishment of local networks. There are currently over 50 of these with a target of 90 to cover the whole country. Many local networks are based in chambers of commerce and similar other already established bodies. Local networks are supposed to recruit new members and service their needs. An annual fee is charged to all members. The local networks encourage the adoption of the MCI national standards, endorse providers, engage in assessment and offer a consultancy service.

As already noted, the MCI work on competence has not gone unchallenged. Rather less mechanistic explorations of the possibilities for using competencies in management development can be found in Silver (1990) and Devine (1990). The latter collection includes accounts of what organizations such as ICI, BP and Kodak are doing with the concept. Jacobs (1989) reports on a survey of the different approaches being used in British companies. In 1995 the Institute of Management produced a report assessing progress since the landmark work of Handy and of Constable and McCormick in 1987. Broadly, progress was noted but major challenges were seen to remain. Notable among these were: organizations both large and small needed to be educated to recognize that investment in management development contributes directly to long-term competitiveness; managers must commit to lifelong learning; senior managers needed to give greater commitment, leadership and support on these matters; and a more coherent infrastructure was needed. It was also recognized that the demands placed upon management development were increasing because much more was being expected of managers. For example, they were increasingly required to focus on the long and the short term; on the local and the international; the internal and the external organization; the operational and the strategic and so on (Institute of Management, 1995: 47).

Factors Shaping the Provision and Effectiveness of Management Development

There has been a wide measure of agreement in Britain that the 'climate' or 'culture' of an organization is vital for successful management development activity to take root. The quality of particular courses may wax and wane but if the underlying climate is perceived to encourage development then this will be the more important factor. Such an observation is, however, somewhat nebulous: what in practice constitutes such an environment and how can it be fostered? This was the concern of a case study in the financial services sector. Sun Alliance are reported (Nixon and Allen, 1986) as having sought over a period of years to foster in-company management development using a variety of devices. They began with individual-based approaches and then in 1980 relied increasingly on OD techniques. But the key lesson from this account of creating the right climate appears to be the demonstrated success of the central development unit whose *example* triggered independent initiatives by divisions who set up their own training and development units. In this way Sun Alliance claim to have succeeded in meeting a key target – to have management development genuinely accepted as a line management function.

What are the most favourable conditions which enable effective management learning and development to take place? While the issue is still hotly contested there are some signs of a measure of consensus around a few vital points. In brief, these are:

1   that management development will be most effectual when it is recognized and accepted as a strategic business activity
2   that the design of management training programmes recognizes the nature of managerial work
3   that account is also taken of the varied needs and capacities of individual managers
4   that education, training, selection, career planning, reward systems, and managerial evaluation are recognized as parts of an interlocking 'system'
5   that evaluation is itself a vital part of the system of development.

But there is another dimension to this whole question of the nature of managerial work. As has been signalled already, the normative basis of the 'true' nature of this work is fiercely contested. While it may be the case that most managers behave in practice in a way characterized 'by brevity, variety and fragmentation' (Mintzberg, 1973: 5) this may not necessarily be the most effective way, the one to which high performers should aspire. Lessom (1990), for example, urges a decisive shift away from the conventional management thinking which leads to this pattern of behaviour. It is based, he suggests, on traditional thinkers such as Fayol, Taylor and Drucker, while in contrast his preferred 'developmental' style draws inspiration from sources such as Schumacher and Yamamoto. Likewise Hickman (1990) suggests that 'managers' and 'leaders' are types at opposite ends of a continuum. 'Managerial types' behave in structured, analytical, controlled, deliberate and orderly ways. 'Leader types' lean to the experiential, visionary, flexible, uncontrolled and creative aspects of work. The appropriate behaviour for current work organizational circumstances, Hickman suggests, is a balanced management–leader work behaviour pattern. Developmental activity thus needs to promote this configuration.

A further aspect of managerial work which is of critical relevance is the extent to which so much of it is done not as an isolated individual but as a member of a team. Working often in increasingly complex technological and economic settings, managers cannot be skilled in all relevant areas: they must therefore rely on teamwork. The theory and practice of successful work teams (Belbin, 1981; Margerison and McCann, 1990) hinges around the idea of complementary roles or, as Margerison and McCann would term it, 'balanced teams'. These latter authors and consultants claim to have identified generic functions which all teams have to perform in one way or another if they are to be effective: these include such activities as advising, innovating, promoting, developing, organizing, inspecting, maintaining and linking.

Management Development as Part of a System

Key sustainable messages are transmitted to individual managers in multifarious and complex ways. The messages conveyed on training courses may be speedily discounted if they conflict with the everyday 'messages' received through task assignment, the selection and promotion process, the reward pattern and many other aspects of the totality of ways in which the management stock is itself managed. An IMS study based on 12 leading cases (Hirsch, 1990) suggested that there is a discernible trend away from the more limited approaches to succession planning, such as just planning one step (or job layer) ahead, towards a wider-ranging development of potential across a broad front. This draws a far larger number of people into the scope of developmental activity and marks a departure from the reliance on fast-track methods for a select group of presumed 'high potentials'. If this trend means that managers who have already experienced a considerable degree of job mobility both within and between companies (Alban-Metcalfe and Nicholson, 1984) will need to rely less on informal sources of information about how to do these jobs, then a great many more managers can be expected to record higher levels of satisfaction in future.

Conclusions

In this chapter we have examined four areas: the economic contexts of Japan and Britain; aspects of Japan's social structures, institutions and culture; Japanese management and enterprise; and the state of knowledge about management education, training and development in the two countries. The literature about Japanese management development tends to be very descriptive. Moreover, it is largely confined to reports about the number and types of training courses attended and the content of these courses rather than how managers use their experiences and respond to them. Equally, most of the literature tends to report on provision divorced from context: hence one gains little sense of how the training and education and development fit within the wider frame of managers' organizational experiences. In the next chapter we start to move the analysis forward by bringing organizational context firmly and clearly into consideration.

3

Management Development Systems in British and Japanese Companies

In this chapter we bring the level of analysis down to sector and organizational level. The eight case study companies are profiled and then an overview is given of the main features of the management development system in each case. Broad comparisons and contrasts are drawn and the organizational contexts are established within which the details described in subsequent chapters can be set. At the very least, we aim in this chapter to outline the kinds of basic features about each of the companies which are required in order to understand the subsequent analyses of their training, development, evaluation and reward practices.

We deal first with the engineering companies Sumitomo and Lucas, then the supermarket retailers Jusco and Tesco, then the telecommunications companies NTT and BT, and finally, the banks Mitsui and NatWest. The concluding section underlines the central themes which will inform the rest of the book.

Sumitomo Electric Industries (SEI)

Sumitomo enjoyed a reputation as one of the best managed companies in Japan. As a consequence it was able to recruit from the most prestigious universities. Indeed, of the 33 members of the board, 22 were from two of the reputedly best universities in the whole of Japan: 15 were graduates of Tokyo University and seven from Kyoto University. SEI also enjoyed a good reputation as a training company. In these and other ways, SEI represented one of the leading companies in Japan and it had in place systematic induction of graduates, much job rotation, planned promotion and many of the other attributes of the classic Japanese company: it was an especially interesting case for these reasons.

Sumitomo Electric had six main operating divisions: Electric Conductor, Power and Cable, Systems and Electronics, Power Line, Communication and Radio Frequency, and Hybrid Products. The last is an innovative division which uses materials produced through new physical and engineering processes: it develops and applies new composite materials in such diverse industries as aerospace, automobiles and construction. The Sumitomo sales breakdown was as follows: wires and cables 52 per cent, special wires 6 per cent, power alloys 11 per cent, brakes 6 per cent, machinery and equipment 4 per cent, engineering work 21 per cent. SEI also had 36 major subsidiaries in Japan and 25 overseas. There were 13,230 employees in SEI including some 1,000 who were on secondment to other firms, but this figure excludes all temporary employees. Of the 13,230 employees, 11,000 were male. The average age of the male employees was 37 but it was only 25 for the females. The average monthly pay of the females was less than half that of the male population. As a manufacturing company it appeared that Sumitomo mainly recruited females direct from school and they were retained until they were married. The males were largely recruited into the lifetime employment system until retirement at age 60 (managers relinquished their posts at 55 unless they were board members).

We concentrated our attention on the Osaka site of Sumitomo. This started operations in 1916 making electric cables. It is the oldest manufacturing facility in the Sumitomo Electric Group. It occupies a large site of some 333,000 m^2 and employs 3,400 people. Today the site produces electrical wires and cables, optical communication systems, radio frequency products and data control systems. In addition an R&D group supports the activities of the operating divisions and also develops local area network systems, superconductors and other high-tech products. The Osaka Sumitomo works is the R&D centre for Sumitomo Electric.

The full board met once a month but there were also three additional executive meetings – including a managing directors' meeting (eight of the main MDs), a weekly executive meeting involving 15 executive directors whose main purpose was decision-making, and a monthly executive meeting whose main purpose was 'study' and discussion.

Sumitomo Electric is unionized. It has one enterprise union which recruits everyone up to and including *shusa* grade – that is, the first grade of management. This coverage means that graduates on their way to the top could well be members for their first 15 years with the company.

A notable feature of training and development in Sumitomo was the consistency which it had displayed for more than 20 years. During this time there had been no significant changes to the system. This was in rather stark contrast to most of the British firms. The emphasis in Sumitomo remained, as it always had, upon the line manager developing his/her subordinates and encouraging in them a wide perspective. Paradoxically, given this line management bias, the training and development system could still be described as centre-led and relatively uniform. For example, recruitment and selection are highly centralized; rotation of managers on a regular basis is very extensive and highly regulated. Yet within these formalized 'systems' the essential development was judged to be occurring primarily through on-the-job coaching. The Sumitomo way therefore was a highly orchestrated system where the real action was nonetheless happening at grassroots level on a day-to-day basis.

Given the multitude of divisions (Sumitomo was a good matched pairing for Lucas in this sense) one might have expected significant differences in development practices. But Mr Tanaka, the senior manager responsible for management development in the corporate headquarters, stated that the variations that did exist were due to local discretion arising from site location in different parts of the country rather than a consequence of the divisional arrangements. For example, he made the point that there were some variations in practice between Osaka and Yokohama even though these sites housed about seven different divisions and groups.

The balance between local and central can be seen in the case of promotion. Annual reports are required by the centre. Line managers' evaluations in these reports carry profound weight and yet, at the same time, the general manager in personnel, was seen as playing a very influential part in the final decisions. The key point was that the expectation that line managers would develop their subordinates was so deeply imbued that there was little need for a stream of policies and interventions from the centre. There was no separate training function, nor were external consultants used for management training purposes. The budget for formal training was itself very small. Mr Tanaka estimated it to be as low as 0.01 per cent of turnover and went on to say that even this was mainly spent on eating and drinking at the events which were held.

Rotation between jobs was a vital component of development and was very extensive. Even in key areas such as R&D there is the same amount of movement as in other parts of the business. We interviewed the head of R&D, who led 160 professionals and 200 technicians. He reported that R&D specialists would spend considerable time working 'downstream' in the production areas relevant to their research and, further, in the marketing of the related products. R&D professionals are associated with particular operational divisions likely to use their research – for example in fibre optics. We were told that even among those specialists working purely in basic research, 80 per cent would have worked in an operational division.

Sumitomo operates a formal appraisal scheme. Appraisal occurs twice yearly and is essentially a form-filling exercise using five-point scales without an interview. Section managers send copies to central personnel and to departmental managers. Furthermore, training activity, whether it be OJT or off-JT, is often followed by evaluations in the form of tests, reports and/or interviews. As each stage is successfully accomplished a 'qualification' is awarded. Trainees are evaluated against a known set of objectives and an evaluation committee comprising his/her own *bucho* and senior managers from other departments review the results. Behavioural aspects such as sensitivity and attitude are given as much weight as knowledge required.

If a person is deemed to require extra skills in say, accounting or marketing, the favoured path is to second that person to one of the relevant departments for a period of three months or so. Practitioners in each area were expected to 'play the teacher' from time to time. The company thus largely looks to its own resources. Emphasis is placed on learning on the job and learning through job rotation (this includes the use of overseas postings and assignment to one of the many subsidiaries). In sum, development of capabilities is seen as a long-term process beginning years before the appointment to a management position.

For more detailed illustration, let us briefly follow through one particular cohort of entrants. In April 1990 there were 900 recruits: 230 graduates with four-year degrees (of whom only four were female); 220 'clerical' appointments with two-year college or senior high qualifications; and 450 factory recruits (of whom 300 were male and 150 female). Some 80 per cent of the graduates had science or technology qualifications. The prime requirements at selection were said to be to identify people who were 'not dogmatic, not geniuses, not eccentric, but intelligent and logical'. The entrants had to 'fit in', we were told; consensus-seekers were preferred. The process of selection was primarily recommendation from university professors followed by a series of interviews – usually including one conducted by a recent graduate from the candidate's university. An evening of drinking and socializing is interspersed with the interviews. One possible disadvantage of the process, it was said, was that Sumitomo people were perhaps too similar: cautious and serious.

For the next 13 years these new graduate entrants will progress together through a series of 'bands' each lasting three to four years. There is no 'fast-track' or 'star' system at this stage. However, after the long induction process the system does become very competitive.

To take a specific individual case example of a retrospective kind: Mr Koiwa was departmental head in the Hybrid Products Division at the Osaka plant of Sumitomo Electric. He was in charge of one of the six product groups in this division. He was recruited in 1961 as one of 60 graduates. When we interviewed him he was responsible for 16 managers and saw himself as head of a 'business' – responsible for quality control, production engineering and design. Despite not possessing an engineering degree he was rotated through production control and similar functions before spending time in sales and investment evaluation. He was expected to make a close study of the whole production process and this is what he says he did. Interestingly he also reported, however, that the OJT system does not continue (as far as he could judge) once people reached management grades: that is, it is a system directed largely at the first 13 years or so of the new entrant's time with the company.

In summary, the general picture at Sumitomo was one of selection and 'competency development' being treated very seriously. The essential learning occurred on the job. This was orchestrated by a powerful central personnel function which helped to plan a series of job moves on a wholesale basis. Formal training was given relatively little emphasis. There was a puzzle about how such a company achieved both specialist excellence and a good standard of general management capability. One explanation might be that while those destined for general management were subject to a long series of planned inter-functional job moves, many specialists were able to stay largely within their specialist area – albeit occasionally being posted for temporary periods to functions such as sales and marketing.

Lucas

Lucas offers a fascinating comparison with Sumitomo. It too is a complex multinational company with divisions and business interests which closely map its Japanese counterpart, and it too had long enjoyed a very high reputation as a training company. By the time we came to undertake our research at Lucas it had reached a stage where it was trying to shed its legacy as an old-style, large, centralized engineering company which had grown (and to some extent declined) with the British motor industry. The story we will tell is of a company which enjoyed a reasonably entrenched position in the marketplace during the 1960s and 1970s, followed by retrenchment in the early 1980s and an associated clear-out of many management development practices. By the late 1980s and early 1990s, the corporation was attempting to rebuild a presence for management development.

The company found its core automotive components business (which included lighting, alternators, switches and the like) suffering markedly as the British motor industry went into decline. Great efforts were made, many of them successful, to broaden the market base. The company had also more recently embarked upon an internationalizing strategy – mainly growing by acquisition of overseas companies. It has now become a world leader in car brakes, is European leader in truck brakes, is world number two in car and van diesel engine management systems, and is world leader in flight control systems.

Lucas had a reputation as a training company especially in relation to the training of engineering apprentices. As we will observe in later chapters, this was not well matched by its endeavours in management development. Internal review by the company had produced the analysis that Lucas managers lacked 'flair'. The history of the company was rather similar to that of the civil service. The emphasis had, for some years, been upon company-wide standards and procedures. This had subdued creativity and individuality. The result, it was said, was that the company now had a large number of middle managers who were basically 'bureaucrats'. As a strategic planning manager told us, 'the system was very good at killing any entrepreneurial activity or proclivity'.

At the beginning of the 1980s Lucas employed some 50,000 people in the UK. A period of downsizing then ensued with overall some 25 per cent of jobs cut. It acquired many overseas companies and now has a worldwide employment total of 51,000. At the time of our research, Lucas Industries PLC had been organized into three main divisions: Lucas Automotive (components); Lucas Aerospace; and a general products division known as Lucas Industrial Systems. It had now become decentralized and even fragmented. The organizational structure was a little more complicated. Within Automotive there were three business streams. These in turn had mini divisions: hence, for example, the electronics stream had an Electronic Products Division. Nominally, each of the separate businesses reported through this structure. Parts of the structure, especially in the pot-pourri of Lucas Industrial Systems, were so complicated that even the general managers of some of the individual businesses said they did not fully understand them. For example, one of them was head of a £6 million business which was supposed to be part of a 'strategic business unit' in instrumentation but just how the separate small businesses 'related' was unknown even to these heads of business.

The company's response to the diagnosis of 'lack of flair' was threefold. It recruited a forceful new manufacturing director who revamped the manufacturing systems. In parallel, it embarked upon an extensive review of its managerial stock and this included an element of psychological profiling and testing. But, perhaps most important of all, it adopted a methodology which it called competitiveness achievement planning. The 130 or so 'business units' were required to benchmark themselves against the world's best. They had also to produce detailed forecasts and strategic plans which would map their way ahead. Market exposure was the theme. Plans which appeared to divisional chiefs as non-viable could, and did, lead to disposal of the particular unit in question. The nature of a competitiveness achievement plan (CAP) can vary from a target of turning one business around in six months to, at the other end of the spectrum, a 15-year development plan for another business where profit might be entirely sacrificed for market share for five years or so, moderate profits only expected for year 10, but market dominance achieved by year 15.

This indicates then that, while Lucas is, in a sense, a conglomeration of businesses, it is a very different animal from, say, Hanson Trust. In Lucas, corporate chiefs had a concept of a technological business: all the various sectors were linked together by the core competencies in sensors, actuation and control. Hanson on the other hand acquires diverse unrelated businesses and 'sucks out short-term profit' with little or no regard for long-term growth or technological development. Lucas sees itself as technology driven and very much committed to strategic planning.

Lucas moved through a phase of what corporate-level management development managers now viewed as 'excessive decentralization' in the 1980s, to a new stance where it sought synergy and, where possible, economies of scale in its activities across the various businesses and divisions. The centre had 'clawed back' some functions: training and development were (to a degree) among these. For example, the corporate level likes to view the top 250 managers worldwide as 'a direct group concern'; moreover, 'we take more than a passing interest in the 2,000 forming the next level down'. 'Audits' of management skills have been done among these managers. As a senior manager observed,

> while we have been trying to get away from the image of 'the Lucas manager' based on the old UK stereotype, nonetheless, management development is the single most important aspect of 'Lucasization' across our acquired businesses. (management development manager, Lucas PLC)

There were difficulties in fitting people into a common grading system. Most especially, managers in newly acquired firms (Lucas was an active player in acquisitions) did not understand what the Lucas grades represented, but generally most were broadly slotted into a common pay system. On fringe benefits, the policy was to follow the norm operating in the relevant territory.

One crucial role which the group level saw for itself was to take full advantage of the group-wide opportunities which existed. Thus we were told:

> Only the group level can provide spectacular career horizons for good people. Hence, we are setting up a 'people of potential' scheme to identify and assist those who have the capability to reach the highest executive levels. It is, however, very hard for us to get mobility of managers internationally, Lucas does not have the culture of an oil company where such mobility is required and accepted as the norm. (corporate planning interview)

Despite these corporate visions the reality on the ground was often very different. For example, the Lucas Industrial Systems (LIS) sector is a collection of businesses which are largely separate from the rest of Lucas. Most of the managers were derived from the acquired businesses and very few of them had any experience of other parts of Lucas even within the UK, let alone overseas. Even the senior personnel specialists in LIS were quite willing to admit that 'we have done almost nothing about management development in LIS; we have a very diverse set of businesses and so it is very difficult to install common systems.' The total management stock in LIS was about 100 'real managers', that is the general managers of the various businesses and their management teams of about six or seven managers per business. In the light of the criticism of the corporate 'patricians' from some of these general managers it is interesting to hear the central view:

> A lot of these small-business managers are relatively unsophisticated and we would normally only see them as superintendents in the rest of the company [that is, in Automotive or Aerospace]; some may turn out to be good entrepreneurs but from our point of view it is extremely difficult to judge the level and range of talents which they have. (central personnel interview)

Jusco

Jusco was one of the top three national chain stores in Japan. It was selected for inclusion in our study because it offered an interesting comparison with the British superstores company, Tesco. Like Tesco, the Japanese company was a successful challenger for top position. It was expanding and was innovative – and training and development were said to be central to its growth strategy. As our detailed reports in subsequent chapters will demonstrate, this proposition can be largely substantiated in practice. We were therefore interested to learn from this case some of the detailed processes which were being introduced and the extent to which it was possible to depart from more traditional Japanese conventions such as the so-called slow-burn career development process.

Jusco was widely known as 'the educating company' in the sector. More than that, it was part of a sector which had traditionally been regarded as lagging behind its equivalent in the UK, but as a company it was possibly breaking with some of the conventions of the solid core of large Japanese corporations such as Sumitomo.

The Jusco company is the largest member of a conglomerate known as the Aeon Group which has some 150 member firms spread over the service industry including chain stores, finance and property leasing. The group name was changed from Jusco to Aeon to reflect this growing diversity. The Jusco company had 12,000 employees and 170 stores throughout Japan. Its sales breakdown in terms of value was: foodstuffs 28 per cent, clothing 22 per cent, household 18 per cent, others 32 per cent. There were six regional businesses with their own headquarters and 15 area business divisions. Each regional business operated a profit centre enjoying a certain amount of autonomy though, as in Tesco, head office maintained control over purchasing, distribution and training. Jusco had joint ventures with Laura Ashley (UK), The Body Shop (UK), Talbots (USA) and the André Group (France). It was a fast-expanding company and was opening shops in Taiwan, Korea, Thailand, Singapore, Hong Kong and Malaysia. In terms of turnover it was one of the top 50 Japanese corporations.

The case of Jusco illustrates the central place which education and training can enjoy. The management education and training provision in Jusco is institutionalized, well structured, and extensive to the point of being near comprehensive. Education and training in Jusco are intertwined closely with the system of qualification grading, promotion and reward. Jusco is distinct from the other three Japanese companies in our sample in placing such emphasis upon promotion based on *merit* rather than seniority. Progress through the grades occurs through examinations, interviews and performance evaluation. Appointments to particular jobs are a secondary issue because one first needs to reach a certain level on the qualification system. Attaining a qualification grade by passing an examination is a necessary though not sufficient condition for appointment to a particular post.

Information about training and development provision was widely disseminated throughout Jusco. The company distributes annually to all employees an education and training programme booklet detailing all the courses of all types and levels. The same booklet lists information about correspondence courses and business-related journals and includes application forms for financial assistance towards learning and development. There are also some comments from those who have attended past courses and the positive effects of courses on their subsequent careers. The sheer level of openness contrasts starkly with the very patchy awareness of training provision in many of our British companies where, for example, local personnel managers tended to hoard this kind of information, and where we found even quite senior line managers ignorant about company training provision. As for the future, the capability development department had as one of its main objectives the development of general managers who could move across the group.

Overall, Jusco as a company is interesting to us because it is a dynamic organization using training and development as key levers in the attempt to bring a lagging sector on par with the best of the West. Education in the United States for some of Jusco's employees plus many study tours to leading American stores was very much part of the Jusco drive towards this objective. It was interesting to observe at close quarters how the company then translated this intelligence into changed practices back home in Japan. Part of the learning was, for example, experimentation with psychometrics for selection and promotion, a departure from the age/wage equations of the past, accelerated career pathing and an experimentation with merit pay for managers.

Tesco

The commercial director of Tesco pointed out that during the past 10-year period Tesco had been transformed into a tight centrally controlled organization. All policy decisions are now made by the appropriate functional director in the headquarters. Stores are seen as operating units – and their managers are 'operating managers' whose fundamental duty is to implement those policies and meet budgetary targets. The change came about as a matter of 'necessity', he argued. The multiple-discount formula of the 1960s and 1970s was not adding value and Tesco was falling behind the competition. A strategic switch was made. The company strategy became directed towards an upmarket, value-added, superstore operation and towards this end there was the closure of some 700 small stores and the opening of 200 new superstores. By 1992 Tesco had 412 large supermarkets and its market share accounted for about 10 per cent of all UK food and drink sales. The company had been growing at a rapid pace for over a decade and even into the early 1990s it was opening on average 25 superstores per annum. During 1992 alone it introduced 700 new product lines. To drive and control this kind of activity new, specialist central functions such as purchasing, quality control, productivity, logistics and the like were created. Tesco employed 58,000 people and by 1996 had overtaken Sainsbury to become the largest supermarket group in terms of overall sales.

The commercial director reports to the main board. Beneath him are a range of 'trading directors' each responsible for a different range of products, their purchase, promotion and new product development. For example, the trading director for the meat business has a budget in excess of £350 million and is ultimately responsible for all of its aspects. The system of monitoring is seen as rather more formal, rigid and tight than that prevailing at Sainsbury's, for example. As some of our interviewees had been head-hunted from Sainsbury's, the reliability of the comparison seemed reasonably sound.

The Tesco 'culture' was one of high expectations, high performance and long hours. A typical example was one of the trading directors who proclaimed proudly, 'I start work at 7.30 a.m. each day and do not finish until 6.30 in the evening – and I expect my staff to follow this example.' Another, a head of a specialist function, agreed that the work ethic in Tesco was very powerful but he was less convinced of its appropriateness. 'There are a lot of bastards out there,' he said, and because the younger managers often took their cue from their bosses 'the bastards were leaving a legacy' that would survive for some considerable time.

The business had changed rapidly in recent years. Just five years previously the average lead time for delivery of stock to stores was four to five working days; now it was 24 hours. Or, to take a further example, just two years ago only nine stores absolutely depended upon computers for 'taking in money' at the checkouts; now it was practically every store. The technical sophistication of Tesco's operation was now impressive. The logistical support had grown extensively. For example, just one division of computer services employed nearly 200 people, half of whom worked on a four-shift system 24 hours a day for all 365 days of the year. Many were highly technical systems programmers and experts in telecommunications.

The emerging management training and development system both reflected and enabled such business developments. A well-equipped management training college had been established in the rolling countryside just north of London. Participants from both the stores and the head office functions saw it as a privilege to attend courses rather than an indication of the need for remedial action. In addition, a whole suite of training courses designed to prepare participants for transition into each main level of management had been devised. The company had used consultants to assist with the diagnosis of its training needs. It had made very considerable progress in offering management development support for most of the major specialisms which it had created, most notably in IT, logistics, accounting and other head office functions. This increasing 'professionalism' had, however, created some tension between the sophisticated systems of the centre and the hands-on day-to-day management out in 'the field' – that is, the stores. The marked distinction between the head office functions and the intuitive, experienced-based 'expertise' of the field managers was a source of some concern, and it certainly made it difficult to generalize about 'management development' as if this represented some homogeneous whole.

The culture of Tesco was interesting and powerful. There was a certain degree of aggression and even machismo. Store managers prided themselves on their entrepreneurship and initiative. They were proud to narrate their career progression from 'Saturday boy' to departmental manager, from there to managership of their first small store, and then typically a rapid series of moves, often across considerable geographical distances, as they went through appointments managing larger and larger stores. The contrasts with the head office specialists were stark. Many of these had come into the company as a career progression within a specific function; their loyalty was often primarily to their 'profession' and thus they were seen as likely to move on if their career path was blocked. The bottom line, from our point of view, was that the construction of an overall management development system which could engage equally with this kaleidoscope of interests and expertise was, perhaps self-evidently, extremely challenging.

Nippon Telegraph and Telephone (NTT)

Nippon Telegraph and Telephone is the major telecommunications service provider in Japan and has many similarities with BT. NTT was a former state monopoly and it was privatized in 1985. The sale of shares to the public was however more restricted than in Britain; foreigners, for example, were not allowed to own the shares and by 1990 the share price was showing a loss on the flotation value. At the time of our research there in 1990, it was Japan's biggest company in terms of assets and number of employees (276,650). (Toyota by comparison had only 65,000 employees.) Of this grand total some 28,000 were in managerial grades and receiving a managerial allowance. Those managers based at head office had on average about five subordinates each; managers in the field, on the other hand, were often responsible for hundreds of employees. Employee numbers were reduced at NTT from 300,000 at the time of privatization in the mid 1980s, but still the company was considered to be overmanned and productivity was viewed as low. Plans for job reductions were less sweeping than in BT: the NTT plan was to use natural wastage to reduce the numbers to 230,000 by 1995. Of the eligible employees, 99 per cent are members of a trade union.

NTT has many subsidiaries and managers are frequently seconded to these. The subsidiaries allow the corporation to enter all sorts of diversified markets which the core business is prevented from entering. In the period from privatization up to 1990, the corporation created an impressive 131 subsidiary companies in which it held at least 20 per cent of the shares. Most subsidiaries are in telecommunications-related areas though some extend into real estate, property leasing, sports and leisure, finance, media and warehousing.

As with BT, however, the main business of NTT is still regulated and it faces restrictions on its range of activities not faced by its competitors. These much smaller rivals are especially active in car phones and long-distance markets. Nonetheless, like BT, NTT still controls by far the largest share of the total telephone market. At the time of our research there were plans by the supervising ministry to break up NTT into separate parts covering, for example, long- and short-distance business. Laws require NTT to provide a standard level of service throughout the company no matter what capital expenditure is involved to reach the distant parts. The Ministry of Postal Services can also intervene in board appointments. The president of the company, who saw it through the privatization process, was removed from office in disgrace during an infamous scandal which surfaced in 1988. This episode triggered a fall in the share price.

There were 37 board members. All but two of the board have joined the company since privatization. Many of them have come from various ministries: thus although there was an injection of outsiders, there was rather less of an inflow of people with a private sector or commercial culture than was the case when British Telecom similarly recruited externally. All but one of the board members are graduates and indeed a very large number of them (22, no less) were from the exclusive University of Tokyo. Such a board profile mirrors the typical top civil servant background.

The organizational structure was in some fundamental ways similar to that found at BT. Beyond the headquarters, there were regions, areas and districts. The regional business divisions in NTT however were given considerable autonomy and operated as profit centres. The consultants McKinsey have reinforced the drive towards decentralization.

Prior to privatization, recruitment into the company was through one of two channels: either a central career route for the management cadre with about 400 entrants per year, or a regional intake of about 10,000 new hires per annum. Even among the latter, only about 40 universities were used as sources for the main technological skills which were required. And about half of the clerical intake came from Tokyo University. Entry was through the civil service examination for these clerical trainees. Graduate technologists however bypassed this method of selection and were mainly recruited through the universities – often by way of direct contact by the company with certain professors. Since privatization the number of recruits has been reduced and the emphasis on graduates has intensified. The civil service written examination has been abandoned in favour of interviews and other more systematic assessment techniques. Mid-career recruitment into the company is still very rare, though less so in the subsidiaries: indeed, for many of these it has become the normal way.

There had been four main changes to personnel practices which were worth noting for the purposes of our analysis. First, there was the introduction of a capability qualification grading system. This represented a shift from a rigid hierarchy of grade, post and person to a more flexible arrangement where grading and salary were attached less to a post and more to an individual. The particular post currently occupied becomes relatively secondary. The new system rests therefore on an effective competency assessment system (*shokuno shikaku-seido*). Eighty-five per cent of large firms in Japan have now adopted this system: it is seen as lending itself rather more to the development of the individual. Second, there was *jinji koka* (roughly translatable as 'personnel rating'). This is a very interesting initiative designed to foster innovative behaviour. Instead of points being deducted from a hypothetical mark as under the traditional system (which induced caution and a fear of making mistakes), this new device means that points are only added for trying something new – even if this does not always succeed. Points are only deducted if nothing new is tried. The system operates through a target and evaluation system at six-monthly intervals. Third, behaviour and attitudes as a manager are assessed as very important criteria. Moreover, guiding, educating and developing subordinates are given priority. The manager's own ability to solve problems is placed in the bottom half of the assessment sheet (incidentally, feedback is not given directly at this stage to the employee, but the coding is entered on a personnel database). Fourth, under the new scheme upgrading is possible without taking on a new posting. Grade progression in the early years is uniform and predictable in accordance with age, but by the age of about 40 considerable gaps will have opened up between the fastest and the slowest movers. The fastest risers can expect to make a board appointment by the age of about 53 to 55.

The concept of 'expert' in NTT is now used to replace that of 'specialist'. This change in terminology is in line with the new career and development philosophy of allowing parallel paths equal in status and increasingly interchangeable between management and 'individual contributor'. Career paths are shaped by the changing organization structure: that is, from the traditional pyramid to series of concentric rings with individuals spinning off into one or more of NTT's 130 subsidiaries and 3,000 affiliates. Managers being developed move in and out of the core organization. Subsidiaries range from large ones such as NTT Data Tsushin with capital of Y10 billion and 6,000 employees, to smaller businesses with capital of just Y30 million and 10 employees. One of the senior managers we interviewed in the personnel department was also chairman of three subsidiary companies each with 150 employees. Under the new 'expert' system a potential manager will be exposed to a whole array of operations in the first 10 years – for example, an accountant will travel across head office in marketing and sales, engineering and the international division – though these moves will usually be organized around his expert area of accountancy. These arrangements mean that individuals do not experience a wide range of merely superficial activity. Above *kacho* level there was more of an opportunity for NTT managers to branch out into other business areas than their BT equivalents.

In summary, the overall contextual setting at NTT was of some relatively contained changes arising as a consequence of privatization. These changes were far less extensive than those undertaken at British Telecom, which we discuss below. And, to put the NTT case alongside the other Japanese companies introduced so far, we can suggest that Sumitomo retains a traditional system; Jusco has moved away from this towards a more merit-based system; while NTT itself has attempted to shift somewhat towards a merit-oriented system but has been less radical in its associated changes than Jusco.

British Telecom (BT)

British Telecom is a large, complex organization. It was originally a part of the Post Office and as such it still had a legacy of quasi-civil-service attitudes and practices. BT was 'privatized' in 1984 and since that date had increasingly been asked to confront the possibility and then the actuality of competition from other providers. While the 'threat' of competition has been extensively used to foster a culture change within the organization, and more particularly to engender a shift from a formal bureaucratic to a more commercial orientation, in reality more immediate pressure in the 1980s had been exerted by the regulatory body, OFTEL, and by continuing political exposure.

A key part of the company's response was a close critical scrutiny of its operations, its structure and its staffing. In 1984 there were 241,000 employees; by 1993 this number had been cut to 171,000. At the time of the research towards the turn of the decade, BT had a three-tier organizational structure. At the top was BT PLC, which comprised three 'divisions': UK Communications (UKC), British Telecom International (BTI) and Communication Services Division (CSD). The first of these was by far the largest – accounting for over 90 per cent of the people employed. At the third level UKC was divided into 30 districts, each of which was a very large business in its own right. There was even a fourth level, the 'terri-tories', which were interposed between UKC and the districts. There were three of these and they were essentially 'span breakers' – that is, they were in effect extensions of head office reaching into the major geographical areas.

A key contextual factor to note in the case of BT is the large number of external appointments made at senior levels in the organization following privatization. As a personnel manager observed:

> They didn't know each other and we didn't know much about them. We aim to educate them about BT and this was one reason for starting the Top 300 programme.

The Top 300 programme started with a three-day session on the UKC business strategy and an exposure to 'the City view'. The idea was to communicate the overall strategy and, to a degree, open it up to wider discussion with a view to engaging greater involvement in it. The Top 300 programme proceeded through various phases covering issues such as customer orientation and was delivered in groups of 15 to 20 at a time. At the time of the research the top 300 managers had attended six parts each. The aims of the programme were said to cover: education, involvement in the strategy, and group building and networking. It was a high-prestige programme, well resourced and involving top global speakers from Harvard and similar elite institutions. The two- to three-day meetings were held in good hotels. The aim was to have a board member attend each of the courses – as part of the course but also making special input. A relevant point to note about this key initiative in the management development portfolio however is that it really grew out of the strategy group and was not initially a personnel or developmental venture. In effect 'the strategy group entered the education of management arena rather than vice versa.'

The districts were responsible for service delivery. There were between 6,000 and 7,000 people per district. Strategic direction comes from head office – in this case from BT UKC. The territorial level 'shared best practice' and monitored district performance and operations. A district could oversee as many as 70,000 people and 9,000 managers, as was the case in the London and South East Territory which we studied.

Management personnel were graded into four 'Levels', the lowest being level 1. Management mobility at levels 1–3 is largely a consequence of individuals applying for posts advertised in the company *Gazette*. There is a central 'hand' in mobility at level 4: succession planning only begins at this level. The 'rules' of the game, it was said, favoured the individual below level 4 where the open internal labour market operated. For example, if an individual successfully secured a post in another district he had to be released from his former position within 28 days even if this meant he would be leaving a half-completed project.

Mobility normally meant transfer between districts and then into headquarters. Rarely was it possible to transfer from head office into the field, and yet operational field experience was usually seen as vital for a future general management position. This pattern reflected the situation in Tesco where there was a similar problem of creating a flow from head office into the 'field'.

The overall picture then, at British Telecom, was of a company in the throes of extensive change – both structurally and culturally. Top management had determined that a major break from past customs was necessary.

Mitsui Trust and Banking

The Mitsui Trust and Banking Co. Ltd, headquartered in Tokyo, had 6,500 employees and just under 60 branches. It was much smaller than NatWest, our British case, but it did carry out core bank functions and did illustrate many aspects of this sector in Japan reasonably well. The company had expanded its operations into many areas including securities, pension trusts, dealing in public bonds and so on. It was one of the biggest players in this sector of the finance industry and was particularly strong in international financing and investments. Its largest shareholders include Mitsui Mutual Life, Mitsui Real Estate, Mitsui Banking, Toyota and Mitsubishi Electrical.

Apart from the (four) auditors, all the remaining 30 members of the board of directors are internal appointees who have worked within the bank all of their lives. All of the senior managers are graduates and they come in the main from the top prestigious universities such as Tokyo and

Keio. Two-thirds of the executives were in fact recruited from just three elite universities. The average age of the board is 57 years. They are mainly graduates in economics and law. Most of them attained the status of *bucho* in their mid 40s and achieved their first board appointment at around the age of 52. The 30 board members also hold key executive positions – either heading up important divisions in head office or as managers of one of the main branches.

Finance sector deregulation in Japan led to some pressure from the city banks to squeeze the trust and banking companies out of the banking and securities side of the business. Mitsui responded with cost-cutting measures such as salary reductions for the post-55 age group. Recruitment into the bank, as is the case in most large Japanese institutions, is through the once a year graduate recruitment straight from their educational institutions. Finance sector recruitment has been highly competitive from the bank's perspective and so considerable effort has gone into this activity. New young entrants are hired into one of two streams: management (which is all graduate entry) and clerical which recruits a mix of graduates and two-year college students. Until 1988 the management recruitment stream had been populated entirely by males. In 1989 there were 164 graduate recruits of whom just three were female. The clerical recruits were all female. Our analysis of the 1996 intake revealed that the range of universities from which entrants were hired was much more extensive than in the past: 23 public and 19 private universities were represented. In the main, it seemed that these new recruits were intending to stay for a full career with the bank.

Mitsui changed its in-company education system in 1988. The existing education section of the personnel department was upgraded into a separate capability development office. This signalled to all members of the company that employee and management development was to have a higher priority. Special attention was given to newly hired graduates in the management (*ippanshoku*) stream. This was to be a mix of planned OJT, self-development and off-JT. The first 21 months were designated as a period of traineeship. The government had increased the retirement age from 55 to 60 in the mid 1980s. The seniority-based reward system meant that this measure increased costs for companies; Mitsui responded by reducing the salaries of the over 55s by 40 per cent and by increasingly transferring older employees into subsidiaries and affiliates. Often these moves were into the top positions in smaller subsidiary companies: the older managers therefore had an incentive to maintain and improve their capabilities even at a late age, which they did by self-development and other learning methods. The government supports such moves in its lifelong education initiative. The Vocational Capability Act of 1985 requires companies to devise in-house vocational capability plans and to designate a responsible person. Through such measures the enterprise becomes eligible for grant support. Further, a reform in the Education Ministry established a Lifetime Employment Bureau which displaced a Schools Bureau and gave attention to the needs of the over-45 age group. The bank had one company union with 72 per cent of employees in membership.

Management training and development activities in this organization were broadly typical of most large Japanese companies. There was a concentration on the sound and systematic induction of graduate recruits. This was organized around a 21-month 'internship' which included an initial period of head office socialization into the company followed by an immediate emphasis on OJT in the branches. Formal training provision for established bank managers was on the other hand relatively sparse. The kinds of programmes on offer at NatWest were not to be found here. In their place, however, was a considerable emphasis on self-development and the expectation that use would be made of correspondence courses. 'Voluntary' study meetings were held on Saturday mornings and managerial employees seemed to feel some obligation to attend.

NatWest Bank

This case is a large and complex organization which, at the time of the study, had a worldwide staff total of some 105,000 people. In the UK, it employed 66,000 staff in a total of 5,000 places of work (branches, business centres, regional offices and the like). Restructuring and reorganization have become a constant feature. For example, in the late 1980s a geographically based organizational tier (known as 'areas') was removed entirely. The core UK banking business, which operated under the name of UK Financial Services, accounted for 80 per cent of all staff in this country. It became organized on a primarily two-tier basis with headquarters playing an absolutely central role in policy-making and 22 regional offices acting as the executive arms stretching out into the field in order to check on compliance by branches and the other units. The most important point to note from our perspective is that, despite the promulgated shift towards more local 'accountability' by the 'businesses', an interventionist and powerful central personnel function remained in place. In addition to the core UK retail banking business there were also a number of other divisions which specialized in such matters as corporate banking and international banking. Despite an expectation (and a desire) that these various businesses/divisions would evolve their own cultures and appropriate practices, a degree of managerial mobility between them was envisaged. The bank was thus trying to be innovative but in a relatively cautious way: hence, for the time being at least, corporate chiefs anticipated the continuance of common conditions of service such as the same pension scheme and the same holiday entitlements – but not necessarily the continuance of the same pay system.

What we were witnessing in this case was the beginnings of a marked shift from the long-standing organization centred, lifetime employment model. Branch closures and staff reductions were beginning. These accelerated in the subsequent years. Cultural priorities began to shift markedly.

The traditional values and mores based around sobriety, caution, long and faithful service, and skill in judicious lending were giving way to a new emphasis on marketing, selling, change, growth targets, performance-related pay, 'customer service' and 'quality'. The cartel-like arrangements between the major clearing banks had collapsed and, with deregulation, these banks were facing competition from new players with far lower cost to income ratios; in consequence banks such as NatWest felt compelled to reorient themselves rather rapidly. The new priorities were cost-cutting and the aggressive selling of a range of new 'products'. This was seen to mean that human resource strategies had to focus attention on individual performance. Additionally, the old-style management development system of slow and steady, all-round development of the rounded, generalist 'banker' was giving way to specialization and the opening up of the internal labour market.

Despite the attempted restructuring, there were many remnants of the earlier history of the bank. The bank had grown to its present size through mergers and acquisitions. Some of these parts still had their own personnel and training functions. Trainers and developers numbering some 2,000 were scattered across the various businesses and divisions. The bank was 'unionized' in so far as it had 16,000 of its staff as members of the bank union BIFU, and another 38,000 who were members of the staff association. The hierarchical and career-oriented legacy is indicated by the existence of the tranche of 10,000 'appointed staff', that is assistant managers who supervised other staff but were not formally on the managerial grades.

The mainstream management development occurred however through the domestic banking division. The average annual intake of 16–18 year olds 1987–90 was 9,000. The manpower planning manager would say what proportion of these ought to have four O level equivalents, what proportion A levels and so on. NatWest was 'capturing' in excess of 5 per cent of the nation's total school-leavers with two A levels; it staffed its middle management ranks with this intake. In addition, the division took 250 graduates per annum and these were destined for higher management ranks. Their career development was looked after by a special central development unit (CDU). School-leaver recruits could occasionally succeed in getting transferred to this accelerated programme. Hence, a key part of making managers for this bank was attaining the appropriate mix of recruits smoothly groomed to match the hierarchical structure. The resulting career competition was described to us as 'managed' rather than all-out and this involved an element of managing expectations.

The core division, UK Financial Services, had a total of 4,391 managers, of whom only 83 (1.89 per cent) were female. As a senior corporate manager put it: 'If you ask me how we develop that lot I have to say I don't really know. To some extent it's still cradle to grave stuff. Some 95 per cent of our present managers will have joined us at age 16 or 18. The way they have been developed up until now has been to push them through in their thousands based on a generalist approach: that system can no longer survive.' The emerging trend was towards the cessation of this generalist pattern and the creation of specialist paths. One division, Corporate and Institutional Banking, had started to recruit directly on its own exclusive behalf. The foundations of an entirely new approach to making managers were being laid and the old edifice was being dismantled.

Conclusions

This catalogue of eight cases reveals, not surprisingly, a complex picture. But certain basic points can be discerned amid that complexity. The first is that at this kind of broad-brush level there are sufficient similarities among the Japanese companies to make it easy to understand why many commentators have felt comfortable about making generalizations about 'Japanese management'. Equally, there were nonetheless sufficient signs to suggest that a number of significant variations exist between the Japanese companies which require and deserve further scrutiny. For example, while Sumitomo Electric had maintained a relatively stable pattern of management development over many decades, this was by no means the case at the retail company Jusco, where some fast-changing initiatives were under way and learning from American practice was intense.

Second, the same kind of broad-brush review also revealed certain patterns and certain divergencies within the British cases. The most notable feature was of discontinuous change. Even the two cases which had previously enjoyed long-standing elaborated management development systems based on the lifetime employment model (namely the bank and the telecommunications company) had commenced a radical departure from that traditional and well-trodden system. Across the four British cases as a whole, it would be fair to say that the single most enduring impression that could be derived from a broad review was one of massive uncertainty about what was appropriate in a rapidly changing environment. There was general agreement that the traditional systems were no longer appropriate, but there was a surprising degree of uncertainty about what should be put in their place.

Third, some interesting differences were discernible between the British cases. British Telecom had in effect swept the deck clean in so far as its old management development system was concerned. NatWest had retained a much stronger central presence in management development activity but was nonetheless reviewing quite fundamentally its future policy and in particular preparing to abandon its previous mainstay – the generalist approach. Lucas, the electrical engineering company, had undergone its 'clean sweep' of management training and development practices earlier in the decade and was now seeking to build an alternative system in its place. Tesco, the stores group, was different again. It was in an early phase of building its systematic approach to making managers. Interestingly, in the 1990s when the 'end of career' idea began to sweep the popular management and business press, Tesco still expressed its prime concern as one of ensuring that it was able to get its fair share of the best graduates and to hold on to them so that it could enhance its management stock at all levels. Using the concepts introduced in the first chapter we can interpret these movements in terms of an overall shift towards a more market-oriented approach to acquiring and managing the management stock and a departure from the organization-oriented model. At the same time, in varying degrees, it would seem that certain companies in both Britain and Japan were seeking to retain some of the advantages of the organization-oriented approach.

These pen-portraits also point to the need for a deeper level of analysis. How, and to what extent, were the 'official' systems in all eight companies enacted in practice? What do the centrepieces of the renowned Japanese system (such as OJT) actually entail in practice? Who does what, how and when? Likewise, from another perspective, what was it like to be on the receiving end of these systems? How did those who were the targets of these management development systems perceive and respond to them? The following chapters examine closely how these choices were confronted and actioned. The analysis begins in the next chapter with an examination of external and internal labour markets for managers and the operation of managerial careers.

4

Managerial Labour Markets and Management Careers

The career is an integral part of the process of making managers. There is widespread agreement, which has been reinforced in recent years by greater understanding of the nature of managerial work (for information on this see, for example, Kotter, 1982; Mintzberg, 1973; Stewart, 1967; 1976; Watson, 1994), that 'management' is not something that can simply be learnt in the classroom or from books. Such is the nature of managerial work – a hectic and fragmented set of activities in which the manager performs multiple roles requiring a high level of interpersonal skills as well as technical knowledge of the organization's activities – that, in the words of Handy and his colleagues, there is a 'consistent belief, common to all countries and to Britain, that the real basis for continuing learning in management is experience at work' (Handy et al., 1988: 5). Commentators differ only in the point of their emphasis. Some stress the importance of a slow and steady progression; others favour the 'fast-track' approach in which experience is acquired at an early age. Some argue that it is best to begin by achieving mastery of a particular function; others believe that it is better to have experience, even involving periods of time in other organizations, of a wide range of activities (for the views of 'successful' managers on these points, see Margerison and Kakabadse, 1985). The key issue, however, is whether the managerial career is planned in a systematic way or is largely 'accidental' (Ascher, 1983). This is very rarely addressed.

The managerial career is not simply a technical question for management development specialists, however. Who 'owns' the career – the individual or the organization – is profoundly important for the working of the managerial labour market. Numerous studies have emphasized the importance of promotion, of 'getting on', to individual managers. The conventional wisdom is that most large companies have sought both to encourage and to capitalize on this to develop an internal labour market for managers which the organization controls. Managers, in other words, are usually recruited young and, subject to appropriate behaviour, are more or less guaranteed promotion internally. They are treated as part of the 'core' and a great deal is done to ensure their loyalty through the operation of the pay system, the pension scheme and other 'fringe' benefits. In the words of Scase and Goffee,

Traditionally, the managerial career is alleged to consist of a meaningful progression through a series of related jobs. This is expected to occur in a relatively routine manner, if only because of the essentially hierarchical nature of large-scale bureaucratic organisations. The criteria for advancement are often varied but normally incorporate considerations to do with length of service, ability and performance. As managers are mobile within such hierarchies, they are rewarded with enhanced income, status and security. (1989: 79)

They go on to quote a number of authors, including Sofer (1970) and Pahl and Pahl (1972), who have stressed the fundamental significance of this promotion process in the work and non-work experiences of corporate managers.

Only recently has the ubiquity of this traditional model come to be questioned. Faced with intensifying competitive pressures brought about, among other reasons, by the growth in an international economy, it is argued that senior managers have been obliged to divest and diversify with considerable internal repercussions. There has been decentralization to quasi-autonomous business units and substantial delayering. Kanter (1989), one of the most influential management 'gurus', talks in terms of the 'demise of "corpocratic" careers' in which managers can expect steady promotion and a job for life; of the 'burgeoning of entrepreneurial careers' in which the emphasis is on the manager's ability to create products or services; and of the 'spread of professional careers' in which the transportable skills and knowledge of the individual manager are paramount. She also refers to 'shifting loyalties' as the attachment of managers to the organization becomes weaker and that to the family becomes stronger.

In practice, of course, the situation has always been much more complicated than the traditional model suggests. The prescriptive literature invariably ignores one essential fact. Much depends, as Handy and his colleagues recognize (Handy et al., 1988), on the type of managerial labour market. This differs markedly from one society to another. Certainly the two countries being considered here have special characteristics which are crucial in understanding how managers are made. Japan is often quoted as the archetypal example of the internal labour market (see, for example, Pucik and Hatvany, 1983). The organization, in other words, grows its own managers and does not normally recruit them from other organizations in mid-career; individual managers, in turn, acquire their experience from promotion and mobility within the organization rather than from moving between different organizations. In the UK not only is there much more reliance on the external labour market – recruitment advertisements in the press, for example, confirm the significance of external recruitment – but the managerial labour market is also highly segmented. Typically, the UK manager will begin his or her career in a function, such as accountancy, engineering, marketing or personnel, which will have its own professional body, entry qualifications, codes of ethics and discipline. For example, accountancy and engineering are so fragmented that there are a number of separate professional bodies which seek to represent each of these functions. It is only later in life that managerial recruits are likely to move into 'general management'. As Alban-Metcalfe and Nicholson's (1984) study of managers' mobility, suggests, British managers have four basic career paths to consider: they have the option of going elsewhere or staying; they also have the option of pursuing a career path within a discipline or function, or becoming general managers.

We have already seen, in Chapter 3, that there are important variations within each country. We now explore these more fully by looking at the types of managerial labour markets, the educational experiences of these managers, the ways they gain entry to their organizations, their subjective experience of managerial work, the systems of career planning, and their views about these systems. Each of these issues is examined in the following sections.

The Managerial Labour Market: Education and Entry

Our British and Japanese managers conformed to expectations so far as their education and age of entry were concerned. As Table 4.1 shows, the Japanese sample had much the higher level of educational qualifications. Aggregating the data (not shown in the table) revealed that not one of the Japanese managers in the sample had entered the labour market before the age of 18 and only a handful had entered by the age of 20, whereas this had been the experience of 45 per cent of the British. Almost all (94 per cent) of the Japanese had degrees, as against less than half (42 per cent) of the British.

Even so, Table 4.1 clearly shows too that, although the Japanese companies were very much alike in the reliance on graduates, there were significant differences between the British companies. Put another way, it was not simply a question of national stereotypes. In NatWest, for example, only 7 per cent of our managers had a degree or a postgraduate qualification. In Lucas, by contrast, 83 per cent had degrees or postgraduate qualifications; the proportion with postgraduate qualifications in Lucas, 38 per cent, is also the highest of the eight companies.

The explanation for the differences rests in the recruitment strategies that our companies were pursuing. The four Japanese companies are typical of the larger Japanese companies generally. Each year they recruit the stock from which the very great majority of their managers are grown direct from university, and not just any university. They draw the great bulk of their recruits from a selected number of the most prestigious national universities such as Tokyo and Kyoto and their private sector counterparts such as Waseda and Keio. These then constitute a 'cadre' which, as a later section will describe in more detail, goes through a fairly standard but lengthy process of development before achieving their first managerial appointment. Each of the four companies has provisions for introducing non-graduates into the managerial cadre – the most notable example being Jusco owing to

Table 4.1 *Educational qualifications and entry age for management* (%)

	Lucas	Sumitomo	NatWest	Mitsui	Tesco	Jusco	BT	NTT	All
Highest educational qualification									
O level or below[1]	10	0	66	0	32	0	27	0	20
A level[1]	7	0	27	8	32	11	10	4	13
Degree	45	73	5	88	36	89	53	64	53
Postgraduate	38	27	2	4	0	0	10	32	14
Age of first full-time job									
Under 18 years	23	0	71	0	35	0	52	0	26
18–20 years	10	0	20	8	39	4	18	4	13
21 years and over	68	100	10	92	27	96	30	96	61

[1] In Japan, the closest equivalent to O levels is graduating from junior high school at age 15, while A levels equate to graduating from senior high school.

the pressure of expansion on its demand for managers – but the numbers, as Table 4.1 clearly demonstrates, are very small.

All four British companies also recruit graduates, but these are not, with the exception of Lucas, the main source from which future managers are chosen. In NatWest most managers emerged from the large number of 16 year old GCSE O level and 18 year old GCE A level entrants it hired every year; the graduates, who represented a small proportion of the total intake, went through a similar process but on a 'fast track'. In Tesco, most managers in the stores emerged from age groups similar to those of the bank, although the recruitment process was nowhere near as structured or centralized; the graduates, who were also a small proportion of the total, tended to go into headquarters functions. In British Telecom, although there had been a sizeable influx of people from outside since privatization, the great majority of managers, that is three-quarters, came from the large number of technicians who were also recruited at 16 or 18 with science O and A levels or who, historically, had acquired technical qualifications such as ONC and HNC on various day-release schemes run by the organization. The graduate intake was of the order of 10 per cent. Only in Lucas did most managers come from the graduate intake. Such graduates were not directly hired in the same cohort fashion as the Japanese companies, however; most were initially recruited into technical and engineering functions and moved on into management positions in a relatively haphazard fashion as and when they desired to change direction and/or vacancies arose.

Table 4.2 also confirms the importance of the internal labour market. In Japan managers in three of the companies had worked for that organization only; lifelong employment, it seems, is very much a reality. Only in Jusco had people worked elsewhere. Interestingly among the British companies it was also in the retailer (Tesco) that managers had the greatest amount of experience in other companies. In the other three British companies more than half had worked for that organization alone, which is a much higher proportion than reported in previous surveys (see, for example, Alban-Metcalfe and Nicholson, 1984, who found that in 1983 less than 10 per cent of the 1,144 managers in a British Institute of Management survey had worked for only one organization). NatWest and British Telecom, it will be seen, had particularly strong internal labour markets. Nearly 90 per cent of NatWest's managers and three-quarters of British Telecom's had worked solely for one company.

Although these differences are not as great as might have been expected, our interviews revealed a very different approach. Our Japanese companies were quite prepared, if a special need arose, to look outside for managers. Sumitomo had done so, for example, to get someone to head a new division. Jusco, by Japanese standards, was doing so fairly extensively to meet the demands of rapid expansion. NTT had felt obliged to make a number of senior appointments from outside following privatization, although not nearly as many as its British counterpart which had gone outside for virtually its entire top tier of managers. Broadly speaking, however, our Japanese companies were firmly committed to the internal labour market approach.

In our British companies this commitment was much weaker. In Lucas and British Telecom, in particular, there was considerable discussion and debate about the balance of advantage between internal and external appointments. Some senior managers argued that they needed to bring in new blood. Indeed, in one of the larger divisions of Lucas no fewer than three of the four key business manager positions had been filled from outside in recent years. Others argued that this would only create disunity. The talent existed, but there was a need to design the right systems to develop it.

Despite the differences in the commitment to the internal labour market, in terms of the length of their careers with their present companies, our Japanese managers did not stand out. Indeed, there were no statistical differences between the two countries. Particularly noticeable are the lengths of careers of managers in NatWest and British Telecom, which were longer than those of their Japanese counterparts. If this lack of national difference seems odd given lifelong employment in Japan, it can be fairly easily explained: the great majority of the Japanese managers, because of their education, entered the labour market at a later age than the British. For example, a 40 year old Japanese manager might have joined the company at the age of 22, whereas a British counterpart of the same age might have joined after working for other companies first; both would nonetheless have had similar lengths of service. Indeed, a point which emerged from the interviews was that it was quite common for the British, faced with a very different labour market from their counterparts in Japan, to be undecided about what they wanted to do on leaving school or university, which led them to shift from one employer to another before settling. This was much rarer in Japan.

In view of the significance attached to early experience in the literature (see, for example, Margerison, 1985), the difference between the two samples in the age of the first managerial appointment is interesting. Not one of the Japanese, it will be seen from Table 4.3, had taken up their first management appointment before the age of 25 and only a handful had done so by the age of 30. By contrast, the great majority of the British had embarked on their managerial career by the age of 30 and a considerable number had done so by the age of 25. Only in NatWest did the first managerial appointment tend to come after the age of 30.

The differences between the two samples, which were statistically significant, were not unexpected. Our interviews with senior Japanese managers confirmed what had been suggested in the literature (see, for example, Handy et al., 1988). A cohort of candidates would be recruited at the same time from university; they would progress, in a fairly structured way, through a series of grades and appointments which will be described in more detail in a later section; and this 'slow-burn' process, to borrow a

Table 4.2 *Career mobility and length of service in management*

	Lucas	Sumitomo	NatWest	Mitsui	Tesco	Jusco	BT	NTT	All
Career mobility (%)									
This company only	58	100	88	100	19	82	76	100	78
1 or 2 others	26	0	10	0	42	15	21	0	14
3 or more others	16	0	2	0	38	4	3	0	8
Mean length of service (years)	16	20	27	20	12	17	22	16	19

Table 4.3 *Age of first management appointment (%)*

	Lucas	Sumitomo	NatWest	Mitsui	Tesco	Jusco	BT	NTT	All
Under 26 years	31	0	0	0	81	11	54	0	22
26–29 years	53	0	7	0	19	46	18	20	20
30–35 years	16	18	63	33	0	35	12	68	31
36–40 years	0	82	29	67	0	8	15	12	26

phrase from Handy (1987), would last not just for a year or two as in Britain, but for many years before they got their first managerial appointment. There are signs of change, notably in Jusco and NTT, where people were being appointed to managerial positions at an earlier age, but this has yet to make a dramatic change to the figures.

Again in the British companies, there was no common pattern. In NatWest and Tesco, as already indicated, people tended to join the organization at 16 or 18 and had to perform a range of routine functions before being considered for management; only recently had NatWest introduced a 'fast track' system for graduate entry. The main difference between these two companies is that promotion is much more rapid in Tesco than in NatWest; a number of the Tesco managers running superstores with multi-million turnovers and a staff of 600 or 700 were only in their late 20s or early 30s. Graduate entry was more common in Lucas and British Telecom, though normally this meant direct entry into the technical and professional functions. There was little evidence of the systematic approach of the Japanese companies. In Lucas, even the type of 'fast-track' system which NatWest, along with British Telecom, had recently introduced was noticeable by its absence. In every case managerial posts, other than the most senior, were advertised internally and individuals applied as and when they arose.

It was not simply a question of national stereotypes then. There are significant differences between the sectors. Again, the retailers stand out; in both companies managers achieved their first appointment to management at an earlier age than in the other sectors. NatWest is also more like the Japanese companies than its British counterparts; managers were unlikely to secure their first managerial appointment before the age of 30.

It is difficult to account for these differences other than in terms of the special circumstances of the sectors. It could be argued that a bank manager, for example, occupies a special position and handles large sums of money. He or she therefore needs to be of a particular age to inspire trust and confidence. Yet, as already indicated, some of our managers in retail were involved in equally large sums of money and were also responsible for literally hundreds of staff. In the circumstances it is difficult to escape the conclusion that it is largely a question of tradition. The banks are long standing, whereas the large superstore is a relatively recent phenomenon. Our two retailers were confronted with rapid expansion which required them to develop systems for developing managers more or less from scratch.

It was evident from our data that there were significant differences in management education and entry between sectors as well as between countries. In order to clarify some of the details of these differences we will now focus on two of the British cases, Tesco and BT. These will help to highlight the dynamics of the way managerial labour markets operate and also allow us to tap into the responses of the human beings caught up in the different systems.

Job Mobility in Tesco

Job mobility was high in the British retailer, Tesco. One of the regional managing directors reported to us that he himself had moved jobs nine times in the past 10 years. Over 90 per cent of managers are promoted internally, the remainder are bought in at mid-career. He gave us some useful insight into how this was done. Apart from advertised vacancies, he and his colleagues made direct head-hunting approaches:

> I have acquired some useful managers from other companies. I have picked up eight from Gateway where people are feeling insecure at the moment. I simply ask around as to who is good and then I phone them directly.

Career planning is seen as a vital task. The regional MD said:

> I am personally heavily involved in succession planning. If I did nothing else but find the good managers to groom I would easily earn my salary. It is the region's responsibility to develop good store managers . . . I get a feel for who is going to go far.

To take another example, the general manager of a southern superstore described his own career trajectory. He was currently top manager in a store with some 600 people and 20 managerial staff. His career had been almost a 'fairytale' success story. He had left school before A levels, and worked as a 'Saturday boy' in a store. He had then spent nearly one year, full-time, at a whole series of stores as a 'gofer' (a general assistant) before gaining a place on one of the junior management training courses. Following a short spell as a staff member in the training centre he took a job as assistant manager in a medium-sized London store. He was then, at the tender age of 21, appointed as manager in his own store. He was moved frequently – short periods of only eight or nine months per store at this stage. This period he described as resulting from Tesco's 'trial and error' approach to management development at that time. Then he 'got lucky' and was allowed three years to 'find himself' at a decent store before being seconded to headquarters for a year working on a project concerning new stores. He was then appointed to his present post. He said that this kind of career pattern was not exceptional in Tesco and that there were some who had moved through the system even more speedily.

As the number of graduates increased, two main career paths were emerging and becoming clear: first the graduate intake, which largely went into specific functions; and second, upward mobility through the stores. For the former, the normal pattern would be to remain within the specialist function for some considerable number of years. Cross-functional moves were possible but this would be much later, and similarly so for moves out into the stores (which in any case were much more unusual). Inter-functional mobility was definitely not part of the early training system.

A few examples will suffice to indicate the kind of mobility in Tesco. The distribution director (logistics specialist) we interviewed had been recruited from a London brewery. A trading director was head-hunted from

Sainsbury's. Two of our interviewees moved on to posts in a building society which was seeking to boost its retail and customer service profile. One of our financial controllers had previously been in two different firms of chartered accountants in the City of London. A quantity surveyor in the estates department (responsible for acquiring new sites) had come from a local authority – and prior to that, a building contractor. An O&M specialist in distribution had had a chequered and varied career before coming to Tesco in response to a national advertisement.

This inter-firm mobility contrasts with the lack of inter-functional mobility within the company. Senior functional specialists told us they would not contemplate a move out of their specialism until they had reached the head of their function and could think at that stage of a wider business management role. There had not been the precedents in any positive sense for cross-functional mobility: where these had occurred it had 'normally been regarded as a last-ditch way of solving a staffing problem'. There was some desire to see this changed. Senior specialists spoke of their desire to have had wider experience. For example, one computer specialist said he would have benefited from a couple of years in finance and a couple in distribution. There was even a suggestion that, in order to break down past resistance to this kind of move, a degree of compulsion might be justified. This, rather interestingly, would approximate to the Japanese system.

But beyond a certain level, cross-functional mobility was thought to be too difficult in the UK. Requisite special knowledge would be too high. In any case most people's prime orientation seemed to be to progress up their functional chimney. In a telling remark about the managerial labour conditions in the UK, one senior functional manager said:

> My main priority for the time being has to be to get to be chief of division. If that proves not to be possible within Tesco then I will have to move to another company and for this my marketability will hinge far more on my specialist roles accomplished and far less on whether I am 'rounded' in business management terms. (Tesco headquarters specialist manager)

Notably, this is a manager who would actually support some corporate-level cross-functional career direction and planning; here he is stating frankly his calculated reasoning given the way the present system operates. To break down the 'Berlin Walls' of functional chimneys he suggested would require positive role models, appropriate precedents and some corporate action.

So far we have been discussing cross-functional mobility within head-quarters functions. But what about cross-fertilization from HQ to stores? There were difficulties here also. The problem was pinpointed nicely and with enthusiasm by a central accountant:

> If I could go into the retailing side at an appropriate level – for example, retail executive responsibility for half a dozen stores – then I would be delighted. The trouble is I don't know the first thing about retailing and so they would probably place me as a mere assistant manager in a store.

So then we asked him about the idea of a secondment. Here again he was dubious:

> I think people are deluding themselves when they talk about secondments in this company. If an HQ person is posted for a year as say an assistant product manager to see how produce is ordered, and then returns to their previous function, there would really be no point.

When asked if he would be prepared to accept a promotion that entailed a move to another function such as marketing (he had previously expressed some interest in this function) he still replied:

> No, I don't think so. I'm an accountant and although I would like to try some other areas such as marketing, I really do not want to stop being an accountant: this is where I see my future. Frankly, if one of these positions [he points to the next grade on an organization chart on his desk] is not going to be available for me in the next two years, then I will move to another company.

Recruitment and Careers in BT

Up to managerial level 3 the districts were responsible for their own resourcing. Similarly, up to that level there would normally be very little movement around the company. But at level 4 and above, it was more widely assumed that a person who wanted promotion would have to be mobile. Within headquarters (in reality a whole series of buildings mainly located in London) there tended to be more movement across different parts of the business. A matter of greater concern was the paucity of mobility between districts and head office.

The main 'mechanism' for job changing was via the company *Gazette*: a weekly job-listing newspaper which contains entries ranging from clerical appointments up to senior management level.

Headquarters personnel had some involvement in district board appointments – especially for district general manager (DGM) or deputy DGM. For these key posts Noel Tappendon, the then personnel director, was usually involved. For appointments to the rest of the district boards the 'head office view' was mainly devolved to the territory level. In practice, most district board appointments tended to be filled from within the territories.

When speaking of recruitment into level 1 (junior management or equivalent) jobs in the headquarters of British Telecom, we asked about the necessity or otherwise of formal external qualifications. An engineering divisional head gave us this reply:

> Formal qualifications are not absolutely necessary. In the advertisements I put out I always say 'professional qualifications an advantage' but it's not mandatory. It does help, though, it shows the attitude of the chap who has put himself out and got his qualifications.

This manager is talking here about professional engineering qualifications. Judging by the pattern of chartered engineering qualifications among incumbent managers, the priority given to these has fluctuated over the years and our various informants confirmed this cyclical character. Yet the sections we are talking about here were headquarters engineering functions – described as 'the cream of British Telecom engineering', albeit not in quite the entrepreneurial way associated with small pioneering companies 'such as Clive Sinclair's outfit'.

Geographical mobility and, by implication, grade hierarchy mobility is hampered in British Telecom by divergencies in quality of life and expenses associated with living in London compared with other parts of the country. British Telecom is a vast organization with large numbers of staff in the capital. Some managers from the provincial towns are reluctant to move to London because of the associated costs and, in turn, there was a staff retention problem in the city. Senior managers based in London claimed their provincial colleagues were able to enjoy a higher standard of living even if they were three or more managerial grades below them.

But being 'hacked off with living in London' was nonetheless generally perceived as a lesser problem than the 'lack of promotion' and the absence of a career structure in the new, rationalized, British Telecom. Departmental managers said it was this factor above all which presented them with their staff retention problem.

Another interesting factor emerged. It is arguably a familiar British complaint but it certainly was re-echoed in British Telecom. To attain senior management positions, it was said, meant sacrificing the intrinsic challenge and interests of practising engineering for a role which involves form-filling and administration. Some engineers were simply not prepared to forgo their interests in order to climb the hierarchy if this was the price: longer hours doing essentially things they didn't really want to do.

It would seem that this kind of problem, relatively familiar though it may be in large engineering companies, is one which sharply marks off the phenomenon and experience of 'management' in British Telecom from that in Tesco, for example. In Tesco, status unambiguously relates to position on the ladder. But in British Telecom intrinsic rewards can flow from 'being the top dog sat around the table with the world's leading contractors and knowing your stuff so well that no one can pull the wool over your eyes' (senior engineer, British Telecom).

One of the changes was the external recruitment of new blood at very senior levels. Executives from favoured entrepreneurial companies such as Rank Xerox, Black and Decker and IBM were recruited. As one insider remarked:

At first people thought, 'Hey, this is going to be great, new ideas will be brought in, it's like having our own Harvey-Jones.' But from my middle-ranking position I have to say that their impact in reality has been zero. I can't think of one guy who has come in from outside who has made any difference to the firm. OK one or two have come in and put the brakes on but anyone could do that; nobody has made me feel better about working for the company.

He then reconsidered and said, there had in fact been some well-respected recruits from STC (a competitor telecoms company). Even these special recruits had found the adjustment problematical, 'these guys were used to having positions of power, but in British Telecom they find that making things happen is not easy – here there are always more forms to fill-in. The world doesn't change anymore when they snap their fingers.'

At district level in British Telecom there were in effect two systems of recruitment and selection in operation. For most positions (that is, below level 4) vacancies were advertised in the company newspaper and it would be left to individuals to apply. Competitive shortlisting and interviewing would then follow. But for the more senior posts, at district board level, the positions are filled 'by appointment'. This means no competitive interviews or applications. Managers are moved between districts, as one said: 'I was brought across from Liverpool, there was no selection procedure, it was just done, that's how it works.'

One in seven management posts were also advertised externally in the national newspapers such as the *Sunday Times* – almost invariably so in the case of positions in sales and marketing. For the rest there is a 'general expectation' that vacancies would be advertised in the *Gazette*. This occurs for 90 per cent of level 3 jobs, for example. But it is not mandatory. If someone in a district was being moved sideways for development purposes or because of surplus of numbers, then advertising is not necessary.

Experience of Management

Like many others, the senior managers interviewed in our companies put considerable stress on 'experience' in the making of managers. In the Japanese companies reference was made to the long and relatively slow preparation of the managers and then the systematic progress through a series of jobs which, combined with on-the-job training, was designed to produce top level general managers. There was also relative satisfaction with the outcome. In the British companies too there was considerable emphasis on experience. Here, however, there was considerable dissatisfaction with present arrangements. A major problem, it was argued, was in developing all-round business managers. A major problem was the segmentation of the internal labour market touched on in the introduction. It was difficult to break down the functional chimneys. In many cases the individual might prefer to stay in his or her function rather than move across. In all four cases, this was compounded by the divisions within the organization. For example, in both NatWest and Tesco, the divisions between head office and the operating units were perceived to be a problem. In Lucas, it was the division between Aerospace and the other divisions.

In the circumstances, it was not unreasonable to expect that there would be marked differences in the experience of our managers – with the

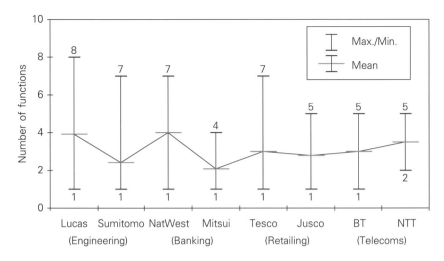

Figure 4.1 *Number of functions ever worked in*

Japanese managers having greater functional experience than their British counterparts. Surprisingly, however, this was not the case. The distribution of the replies to a question asking if they had worked in any one of 12 common managerial functions is shown in Figure 4.1. It will be seen that in two of the sectors, engineering and banking, the British managers reported having worked in the greater number of different functions. In retailing the figures for Tesco were very similar to those of Jusco. Only in the telecoms was the Japanese figure higher than its British counterpart.

One possibility was that the explanation lay in the distribution of the replies. That is to say, the high British average might have been due to a relatively few managers having a very large amount of functional experience. In fact, the distributions were approximately normal in all eight companies. Also, as Figure 4.1 confirms, the maximum number of functions quoted did not differ very much between the two countries.

Another possibility was that the distribution might be explained by the differences in the age at which our managers entered management. It has already been shown in the previous section that, on average, the Japanese took up their first management appointment later than the British. Conceivably the Japanese managers simply might not have had enough time to become involved in as many functions as their British counterparts. This did not prove to be the case either. Indeed, the British lead held for all categories of age of taking up the first management appointment. In short, the results were statistically robust, which means that other explanations have to be found.

Little serious analysis has been undertaken into the precise nature of management functions and so a check was made to ensure that there were no fundamental differences in the meanings which our managers in the two countries attached to particular labels. It could have been, quite simply, that our Japanese managers recognized fewer labels than their British counterparts. Planning, for example, might not have been seen as a separate function in the Japanese companies. In the event, a detailed analysis of the replies to each of the 12 functions in turn suggested no major differences in perception. In six functions, at least one manager in every company reported having worked in it in the present organization. In a seventh, finance, it was the British companies which stood out; no British Telecom manager reported having worked in this function. In two, the Japanese companies were divided: two had representatives and two did not. In a further two, one British company and two Japanese companies did not have representatives. Only in one of the functions listed, that of 'management trainee', did no manager in three Japanese companies report having worked in it. As an extra precaution, therefore, the figures were recalculated to exclude this function, but the overall pattern of replies remained much as before.

Our next step was to look at the figures a different way to see if, function by function, more British or Japanese managers reported having worked in it. Not surprisingly in view of what has already been said, the British figure was higher for 'management trainee'; it was also higher for administration. But the Japanese reported more experience of finance, sales and personnel and, when the figures were studied by pairs of company in each sector, more experience of what might be thought to be 'core' activities: production and R&D in the case of engineering, and 'sales' in the case of banking and retail. These points may be significant in themselves: it could be that the Japanese managers have more experience of the functions which are really important to the particular business. For present purposes, however, they simply suggest that the figures are not distorted by national differences in the definition of a function.

There is perhaps one qualification to this generalization which emerged from our detailed interviews. It concerns the definition of job titles in NatWest. A normal part of the career path in this company would involve a spell as an 'administration' manager in a branch; this would be concerned with personnel and routine matters internal to the bank, as distinct from relations with customers. Managers in NatWest might therefore have said that they had worked in personnel as well as administration, whereas their Japanese counterparts might not have done.

Even so, although there are variations between the sectors, one thing stands out. It would be wrong to see wide functional experience as central to Japanese practice. This does not mean that experience is unimportant, however. Just as important as functional experience, if not more so, is experience of different divisions of the company's activities. In all four of the companies there is a long-established practice of rotating managers between jobs in different divisions to broaden their knowledge of the company. This does not necessarily imply a change of function, however. One of the specialist accountants among our interviewees, for example, had spent extended periods in two different works as well as two different head offices in his time at Sumitomo; two of our interviewees, one at Mitsui and the other at Sumitomo, had spent periods as full-time officials of the company trade union. Such job rotation, as will be explained in more detail in the next section, is a critical element in making managers in our Japanese companies.

Certainly, the answers to a question about the number of divisions in which a manager had worked seemed to confirm the importance of this type of experience. In three of the Japanese companies, every single one of our managers had worked in at least one other division and more than 90 per cent had worked in three or more; in the fourth, Sumitomo, 80 per cent of managers had such experience. In the British companies, the highest score for working in one other division was 76 per cent; this was in British Telecom. More than half the managers in Tesco and about a third of those in Lucas and NatWest had never worked in another division. Relatively few of our British managers, outside of British Telecom, had worked in three or more divisions.

Our detailed interviews also threw a great deal of light on these issues. In the case of functional experience, it is clear that not a great deal of confidence can be put in the quality of experience gained by our British managers. Many of them, it will be remembered, had left school at a relatively early age; the fact that they had worked in a number of functions was very often an accident rather than planned. Similarly, graduate recruits may have spent some time in a range of functions as part of their initial induction. As will be seen in the next section, there was very little disagreement between the managers and their superiors about the significance of functional chimneys. Most recognized the problem but, in the absence of any serious career planning, functional specialists in particular saw personal advantage in the present arrangements: it gave them an alternative career path into other organizations.

There was also widespread recognition of the barriers posed by the divisional structures in the interviews with our British managers. In NatWest and British Telecom there were perceived to be barriers between headquarters and the regional or district organizations; in NatWest, for example, a number of managers graphically waved the internal telephone books in front of us to demonstrate how they felt about what they perceived to be an inordinate growth in the size of headquarters and the lack of contact between it and the branches which were supposed to be making the money. In Tesco, as well as alluding to the same 'headquarters–regions' problem, a number of respondents spoke about the 'Berlin Wall' which existed between the stores and distribution; it was virtually impossible for a store manager to get experience of managing distribution and vice versa. In Lucas, many managers referred to what in their eyes were the wasted opportunities afforded by the presence of a large number of small businesses in one of the divisions which might have been used to develop general managers; the trouble was, they said, it would be difficult to make one's way in the two larger divisions if you were to step outside.

Such points, for the most part, did not figure in the interviews with our Japanese managers. In the case of functional or specialist activities the main concern was that it was proving increasingly difficult to ensure that individuals had the necessary knowledge. The internal labour market meant that those following functional or specialist career paths did not think, seriously, of exploiting any 'professional' skills they had in the 'open' market. The issue of the divisions did arise, but it was equally basic. If there was a problem, it was the reluctance of divisions sometimes to release good managers. Our impression, however, evidence for which will be given below, is that headquarters personnel had greater 'clout' than their counterparts in the British companies to bring this about.

Career Planning

Our concern was not only to establish the nature and extent of experience, but also to investigate how far this was planned or was acquired haphazardly. Our general expectation, admittedly from the relatively few existing studies of the issues, was that the Japanese companies were much more likely to plan the careers of their managers than the British. Certainly our interviews with the management development specialists in the Japanese companies confirmed our expectations about them. Each of our Japanese companies had very clear and often long-established systems for grooming their managers. Even though our four companies operate in very different markets, and so might have been expected to have developed diverse arrangements, the key features were very similar and reflect practice in most large Japanese companies (see, for example, Pucik and Roomkin, 1989: 261–6).

Accompanying the system of lifelong employment was a dual system of promotion 'ladders' working side by side which is not dissimilar to that found in the armed forces or the civil service in Britain before the report of the Fulton Commission of Inquiry (see, for example, Kellner and Crowther-Hunt, 1980). One of these is often referred to as the 'status' ladder, but perhaps is better described as the 'qualification' ladder. This is the basic ladder which every manager has to climb. The other might be thought of as the 'appointments' ladder and comprises specific positions and jobs. The two ladders are related but not rigidly so. Thus a manager will have to have achieved a certain level on the qualification ladder to be considered for a particular appointment. Achieving such a level of qualification, however, does not guarantee the manager an appointment normally appropriate to that level. Indeed, a not inconsiderable number of managers in our companies who had achieved managerial 'qualification' did not have functional posts.

For example, at Sumitomo progression involves a mixture of seniority and merit. Managers usually have to spend a minimum number of years in each of the first four grades on the qualification ladder before becoming eligible for promotion to the next one. This explains, going back to the previous section, why our managers very rarely took up their first managerial appointments until well into their 30s; it takes 13 years to reach the end of the grade of *kanrishokuho*, which translated literally means 'candidate to management'. Once the minimum service requirements have been satisfied, progress from one grade to another depends on merit which is determined by the systems of evaluation discussed in more detail in the Chapter 7. Typically, then, a group of managers who entered the company together will move more or less as a cohort until their mid 30s; thereafter the speed of their advance can differ. Even when relatively well advanced in their careers, many of our respondents confirmed, Japanese managers would compare themselves with, and measure their progress against, colleagues who had joined in the same year. In the top four grades the length of service is also important, but the time limits are less rigid and merit is given more weight.

The systems of the other Japanese companies differ in detail only. For example, the number of grades, together with the minimum service qualification, may differ. In NTT, before privatization, the arrangements were very similar to those in the civil service in that the relationship between the two ladders was much more rigid; the arrangements introduced in 1985 allow for greater attention to merit. In Jusco, the arrangements allow for the most rapid promotion, which reflects the company's recent expansion and the need to increase its managerial stock very quickly. Interestingly, too, to move through the 'qualification' grades, Jusco managers have to pass a series of examinations as well as satisfying the other requirements of the evaluation system posed in interviews and the personnel rating. Personality assessment is also an integral component of the promotion at more senior levels.

A second feature which the four companies share is job rotation. As other commentators (see, for example, Rohlen, 1974; Yoshino, 1968) have observed, the arrangements for job rotation are fairly formal. Usually, for example, job rotation takes place at regular intervals. In Sumitomo it was five years; in Jusco it was two or three years. There are also fixed points in the year when rotation takes place. In the case of Sumitomo, for example, those who are eligible for transfer are rotated in either January or July. Rotation also continues well into the manager's career; it even occurs at the *bucho* level, which is roughly equivalent to the general manager of a major unit in Britain.

Such are the nature of the activities of our four Japanese companies that secondment was also widely used. Secondment was especially important in the case of the bank. The recent extension of the retirement age from 55 to 60, as will be discussed below, was causing particular problems. Secondment to corporate customers, as well as providing valuable experience, was a way of relieving some of the pressure.

Not surprisingly, a third feature which the Japanese companies have in common is a very high level of centralization of responsibility for the management stock. In each case a so-called 'capability development office' in the personnel department at headquarters exercised overall supervision not only over training and development but also over every aspect of their terms and conditions of employment. This was even true of Sumitomo, which is a multi-divisional company, and Jusco, which is essentially a federation of quasi-independent companies. There was also a very high level of involvement of senior managers in the decisions which were made. In Jusco, for example, it was the president himself who chaired the panel which makes the final decision about the upgrading of individuals into the management grades. Decisions about the job rotation of senior managers would also involve board members, as would any differences of view between the capability development unit and divisional managers about job moves at lower grades.

A fourth feature, which is essential to the others, is the existence of a very detailed personnel database. Sumitomo, for example, was able to undertake at our request a computer search of the cohort of managers who had entered the company in 1969. Of the 68 who did so, 22 had arts backgrounds and had gone into the 'administrative' stream, and 46 had engineering degrees and were placed in the 'technical' stream. As well as detailed summaries of the education and training courses they had undertaken, the records also contained details of their job rotation. Those in the 'administrative' stream had been rotated fairly regularly between a range of function areas such as planning, marketing, personnel and accounting. Of their colleagues in the 'technical' stream, only five had stayed in the same function, which was R&D; the remaining 41 had been rotated between, for example, R&D and production or between engineering and clerical. In each case the rotation had been fairly regular, that is every two to three years.

Interestingly, the twice-yearly personnel rating evaluations which, as the next chapter will show, provide a fairly detailed assessment of the individual's abilities, had not yet been computerized, but there were plans to do this. The information certainly existed in document form, however, and was kept by personnel at headquarters.

As for individual involvement in career planning, in three of the companies, Mitsui, Jusco and NTT, each year the managers could express their views about their next appointment in a self-reporting form, which was separate from the evaluation process, for endorsement by their immediate superiors. Several of our interviewees at *kacho* level considered that their managerial appointments, so far at least, had accorded pretty well with their own preferences. Some of the older managers in our sample, however, said that at their level there was little point in expressing a view; they recognized that they would have to take up the position for which the company needed them. In the cases of Jusco and NTT there was some talk of developing new systems to allow for more individual involvement. In both these cases there was a feeling that this was going to be necessary for the future as today's younger employees were going to expect this to happen as they progressed in their careers.

The information from the management development specialists in the British companies suggested a much more varied pattern than the traditional stereotype. Thus NatWest shared some of the characteristics of the Japanese companies. Large numbers were recruited at 16 and 18 and worked through a series of assignments; graduates did the same only in a fast-track system. As with the Japanese, it was a 'slow-burn' system, which explains why many of our sample did not take up their first managerial appointment until they were in their 30s. The key to career planning was the system known as 'tiering'. Using this device all individuals embarking on a career in the bank were 'streamed'. This was done by attempting to calculate the highest grade which each individual entrant might be eventually expected to reach. As one senior corporate manager said to us, 'everything we do in management development at NatWest comes down to the tiering system.' To understand the 'tiers' it is necessary to understand the managerial grading system. The top eight grades (with the numbers of managers in each grade) are as follows:

MX	12
MA	56
MB	64
MC	107
MD	493
ME	598
MF	1,644
MG	1,427

MX was the very highest grade and it contained the chief executive and similar top managers who were above and beyond the job evaluation system. The tiers reflect these grades. A person expected to reach the top grades would be given an E tier; if a person was tiered S then it would be assumed that eventually the person would reach an MC or MD grade. A B tiering implied an expected attainment of one of the lower management grades. At the time of our research there were 350 aspirants with E tiers, 770 with an S and 2,100 individuals with a B tiering. They were to be found in different grades because they were 'coming through the system'. Disillusionment among those not privileged with the highest tiering was said not to be a problem

> because they are 'conditioned' from the day they join us. . . . In any case, those who are still clerks at 32 years of age get the message. OK so we lose quite a few, maybe 10 per cent per annum, and we also lose some B tiers, but we can live with the numbers we are losing. It is rather different for the top-tiered staff, we have a desperate need to retain these, hence we move them through the system as fast as possible. (senior personnel manager)

Interestingly, the operation of the system varied depending upon the region. In the then booming Thames Valley the bank found it necessary to recruit three times as many people and to push them through much faster (to counteract poaching and labour turnover) than was the case in more stable environments such as the Midlands.

Movement of managers between divisions was rare and was thought to be even less likely in future as areas such as corporate and institutional banking became more specialized. One estimate given to us was that possibly the top 10 per cent of tiered managers might be given this sort of mobility in order to prepare them for general management. One consequence of the increasing specialization was that domestic banking was being milked of talent as areas such as corporate banking had grown. The bank promoted 15,000 people in 1989 and some motivation was thought to stem from this fact. And domestic banking did have 100 business centres which offered opportunities for ambitious people. There was, however, some disillusionment among those who were 'trapped' in linked branches out on the periphery.

In the 1980s the bank was recruiting on average about 250 graduates per annum. What would happen to these? One central management development manager gave us his answer: 'We have been reviewing the cradle to grave policy for some time, but we nonetheless expect the bulk of our people will continue in this mode; we like to grow our own timber.' These arrangements were highly centralized. A 'central development unit' was responsible for the careers of those with the highest tiers.

The other companies had adopted a much more fragmented approach which, in part, reflected the strength of the functional and divisional arrangements already discussed above. In Tesco, for example, recruitment for the stores was organized on a regional basis. In Lucas, there was a recognition that there was little systematic career planning for the reasons which will be discussed in more detail below. A major problem was that the centre was only re-establishing a relationship with the sectors and divisions. They did not even have a database, though there had recently been a major audit of senior and middle managers.

In many respects British Telecom was perhaps the most interesting case. As some of our respondents pointed out, being part of the civil service, many of its practices had historically been very similar to those of our Japanese companies. Thus managerial careers had been highly structured and responsibility for them centralized at headquarters; younger managers, for example, had been required to spend minimum periods in a particular grade before applying to a selection board to be judged suitable for consideration for appointment to the next grade; the passing of examinations was also required to go beyond a certain level. In recent years, particularly following privatization, much of this system had been abandoned and responsibility for management development generally decentralized to the regional organizations. A set of new practices was under discussion and, depending on which manager was being interviewed, many were supposed to be in place. In practice, however, our impression was that, like Lucas, the company had thrown the baby out with the bathwater; its supposedly 'sophisticated' new personnel database, for example, could give us no information about managers' job changes.

As for individual involvement in career planning there was very little evidence of this taking place. British Telecom had recently introduced a system of personal development planning which was going to be the cornerstone of its approach as far as senior managers were concerned. The personnel director of Tesco felt that this might be the next step for his organization as well. Questions about individual involvement in career planning simply brought a sigh in Lucas and positive opposition in NatWest. Only where individual managers had taken the initiative were individuals seriously being involved, but these cases were relatively isolated.

In the circumstances, the replies from our managers to a question about the presence of career paths produced very surprising results. As Table 4.4 shows, in the banks and retail our British managers were more likely to perceive the presence of career paths than their Japanese counterparts. In engineering and utilities, although there was less certainty about career paths, there were no significant differences between the managers in the two countries.

Because of these results, further analysis was undertaken. The four categories of answer in Table 4.4 were collapsed into two: 'clear or broadly recognizable' and 'traces or none'. We then examined the issue statistically, using loglinear methods which are described in Chapter 7 and in Appendix A. When we looked at the relationship between presence of career paths, country, and sector, we found that there were no simple 'country effects' in evidence. Instead, only the most complex model representing interactions between all three variables, that is country, sector and company, was able to produce meaningful results. In other words, the pattern of replies very much depended on which individual company a manager worked in. There was no clear tendency for the British companies to differ as a group from the Japanese or the banks or for the other sectors to have a common pattern. The perceived presence of career paths was highly company-specific: there was no one single model.

It is tempting to dismiss the answers to a single question. In our survey, however, the managers were also asked a separate question about whether there was 'any system of career planning'. Table 4.5, which gives the results, suggests a pattern of responses not dissimilar to those to the question about 'career paths'. That many managers in some of the British companies should have responded negatively was to be expected in the light of what was known. Much more surprising, at first sight, are the responses of our Japanese managers. In three of the four companies our Japanese managers were less likely to report the presence of a system than their British counterparts; the difference between the banks in the two countries was especially marked. Only in telecoms, by a relatively small margin, did more Japanese than British managers report the presence of a system.

To make sense of what are quite startling results, it is necessary to refer to data from our interviews with the Japanese managers. Put simply, the

Table 4.4 *Clarity of career paths for management* (%)

	Lucas	Sumitomo	NatWest	Mitsui	Tesco	Jusco	BT	NTT	All
Clear	3	10	32	4	23	7	15	8	14
Broadly recognizable	36	28	42	12	35	26	39	68	36
Traces	32	41	24	56	19	52	33	20	34
None	29	21	2	28	15	15	9	0	14
Other reply	0	0	0	0	8	0	3	4	2

Table 4.5 *Presence of system of career planning for management* (%)

	Lucas	Sumitomo	NatWest	Mitsui	Tesco	Jusco	BT	NTT	All
Yes and:									
Works very or quite well	9	21	63	24	35	15	0	22	25
Works poorly or unsatisfactorily	44	0	27	4	17	7	24	11	18
No	39	52	5	64	42	63	64	54	45
Don't know	9	28	5	8	8	15	12	13	12

Japanese managers tended to see career planning in personal terms: they interpreted our questions, in other words, to be asking whether there was any means for them to plan their own careers. Many answered that there was no such means because their job moves were planned by someone else. It was common to be moved with little notice and with no chance to have one's own wishes taken into account. A manager would certainly know that the norm was to stay in a certain position for so many years and would thus be able to predict when he would be moved; and he might have some idea of where he might go. But he would have no direct role in this decision.

This interpretation is consistent with one of Lincoln and Kalleberg's (1985: 754) observations. In their discussion of the celebrated *ringi* system of decision-making, in which a junior manager drafts an initial proposal and other managers then amend and eventually endorse it, they point out that there is apparently a high level of delegation of authority. Yet, in fact, although this system integrates managers into the company, it offers little real decentralization of decision-making authority. In like manner, although our managers were fully integrated, they had little real choice in the development of their own careers.

Of course, being able to identify the presence of a system of career planning does not mean that managers are necessarily satisfied with it. So, in a further question, those managers who had said that there was a system were asked how well it worked (Table 4.5). Given that many were unable to identify a system, the numbers were small, but the pattern was indicative. The responses from our four Japanese companies were very similar: there may have been little career planning in the sense that our managers defined it, but they were reasonably satisfied with the results. Indeed, the tendency for the Japanese to report higher levels of satisfaction was statistically significant in Sumitomo and NTT.

In the British companies there was again wide variation. Managers in NatWest were most favourable followed by those in Tesco. In Lucas and British Telecom, however, most managers denied the presence of a system or felt that the system worked badly. For example, all six of the Sumitomo managers replying said that the system worked well or quite well; by contrast, no fewer than 13 of the 17 Lucas managers who responded said that their company's system worked poorly or unsatisfactorily.

As a follow-up question, bearing in mind the emphasis which a number of recent commentators have put on changes in the managerial labour market, our managers were asked about trends in horizontal job moves and promotion. Overall, it will be seen from Table 4.6, the pattern is fairly clear. More managers reported an increase in horizontal job moves than a reduction or stability; over half the managers in six of the eight companies reported an increase in horizontal job moves. Similarly, more of our managers reported a reduction in promotion opportunities than an increase or stability; over half the managers in six of the eight companies reported a reduction in career opportunities. Significantly, however, in both cases our

Table 4.6 *Perceived trends in horizontal job movement and promotion* (%)

	Lucas	Sumitomo	NatWest	Mitsui	Tesco	Jusco	BT	NTT	All
Horizontal job moves									
Increase	37	57	75	58	54	48	53	57	56
Same	50	37	20	42	33	30	31	29	33
Decrease	13	7	5	0	13	22	16	14	11
Net change[1]	+24	+50	+70	+58	+41	+26	+37	+43	+45
Promotion opportunities									
Increase	26	3	12	20	20	18	21	28	18
Same	52	43	20	36	24	26	30	36	33
Decrease	23	53	68	44	56	56	49	36	49
Net change[1]	+3	-50	-56	-24	-36	-38	-28	-8	-31

[1] 'Net change' is the percentage reporting increase minus the percentage reporting decrease.

companies were equally divided; more than half the managers in two companies in each country reported a reduction in promotion opportunities.

Putting together the results of Tables 4.5 and 4.6, suggests that the degree of satisfaction with the arrangements for career planning does not seem to depend on views on the availability of upwards as opposed to sideways moves. Two sectors stand out. The first one is the engineering sector: fewer managers reported an increase in horizontal job moves and a reduction in promotion in Lucas than in Sumitomo. The second is banking: more managers reported an increase in horizontal job moves and a reduction in promotion opportunities in NatWest than in Mitsui. In Lucas, it will be remembered, there was considerable dissatisfaction and in NatWest considerable satisfaction with the arrangements for career planning. In short, in the light of the growth in the range of products sold by the banks there were more different types of jobs open to NatWest managers, and they welcomed this, even though upward promotion was limited. In Lucas, by contrast, dissatisfaction with career planning stemmed from the organizational dislocations explained in Chapter 3.

Looking to our detailed interview data, the major expressions of dissatisfaction among the Japanese were to be found in the bank. As already indicated, the retirement age had recently been increased from 55 to 60. Three of the companies – Jusco being the exception – had a particular problem in that they had a considerable surplus of managers at the older level which reflected recruitment at the time of the so-called 'bulge' generation in the late 1960s. In each case managers relinquished their posts at 55 (unless they were board members). In Mitsui, salary reductions of some 40 per cent occurred for those over 55 years. There was however some encouragement for as many as possible to think in terms of a second career – perhaps in one of the bank's corporate clients. In Sumitomo, managers over 55 experienced a 30 per cent cut in salary. Here, however, they had an opportunity to remain on the payroll until aged 65 at half pay. In NTT the older managers were even guaranteed two years' employment in a subsidiary. Only in Jusco was there no automatic salary reduction: salary in this company was dependent on performance.

NatWest and Tesco, it will be remembered, had the highest numbers of managers reporting the existence of career paths and a system of career planning. Interestingly, in both cases, there was dissatisfaction among some of the younger managers who expressed concerns about the traditional practice of promoting good people out of the branches and stores into head office; in their view the system was going to have to be changed in order to keep good people in the 'front line' where the money was being earned. Overall, however, most managers, especially the older ones, were reasonably satisfied.

In Lucas and British Telecom, by contrast, the situation was very different. In both cases the companies had experienced considerable changes in recent years. Lucas, it was generally recognized, had gone too far down the financial control route in the first half of the 1980s with the result that many of the headquarters functions, including management development, had been disbanded or downgraded in importance. Many managers recognized the recent initiatives that had been taken to promote management development. So far, however, most believed that it had not gone beyond the organization of courses; the older ones especially looked back to what they believed to be a 'golden age' when the situation had not been so very different from that in NatWest. In British Telecom the situation was fairly similar. British Telecom had experienced first, under public ownership, an intensification of commercial pressure, and second, following privatization, major reorganization which, as in Lucas, resulted in considerable decentralization. Rightly or wrongly, many of our managers thought that the major changes associated with privatization, and before that with 'commercialization' under public ownership, had disrupted traditional career paths and promotion expectations.

Conclusions

Our findings confirm some aspects of the traditional stereotypes and qualify others. Thus, our Japanese companies recruited the great bulk of their managers from a graduate population which were taken on direct from university. By contrast, relatively few of our British managers were graduates and the pattern of their backgrounds was much more varied than their Japanese counterparts. Especially pronounced were the different arrangements for career development. In Japan there were very formal arrangements for the planning of the careers of individual managers such that very few of our Japanese sample arrived in their management posts before the age of 30; there was steady progression though a number of well-established positions and very formal arrangements for job rotation which crossed divisional boundaries. In Britain the arrangements were much more haphazard. In most cases managers applied for jobs as and when they arose; the result is that there was little pattern to the age at which managers took up positions. There was also less mobility between divisions than in Japan. Indeed, divisional boundaries were as important as functional boundaries.

   In some respects, however, it is necessary to qualify the traditional stereotypes. Our Japanese managers did not have experience of a wider range of functions than their British counterparts. Any experience of the business they achieved came mainly from working in a number of different divisions and different aspects of the same function. Also, although there was career planning, it emerges that these managers did not feel involved in this planning; in other words, it was the organization that 'owned' their career. As for our British companies, the internal labour market seems to have been stronger than most previous studies had suggested. Most managers in the sample had spent their careers with the same company and their length of service was roughly the same as that of their Japanese counterparts.

It must not be forgotten either that there were very significant differences in the experiences of 'management development' in these companies. There is certainly no one single pattern. Most of NatWest's managers, for example, started in the organization at 16 or 18 and worked their way fairly slowly in almost 'Japanese' fashion before achieving their first managerial appointment in their late 20s or early 30s. Tesco and British Telecom had also recruited their potential managers early. In Tesco and British Telecom they also got their first managerial appointment much earlier. In Lucas, by contrast, the majority of managers were graduates (indeed, Lucas had the largest number of managers with postgraduate qualifications) and for most the first managerial-level appointment came at a rather later age. In short, significant choices were being made.

In Japan too there were differences. In Jusco the system of promotion was much speedier than in the other companies and meritocratic factors were brought into play at a much earlier stage. Sumitomo Electric and Mitsui Bank had preserved the most stable systems, whereas NTT was scrutinizing its traditional career planning systems as it began some fundamental restructuring following privatization.

To return explicitly to the themes we raised earlier. While assumptions about careers were being reassessed in some of the eight companies, there was also sufficient evidence to suggest that the idea was by no means as dead as some popular commentators have asserted. Moreover, the concept of a lasting link with one firm also remained a core belief. Japanese companies had qualified the meaning of the lifetime model by imposing conditions on post-55 employment, but they were showing few signs of abandoning the model completely. In the UK, 'downsizing' had represented a clear challenge to the cosy assumptions of lifelong security and career growth in exchange for loyalty. But even here there were few signs of any clear alternative model. Optimists have posited the idea of 'employability' and the 'passport' for movement between jobs offered by the building of a portfolio of skills. Another way of looking at this is to use Dore's framework: the recent movements in the British cases could be seen simply as a further emphasis upon the 'market-oriented' tendencies already inherent in the British context. In any event, the optimists' scenario is very dependent upon the skill formation processes which managers can enjoy. We turn the focus on to these in the next two chapters and we also return to the wider theme of the future, or lack of future, for the idea of organizational careers in the final chapter.

5

Training and Education

In the preceding chapters we have examined the recruitment and selection of managers, their career paths and the systems of career planning which they experience. It has been shown that, although there are some differences which are explicable by national-level characteristics, other features are more clearly traceable to sectoral and organizational variables. In the light of these findings it is interesting to anticipate what patterns of comparison and contrast we might expect to uncover when we turn to examine the provision of managerial training, education and development in the sample of companies. Previous comparative literature has suggested that British managers have been located very close to the bottom of international league tables when measures in these areas have been taken, while Japan comes towards the top (Constable and McCormick, 1987; Handy et al., 1988). We might expect therefore that the Japanese managers would report rather more personal experience of training and development than their British counterparts.

One limitation of previous work is its focus on national averages, with little sensitivity to sectoral variations. It would therefore be very difficult to predict which of the companies within these two countries would, on sectoral grounds, offer the greatest training provision. What was already previously well known was that, in the main, larger companies provide more training than smaller ones (Mangham and Silver, 1986). As all of our case organizations were large, this indicator was of little help. Similarly, beyond the general issue of the amount of training (whether measured by the level of expenditure or the number of training days) there was little guidance in the literature as to the preferred modes of development between sectors or companies. For example, could one expect more reliance on on-the-job training and mentoring in a public utility than in a private sector engineering company? How do banks contrast with supermarkets in their management training practices?

If the comparative literature is of little help, perhaps the generic material on management development offers some clues. A previous comprehensive review of the management development literature (Storey, 1989; 1990) had shown that it could be grouped into four main categories: definitions of the nature and functions of management development, that is, conceptualizations of the processes and interpretations of its various purposes; descriptions, and even more so prescriptions, of what should be done in course provision and the like; studies of the nature of management and managers and the implications for development; and finally management development in relation to the changing organizational, economic and international contexts. We updated this review from 1989 to 1994. This indicated that the vast majority of books and articles continued to concentrate on practices and prescriptions. The analysis of 'competencies', which had been identified as an emerging major issue in the 1989 review, continued to be represented as a major theme. Mentoring also continued on an upward trajectory – at least as a subject for discussion – and so did the issue of cross-cultural management development and the whole theme of 'international management development'.

Much of the recent literature makes generalized and often thinly substantiated assertions about the changing business environment and the claimed implications for management development. Thus, we are told that in the 1990s the challenge is for continued investment in management training and closer involvement between business schools and corporations (Heisler and Bentham, 1992). Further, it is claimed that fundamental changes in the business environment have ushered in a 'new era' and an accompanying 'new paradigm' for management development which focuses on 'anticipatory learning' in place of traditional 'maintenance learning'. By helping to design management education and training programmes that translate policies into 'effective learning and action', we are told, management development specialists 'will be indispensable participants in the struggle to compete against new global players' (Fulmer and Graham, 1993). Much of this literature seems to rely more on wishful thinking than upon sound research. 'Challenges' for the coming decade have been enumerated. These often read like projected lists from a familiar and well-worn agenda – 'teamwork', 'globalization', 'technology and information systems', 'leadership' (Fulmer, 1992). Likewise, the attributes of management leadership for the new millennium are said to be 'vision, integrity, trust, commitment, risk taking, visibility' and the like (Capowski, 1994).

There is clearly a need to go beyond such star-gazing. But to what sources can one turn? It is possible to find reports of empirical surveys but almost invariably these are the products of mailed questionnaires directed at human resources directors and management development specialists. For example, Vicere et al. (1994) report a survey of managers responsible for executive development in a sample of American *Fortune 500* companies. This produced the finding, not surprising given the methodology, that management development was being accorded 'an increasing emphasis' compared with 10 years previously. The sole reliance on data from management development 'champions' we find highly problematical (see also Royal Society of Arts, 1994).

Another popular theme in the existing literature is the role of women. Factors impeding or advancing women's development and access to training have been much researched (Burke and McKeen, 1994; Ohlott et al., 1994; Ragins and Scandura, 1994; Tharenou et al., 1994). Training has been found to benefit men more than women (Tharenou et al., 1994). Mentors and sponsors were helpful to women but were generally less available to them (Burke and McKeen, 1994). From a different direction, Ragins and Scandura (1994) examined men and women who acted as mentors. Women reported outcomes and future intentions which were very similar to those of the men. It has been suggested that one reason why so few women have been promoted to senior management positions is that they receive fewer developmental job opportunities. Ohlott et al. (1994) tested this idea by surveying male and female managers about their developmental opportunities. They suggest that men receive more task-related developmental challenges. Our own sample of managers in eight organizations reflected the gender bias of the management population in these companies and we were not able to shed systematic new light on the causal influences.

By far the largest amount of recent management development literature relates to prescriptions about how it might be accomplished more effectively. Outdoor training is evaluated and recommendations are made (Irvine and Wilson, 1994). Fast-track programmes designed to accelerate the development of individuals identified as having executive-level potential have been reviewed and advice for improvement has been given (Field and Harris, 1991). Action learning is an old favourite and continues to attract supporters (Henderson, 1993). The relative merits of assessed and certificate-granting courses compared with non-assessed training have also been weighed (Simpson et al., 1994). Going one step further, accreditation of prior learning (APL), although much championed by the Management Charter Initiative, has been found to be little practised (Preston and Smith, 1993). Mentoring has attracted considerable attention and enthusiastic support (Akande, 1993; Antal, 1993; Hamilton, 1993). There is plenty of advice available on how mentoring schemes might be improved but the guidance, it has to be said, is fairly self-evident, such as ensuring better clarification of purposes, recognition of the multi-faceted nature of the relationship and so on (Gibb and Megginson, 1993).

Research by occupational psychologists in the area of training and development has focused mainly on the significance and implications of individual differences for the management training process (Drath, 1990; McClure and Werther, 1993). The present study is not concerned with differences between individuals, so that this literature, too, offered us little guidance.

Recent work on management 'competencies' has ranged from how to make competency assessments more strategically relevant to the organization (Tovey, 1993); through advice on competency-based action learning (Smith, 1993); to a reframing and widening of the scope of meaning associated with competencies which takes the concept beyond the MCI's usage (Brown, 1993; Holmes and Joyce, 1993; Zimmerman, 1993). Iles (1993), for example, widens the concept beyond the individual job to embrace the career stream and the wider organizational context. Most of all, the management development literature is replete with reports of allegedly successful new programmes in single companies (see, for example,

Downham et al., 1992; Mole et al., 1993; Smith, 1992). Invariably, these near-anecdotal accounts repeat the usual litany of prerequisites such as the need for top management support and alignment with business needs. Far less common is any genuine objective analysis of content and process or longer-term evaluative review. In the light of this literature, we had little guidance on the key analytical issues of how and why training provision varies in both extent and form. Nor was there much help from the prescriptive literature as to the conditions which promote or retard training activity: the common presumption is that training is simply a good thing. What could be found in this literature was the general assumption that there was more systematic training in Japan and that there was an increasing emphasis on 'competencies' in the UK. We assess these points and also explore the varied meanings of management development in the companies in our sample.

Our first task therefore was to compare the kind of training provision offered by our sample of companies and to record the various reactions to it from our sample of managers. The poor training record of British companies is legendary. In general therefore one would expect to find a marked (adverse) contrast between the British and the Japanese companies. In fact we found that in some respects our British sample reported more training than did their Japanese counterparts. They also reported higher levels of satisfaction with the training that they had received. This led us to consider the different meanings given to the term 'training'. We argue that Japanese managers carried out many learning activities, often in their 'own' time, but that they did not necessarily single these out as discrete training activity. As for attitudes, the British 'lead' may have reflected relatively low expectations, with almost any serious attention to training being valued highly, while the Japanese were more likely to take a significant amount of training and development for granted.

We look first at the overall contrasts between firms in the pattern of training. We then consider each firm in turn, developing a more detailed portrait of training provision and its links with wider aspects of managerial careers and organizational context. This detailed picture provides the evidence for the argument that training was indeed deeply embedded in the Japanese firms. We think it useful to provide chapter and verse on this point. Where relevant, we include commentary from managers themselves but do not repeat more general evaluations of careers and development experiences, which can be found in other chapters.

Extent and Nature of Training

Experience of Training

We asked each individual about their own personal experience of seven different forms of training and development. The list was as follows: (1) in-house training by internal trainers, (2) in-house training by external

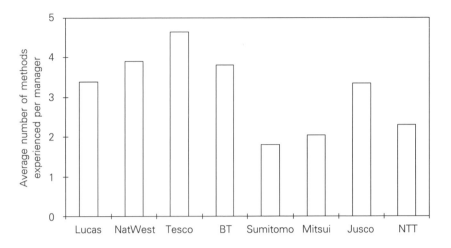

Figure 5.1   *Experience of training*

trainers, (3) off-site training by internal trainers, (4) off-site training led by external trainers, (5) on-the-job training, (6) mentoring/coaching, (7) special job placement (see Question 38, Appendix B). We also asked whether, irrespective of their own experience of these techniques, they were aware of the use of these methods for other managers. We begin here by focusing on the results relating to reported personal experience.

The first measure we took was the simple mean number of training activities experienced. Making comparisons across companies and countries, the results emerging from this measure were a source of surprise. As Figure 5.1 shows, in each of the four pairings the British managers claimed to have personally been exposed to a greater range of training experiences than did their Japanese counterparts.

Thus, for example, the Lucas managers said they had, on average, personally experienced some 3.4 of the range of training methods whereas their counterparts in Sumitomo reported only 1.8. As the figure also reveals, the two retailers were the most active trainers in their respective countries according to this measure.

There could be the possibility that the British 'lead' across the companies as a whole was distorted by a preponderance of replies on just a few categories of training. Hence, we ran through the data to check this; but this revealed that the tendency for the British managers to have personally experienced a particular training device held up on each of the seven listed types quite separately. Most surprising of all was that the difference was sustained even with respect to the supposed forte of the Japanese: on-the-job training.

In broad terms, OJT is an integral part of organizational life in Japan. As a systematic, conscious process OJT is usually regarded as well established in most of the large companies though it is mainly targeted at people in the early phases of their careers. To a large extent, everyone could expect to receive it as part of their development. Most of the larger companies regard OJT of younger employees as one of the main methods of in-company education, training and development. With regard to the 'informal' variant of OJT in Japan this is naturally less easy to identify. Japanese organizational members tend to observe that the practice of watching and learning from their bosses' behaviour is common. It is often said in Japan that subordinates grow into managers by 'watching their superiors' backs'. The open-plan office arrangements, where, up to *bucho* level, managers are exposed to their subordinates, allows plenty of scope for this sort of informal learning.

At the managerial levels above *bucho*, OJT takes place also, though rather less formally than is the case for junior staff. Superordinates are practised in assigning certain tasks to their subordinate managers where part of the objective is to allow for learning and development. The opportunity to talk through problems associated with assignments is more readily afforded than is perhaps the case in Britain.

Nonetheless, despite the embeddedness of OJT in large Japanese corporations, its use was found not to be universal in our study. The most notable and remarkable exception was uncovered in the case of NTT. Here, in just the sort of setting where one might have reasonably expected OJT to have been flourishing over the years, the senior training manager reported to us that OJT was only now being placed on his list of priorities for future action. In fact, this manager had just drafted a paper outlining the benefits of OJT and a series of recommendations about how to implement it within NTT. As we will see, this concern reflected a substantial shift in training provision following privatization. The more general interest of the case lies in its illustration that Japanese training systems are not immune to the pressures of a changing environment, a point to which we return in the conclusion to the chapter.

Subjective Evaluation of Training Provision

Managers were asked to say whether each activity that they had personally experienced had been valuable. Respondents were given three categories of evaluation: 'very valuable', 'fairly valuable' and 'not valuable'. We aggregated the replies so as to form an 'index of satisfaction' with training. We scored 'not valuable' as 0, 'fairly valuable' as 1 and 'very valuable' as 2. We then divided the total score by the number of forms of training on which each manager commented. The overall mean of 1.34 showed that managers generally tended to the more favourable evaluations. To allow for possible biases in that, say, British managers may have commented on different types of training from those experienced by the Japanese, we looked at scores for each type separately. The results were similar to those for the overall measure, which incidentally adds weight to the assumption that we can indeed add the scores. The outcome was surprising. As Figure 5.2

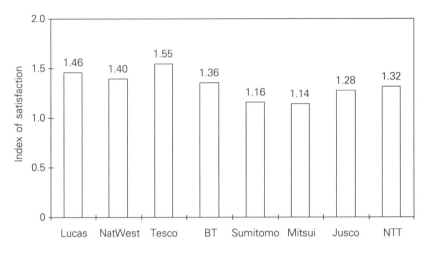

Figure 5.2 *Perceived value of the training received*

shows, the British managers uniformly rated their training as more valuable than did their Japanese pairings.

A test (using analysis of variance) found that there were no sector-based patterns on this measure but that there was a clear difference between countries. As the figure shows, all the British samples returned higher scores than the Japanese ones. The most satisfied group of managers out of the total of eight companies were those employed by Tesco. Lowest levels of satisfaction were recorded in Sumitomo and Mitsui. Particularly notable were the results concerning on-the-job training. Here the differences were especially pronounced, with managers in Lucas and Tesco being especially favourably disposed to the technique, and managers in Sumitomo and Jusco being very lukewarm. At Lucas, 9 out of the 12 managers commenting on OJT said that it had been very valuable; at Tesco, the figure was 15 out of 17. Corresponding figures for Sumitomo and Jusco were 9 out of 20 and 9 out of 24. Statistical differences between the two firms in each sector were clearly significant.

The perceptual aspects of these unexpected differences are perhaps easier to explain than are the reported levels of activity. It may be that the Japanese score OJT lower precisely because they take it rather more for granted. In contrast, in Britain, OJT is still seen as something of a novelty and it even has a certain exotic mystique. Hence, the British were more inclined to enthuse about it even if its appearances are as yet fairly small-scale. Lucas Industries offers the clearest example of this. Following the virtual abandonment of managerial attention to training in the early 1980s, it once again rose through the agenda from the middle of the decade onwards. In the face of this, our sample responded very favourably.

Of course there is also the possibility once again of the culture factor playing a part. It may be that the Japanese tend to be fundamentally more self-critical and are thus less likely to report that training had been very valuable to them.

But if the Japanese simply take OJT for granted, why did they not report its presence more often? One possibility is that because OJT is so embedded as part of everyday life the Japanese respondents may perhaps have had more difficulty in isolating and identifying specific occasions when it had been seen as manifest. In contrast, British managers may have lower thresholds of awareness concerning what can be seen to constitute a training event or experience. Whatever the true explanation for this surprising result, the collateral information that we collected in Japan did suggest that systematic training and development were widely practised. In the light of this, it would appear that the *post hoc* explanation that we mount above concerning perceptual thresholds provides, for now, the best account of these findings. It hardly needs emphasizing that we see further investigation of this point as deserving priority attention in future research.

Amount of Time Devoted to Training

We asked all respondents about the total number of training days that they had experienced over the previous two years. This was computed as an annual average. Again, to our surprise, higher figures were reported in Britain compared with Japan across three out of the four sectors (engineering, banking and telecommunications). The only exception was retailing, where the Japanese reported very high figures. But, this Jusco sample was the least reliable of the eight company samples because it had been drawn from managers going through a training programme. At the other end of the scale we uncovered the remarkable result that 61 per cent of Sumitomo managers claimed to have spent less than one day per annum on formal training programmes. The full results are shown in Table 5.1.

The Japanese scores once again ran counter to all expectations. Apart from the case of the Sumitomo managers, we found 50 per cent of Mitsui managers and 36 per cent of NTT managers reporting that they had spent an average of less than one day per year in formal training during the past two years. It has to be remembered that these are large leading Japanese corporations. Indeed, Sumitomo itself is renowned in Japan as a 'training company'. Yet our data show that only 8 per cent of its managers reported having spent six or more days per annum in training: this contrasted starkly with the 59 per cent of Lucas managers reporting such a level of training.

It is possible that replies to certain apparently basic questions cannot be taken at face value. This takes us back to the culture-contrast argument discussed in the introductory chapter. In this context it is worth noting that we had all the questions checked with experts in Japan before conducting the study. Faced with these surprising results we have been able to construct an *ex post* explanation: training may simply be seen as less of a discrete, identifiable activity in Japan than has previously been thought. There is a

Managers in the Making

Table 5.1 *Average number of training days per annum* (%)

Number of training days	Lucas	NatWest	Tesco	BT	Sumitomo	Mitsui	Jusco	NTT	Overall average
Less than 1	13	20	7	0	61	50	0	36	22
1–5	28	37	23	48	32	33	4	52	32
6–10	50	32	50	33	4	4	15	8	26
11–15	6	7	15	9	0	8	31	0	10
16 and more	3	5	4	9	4	4	50	4	10

further possibility. 'Management training' in Britain and Japan may follow very different patterns. Not only may development operate in a far more subtle manner in Japan, it also seems to be the case that formal training is concentrated during the early years. Thus 'managers' and indeed all capable persons are trained and developed in accord with a systematic pattern with the formal training being front-loaded. In Britain, 'management training' is something 'bolted on' at a later stage for a certain select coterie. It is often designed to be applied at the critical transfer stage from one grade level to another. But in practice, British managers are expected to 'catch up' with key courses which, owing to other pressures, they had missed at the actual time of promotion or pre-promotion. Hence, in drip-feed fashion, management training in Britain was frequently seen as a matter of 'going on courses', and four to six days per annum – that is, one or two courses – was seen as broadly the norm and the appropriate amount.

There was also a further factor at play which would help to explain why British managers reported more training days over the immediately preceding two-year period. The period of fieldwork, 1988–90, coincided in Britain with the launch of major corporate programmes relating to 'total quality management' (TQM), 'culture change', 'customer service' and 'performance excellence'. In manufacturing, in addition to the above, new production planning systems were introduced, most notably manufacturing requirements planning (MRP) and MRP II. All of these 'programmes' were typically launched with a major effort to raise 'managerial awareness' in respect of these initiatives. In British Telecom, for example, there had been massive investment in TQM and so it was hardly surprising that not a single manager in our sample had escaped the accompanying managerial training programme.

Running alongside these special programmes, the late 1980s was also a period of high awareness of the issue of management training and development in Britain. The Management Charter Initiative, to mention just one major development, had put the theme high on the public agenda. In other words, the fact that the timing of our survey coincided with a major upswing in attention to (and probably provision of) management training and development in Britain may go some way to account for the discrepancy – favourable to Britain – in results between the two countries in this survey.

Another possible reason for the finding about the relatively little time spent by Japanese middle managers as measured by 'training days' could conceivably be traced to the way the question was put and understood. In the Japanese translation of the questionnaire (Appendix B), question 54 asked about the number of days spent in 'off-the-job training'. Our Japanese advisers suggested to us that this would probably be interpreted as attendance at any kind of course arranged by the company or attendance at courses at the instigation of their company. Our information gleaned during the interviews was that, as indicated above, these were by no means annual events for most well-established managers.

Relatively junior managers would attend pre-appointment courses, and *kachos* would often attend a course to see how they were measuring up. But by the time they reach *bucho* it becomes much rarer for them to attend company-organized courses.

The difference in wording between the two versions of the questionnaire is probably not so critical, however, for it seems likely that the British sample too would interpret 'training days' to denote off-the-job training. In other words, although the phrase about off-JT was not explicitly inserted in the British questionnaire it would almost certainly be understood to be implicit in the construction of the question.

The variation in the pattern of the findings serves rather to point up a key feature of Japanese training and development – namely that for established managers 'self-development' is regarded as far more important than 'training' *per se*. Self-development in Japan takes various forms. Most often it takes place outside the firm. The Japanese questionnaire contained two questions which asked about the kinds of things these managers did in the way of self-development and the number of days which they spent on it. It was revealed that most of the sample were undertaking a range of activities on their own initiative.

The phenomenal increase in the number of private specialist organizations and associations catering for external 'open seminars' and for 'discussion/study meetings' is testimony to the demand for this service and to the level of activity. Much of this growth has taken place in the past three years or so. It needs to be emphasized that the Japanese managers would not count this form of development in their 'training days'. Hence, much Japanese management training and development is 'hidden'. Moreover, formal training programmes are typically not seen as the main route to 'development' for Japanese managers.

We have raised the possibility that Japanese training was relatively focused on self-developmental aspects and that it tended to be concentrated in the early parts of a manager's career. In order to gain a closer understanding of training activity in organizational context, we now examine the details in each case study company. This account has two main purposes. First, how does the celebrated Japanese system actually work at the day-to-day level? It is useful to describe developments in some detail. Second, what analytical themes emerge? We identify the key themes at the head of each section.

The Retail Sector

We begin with Jusco, which is perhaps the most developed case of a 'training company', to illustrate the theme of a strong commitment to training. The case also shows how links between training, manpower planning and business strategy are developed. The comparison with Tesco suggests that a training culture can emerge in Britain in the appropriate conditions.

Jusco

Structures of Training   The case of Jusco, the Japanese multi-store, well illustrates the central place which education and training often enjoy in the Japanese corporate context. The company motto is, 'Education is the most valuable welfare benefit which the company can offer to its employees.' This has been embedded in the company's values for all of its three decades. During the 1970s, when expansion was relatively easy, a focus on human resource development required considerable foresight. Today when competitive conditions are tighter it is considered that the prior investment in the human resource has given the company a crucial competitive advantage. Jusco is known as 'the educating company' in the sector.

The management education and training provision in Jusco is institutionalized, well structured, and extensive to the point of being near comprehensive. Table 5.2 illustrates the scale and nature of this provision at the time of our study.

As can be seen from this table, the Jusco system encompassed on-the-job training (OJT), off-the-job training (off-JT) and more general education. The scheme covered capability development for all categories of staff (nonmanagerial as well as managerial) but the provision for management training was particularly extensive.

Education and training in Jusco is intertwined closely with the system of qualification grading, promotion and reward. Jusco was distinctive among the Japanese companies in our sample in placing such emphasis upon promotion based on merit rather than seniority. The qualification system is shown in the left-hand column of Table 5.2. Progress through these grades occurs through examinations, interviews and performance evaluation. Appointments to particular jobs are a secondary issue because one first needs to reach a certain level on the qualification system. Attaining a qualification grade by passing an examination is a necessary though not sufficient condition for appointment to a particular post. Generally speaking, however, remuneration reflects grade rather than the given post.

An illustration will help to clarify the link between these systems. At the pre-management grade of *shuji* (see level 5 in the left column of Table 5.2) one applies for a candidacy examination which is in two parts. Part one comprises questions based on half a dozen set books, while part two poses questions designed to elicit understanding of the company's own policies, practices and range of activities. If successful at this examination and at a subsequent interview the candidate is placed on a 'candidacy' list for the next grade during which time he/she has to submit an essay once a month. In addition a further panel interview has to be negotiated. Following success the person is made a *fuku-sanji* and given a course of post-upgrading education (see second column of Table 5.2).

Further upgrading to *sanji* is dependent upon a personal recommendation from the divisional *bucho*, and the satisfactory completion of a personality test – the Minnesota Multiple Personality Inventory. Managers of

Table 5.2　*Jusco training system overview*

Qualification grades (1 = high; 10 = low)	Education for upgrading	OJT	In-company courses	Off-JT		
				External courses	Jusco specialist education	Manager courses
1	Post-appointment course	All grades: Job-related manuals Coaching Observing manager	Store managers' courses	All grades: In-Japan courses Overseas courses, mainly USA	All grades: Jusco University and Jusco Postgraduate School	Management grades: Overseas courses Seminars
2 (Management)	Pre-appointment course		*Bucho* and *kacho*			
3 (Management)	Post-appointment course		Merchandising / Finance and accounts			
4	Pre-appointment course		Work design			
5	Upgrading course of study					
6	Upgrading course of study		Sales training / Problem-solving courses			
7	Upgrade course		English language			
8	Post-upgrade course / Follow-up course					
9	New recruit orientation					
10	Entry					

large superstores and heads of central departments are drawn from the *sanji* grade. Again pre-appointment and post-appointment education and training are a routine part of the process.

As the third column indicates, quite apart from the qualification development system and grades there is also provision for level-related OJT. The most important component here is a 'sales expert system'. Through OJT and self-study, employees are trained and educated to be fully conversant with matters relating to the merchandise, dealing with customers, merchandise presentation, stock control, ordering and sales management. For each of these a comprehensive set of manuals has to be absorbed; progress is monitored on a monthly basis and the results are recorded. Success in practical activity and OJT is a prerequisite for entry to the sales management examination.

The success of the employee is seen as a reflection on the competence of the superior in the task of developing his subordinates (a key responsibility for any *kacho*). The latest information that we could collect showed that, at the end of 1989, some 98 per cent of graduate entrants acquired the category 6 sales expert qualification and 70 per cent succeeded also at category 5. The sales expert system, it is worth noting, offers a route into senior positions for the non-managerial intake – that is those recruited locally. This system of development had been successful in motivating female employees recruited locally. At the time of our study some 50 per cent of category 5 sales experts were women. The importance of the Jusco sales expert system is that it is a well-established and well-planned OJT method through which the majority of Jusco employees are systematically trained. The curriculum is regarded as of a high standard and arranged progressively. The Ministry of Labour designated it an officially recognized in-company examination in 1985, thus giving it a respected status; it was the first such designation in the retail and distribution sector.

There is another key training feature worth attention in Jusco: the 'Jusco University'. This is a three-tier programme of study organized by the capability development department at the central office in Tokyo. It is, in effect, an institution which is designed to develop specialists for middle management levels, though the 'graduates' are not confined to the particular specialist area they may have studied. For some functional areas, such as personnel, the Jusco University's educational qualification is a precondition. Jusco University has been in operation since 1969. Twenty years later, in 1989, the entry qualification of a university degree was removed. Also at this time successful graduates were guaranteed an appropriate posting within two years of qualifying. It is here that the close interconnection between the company's training system and its manpower planning system can be clearly seen.

All of this is supplemented by a so-called 'Jusco Postgraduate School' which is open to those who have reached the rather senior level of the *fukusanji* grade. It is designed to groom future top management. Entry is by recommendation and interview. Graduation is by course work, dissertation and a final viva voce. The course is of two years' duration and comprises a mix of distance learning and seminars. To illustrate the significance of this course it is worth looking at the composition of the members attending it while we were conducting our study in 1990 and at the type of project work in which they were involved. There were two *fuku-san'yo* and 17 *sanji* who were presidents of subsidiary companies, managers of very large stores, or *buchos* at head office. The remaining 18 were of *kacho* grade and were managers of medium-sized stores. Often the *bucho* level is where ideas for new business originate, and by putting them through this kind of course the originators of such ideas were sometimes being prepared for appointment to run subsidiaries to bring these ideas to fruition. Here we witness the close link between education in Jusco and its business strategy. The Aeon Group as a whole is keen to use this new business start-up route as a means to diversify the company.

Off-the-Job Training and Self-Development   In addition to the above patterns of highly systematic long-term training provision, there are shorter injections of off-the-job training available in the company. For example, at the time of our study all newly appointed *kachos* and *buchos* underwent a short introductory training course of approximately three days. Similarly, all mid-career recruits (264 in 1989) were placed on an off-JT programme with the accent on orientation into the company. Then there are the overseas seminars of some 10 to 12 days' duration, which are held mainly in the United States. About 100 managers a year attend these. In 1989 a special one-off event was held which involved 500 managers being sent on a tour of US stores. In addition, younger managers with potential are eligible for attendance at prestigious postgraduate schools in America. These courses include the 13-week Advanced Management Program at Harvard Business School and various one- to two-year MBA programmes. The main off-JT management courses are shown in Table 5.3.

At home in Japan, the company sponsors some 22 manager education courses at both private training/consultancy centres and universities. The courses range from business strategy seminars to courses on 'store opening strategies', merchandising, and 'top executive development'.

In addition the company encourages self-development through various support mechanisms. It promotes the idea that up to 10 per cent of each person's individual salary should be used to fund self-improvement. It also provides a large number of correspondence courses (121 were available at the time we were there). Significantly, those who have completed courses with good results have their names recorded by 'personnel deployment' and this information is used in manpower planning and appointments. The 'basic management' course has a three-month duration and its contents cover the range of management techniques; there is even a course on 'strategic OJT'.

The close link between business strategy and the company's training and development provision is perhaps nowhere better demonstrated than in the

Table 5.3 *Jusco overseas off-JT courses for managers*

Course name and target	Duration	No. of participants	Location
Pegasus American seminar, basic course: (a) Merchandising planning, headquarters (b) Senior merchandising managers in area, business divisions and subsidiaries	10 days in April	15	West Coast USA
Pegasus American seminar, advanced studies: Top merchandising and sales directors	12 days in April and 12 days in September	5–10	Tour all USA
Santa Clara University fashion marketing seminar: (a) Merchandising headquarters staff (b) Senior managers in area, business division and subsidiaries	11 days in October	15	West Coast USA and New York
University of Southern California food marketing seminar: (a) Middle managers in area, business divisions and subsidiaries (b) Store managers and food sales *kachos*	10 days in April	15	Los Angeles
US West Coast tour of stores, Tsukiyama seminar: (a) Regional business division *buchos* (b) Top directors, subsidiaries	10 days in November	15	West Coast USA

realm of internationalization. Jusco is rapidly expanding into South East Asia and the US. In support of this the company is taking active measures to develop its human resources to allow this plan to come to fruition. For example, there are international business courses at the Jusco University; all students on all courses are tested in English conversation; and secondments to overseas stores are fully established.

Evaluation Overall, the most impressive features of training and development in Jusco are the scale of provision, its internal integration, the integration with personnel policy (especially in relation to manpower planning and deployment), and the articulation with business policy. Jusco is relatively distinct from the other Japanese companies in that its system is rather more merit-based than seniority-based. The qualification system allows specialists to rise through the organization without being appointed to managerial posts. The case represents a radical modification of the classic Japanese personnel model rather than a total break from it. This seems largely due to the special circumstances of the retail environment in which the company operates, with very rapid change and expansion being the norm. In these conditions early and rapid identification and development of talent have been essential. The habit of learning has now seemingly become embedded in the organization. At the same time the pace of change and flux is illustrated by the point that some respondents revealed that about half of those colleagues who had joined with them had now left the company. Another important feature is the way the central capability department is changing its key focus of attention from primarily addressing the needs of store management to wider generic management capabilities, as the nature of the Aeon Group changes with expansion into a wide range of sectors (for discussion of Jusco's place in the Aeon Group see Chapter 3).

Tesco

In some ways, the picture at Tesco was comparable. There was an over-whelming view among the Tesco line managers that the company training provision was very good. They reported that they were able to access the training they needed both for themselves and their staff. Invariably, they said that when they put people's names down for a course then they did gain a place on that course. If there was a hesitation about unqualified endorsement of the whole system it arose from an anxiety that the insularity of in-company courses limited exposure to fresh ideas. Relatedly, there was some doubt about how much one could learn from one's colleagues who were not specialists in one's own field.

Indicative of the way training provision can fluctuate was the case of the Computer Services Division at Tesco. Prior to the improvement in central training this division was running effective training of its own, part of this in conjunction with the Henley Management College. Since then that movement had been lost so that while overall company training had improved, this division's training had deteriorated. In addition, department heads have their own training budgets. They use these as they see fit: this includes sponsorship, for example, on Open University courses.

With the increasing number of management entrants in retailing having university degrees, some tension was created in the traditional system. Managers without degrees saw the 'graduate question' as an increasing problem. Some were considering distance learning of MBAs as a way to gain credibility. The company had an arrangement with Stirling University which had a distance learning MBA with a retailing slant. For those managers with undergraduate degrees in business studies this MBA was viewed as a problem. One such manager pointed out that he viewed his undergraduate degree as more valuable but that an MBA would 'open doors' within the company. Nonetheless, he was not prepared to undertake the Stirling University MBA because of the extra intrusion this would make at a time when he was already working very hard. He said that he would, however, do a full-time MBA if the opportunity presented itself.

A generally more systematic and professional approach to training within the company had been a pronounced feature of recent years. Senior line managers acknowledged this though they said that perhaps the company was rather better at managing the training requirements associated with big one-off projects – such as Checkout Plus, the new electronic point of sale (EPOS) system – than it was at ensuring consistent routine training.

Each regional office had a training centre and there were regional training managers with a training staff of about three training officers. Some 80 per cent of stores also have their own training managers. There is also a central company training director and a Tesco management college at a country house at Ponsbourne. This house has been converted into a fully equipped residential training facility. The bread and butter activity here is the three-week courses for new managers in 'essential management skills'. To this extent, the Tesco management training provision is similar to that offered by Jusco. There are differences in training provision, however. More senior managers, such as those at regional executive level (typically there are five of these in each region), are sent to external management colleges such as Ashridge. Also it seemed normal for three or four managers in each region to be participating in MBA programmes.

Training and education appeared to be important issues in Tesco – certainly to a degree unusual in most British companies. As one regional manager remarked:

> Training is seen as critically important right up to my level at least. We now have, as a result, among the best middle managers anywhere – and they are all home-produced. There has also been another consequence. Our staff now think completely differently from the way they did 10 years ago: back then we had sheds full of stock, now we replace stock daily. Also we now definitely see people as a resource, the whole style has changed.

A further parallel with Jusco was the attention being paid at Tesco to the policy of developing women managers. The claim was that now more women are being promoted than men. Here again the 'special programme' nature of the British context was evident. For example, in one region the managing director had decreed a 'special effort' to train first-line managers – particularly female ones. The aim was to ensure that every one of the approximately 900 supervisors in the region received some training.

Tesco store managers generally expressed satisfaction with the training which they had received and which was currently on offer. Most of the managers we interviewed could cite at least some of the training programmes they had attended. However, most agreed that the company's training function and provision had only became proficient in the last three or four years. The central training and development department was seen as having improved markedly over that period. It had an annual budget of some £13 million. Interestingly the department grew in stature as the business as a whole became more evidently successful. The direction of causality here was very uncertain. The more successful Tesco became as a business, the greater was the felt need for a professional personnel and training function.

The point was made that training in Tesco (beyond the basic management skills course) was too linked to the grade hierarchy. One grade 18 manager expressed frustration that the next logical course (at Ashridge) was open only to those on a grade 19.

The widespread view that training was now far superior to what it was previously has to be set in the context of the previous paucity. Senior managers felt that a large and successful company simply had to improve training in order to ensure a better population of managers. Notably, there had been no attempt to measure what pay-back any particular training package had made.

The availability of courses in Tesco was universally seen as unproblematical. There was rather less certainty about the value of internal courses. And in catch-22 fashion there was some hesitancy about the relevance of external courses to Tesco's particular needs. One trading director said his division was breaking through this impasse by getting line managers to develop training packages 'which fit our specific needs'. This, he judged, would ensure that training was integrated with the company's business requirements.

As for training for store managers it may be best to illustrate by taking just one fairly typical case example. The general manager of one of our large superstores was aged 33 at the time of our interview with him. He had left school with A levels and had joined Tesco as a management trainee. He had then been posted to a bewildering number of different stores, serving as assistant manager in eight different stores in quick succession, each posting lasting only about 12 months. He had spent some time at the company training centre at Ponsbourne but, apart from that essential management skills course, his only additional management training had been on various specific courses relating to innovations in new technologies such as a new computer ordering system.

During his period as a trainee he had experienced a mix of on-the-job training and off-the-job modules. He had additionally attended a series of technical modules such as on employee relations and effective presentations as well as a leadership course which included 'outward-bound' elements. More recently he had attended the senior management development (SMD) programme. He saw the helpful feature of this as that it was attended by store managers and their head office equivalents in equal numbers, thus forging mutual understandings. This manager had also started the Stirling distance learning MBA. He observes that this gives him some appreciation of the role played by head office because though he has spent his career in retailing he claims little knowledge about what head office actually does. Meeting corporate staff he has again found stimulating and he now claims a wider business appreciation.

Table 5.4 *The new Tesco management training system*

Level	Course	Duration
School-leaver entry	Trainees' courses	12 months
Supervisors/junior management	Supervisors' course	12 months
Assistant store manager/ store manager	Retail management	12 months
Retail executive	Senior management development (SMD) programme	
Grade 19	External executive programmes, e.g. Ashridge Management College	3 weeks

Of course the problem with taking a life-history approach to describing the training provision is that during the course of time the training which a company provides can change – sometimes radically. Hence it is worth reviewing provision at the time of the study. This, it should be noted, was widely regarded as superior to how it was in the past (the improvement is traced back just three years). We describe it here in the 'ideal' terms it was described to us. In this account the progressive training provision dovetails with career progression. In reality not every individual will necessarily experience it quite in this manner. At the introductory level, there was a 12-month course for selected school-leaver entrants. Then beyond that there was a 12-month supervisory and junior management course. The third step was a 12-month retail management training course. Having emerged from this, managers were ready for appointments as assistant store managers. While serving in this role there was a management development course designed for those seeking appointment as general manager of a store. Having reached this level the SMD course is available which could lead to a retail executive position. And then for the more senior post holders there are the Ashridge-type programmes which are expensive, three-week residential events designed to give top-level 'polish' to the top flight of Tesco managers who are still moving upwards. The system is summarized in Table 5.4.

In summary, management training in Tesco vastly improved during the three-year period leading up to our study. The availability of training courses was universally agreed to be unproblematical. In addition, the company had acquired a well-equipped training centre. The course provision was well structured with, on the face of it, a sequential series of programmes which could take a management trainee from induction through to assistant manager, general manager and then executive level with a course to fit each critical stage. As we noted, however, as this is a newly devised structure, no one in the company had actually been through the system as a whole. The conditions promoting this development were clearly the move of Tesco towards the top of the food retailers' league, and its associated wish to provide a high-quality service. Given the record of other companies within the British context, there must, however, be a question mark over the long-term survival of this new structure.

The Engineering Sector

In this section we compare management training provision in Sumitomo Electric and Lucas Industries. We start with Sumitomo.

Sumitomo

First, the Sumitomo case illustrates some points similar to those we described at Jusco. Second, the company underlines the long-term stability of training systems in Japan, which contrasts starkly with the very uneven experience of Lucas. Third, Sumitomo can be taken as an exemplar of large manufacturers in Japan. Finally, the firm illustrates some of the tensions felt by such firms; as we will see, there was concern that training produced managers who were too similar to each other and too inflexible, and also that senior management development could be taken further.

The Training System In Sumitomo, the system for the training and education of managers was founded on the systematic annual recruitment of cohorts of high-quality graduates (numbering some 200 per year), their retention for a lifetime of employment, and their progress through a systematic, integrated and long-established training and development programme which extended over many years. The lifetime employment system was very much in operation: indeed, this case illustrates just how rigidly the policy was followed. In the 20-year period between 1965 and 1985 the company made on average only one mid-career appointment from outside every three to four years. There were occasional exceptions. In the 1980s with expansion into some new areas it became necessary to hire 40 engineers in mid-career, but routine appointment of managers at this level was almost unknown. Only one external management appointment was made between 1987 and 1989 (although in 1989, 10 project managers were appointed).

The company philosophy as expressed by senior managers was that the most vital thing was to instil in individuals the desire to learn. It was the responsibility of every *kacho* to stimulate this habit through close personal coaching in the first seven years or so of appointment. There was even a claim that there was daily contact between trainee and superior. Goal setting and goal achievement were said to be central. Additionally, it was claimed that the emphasis was on self-development and coaching. What was undoubtedly the case was that, to underpin these, there also existed an infrastructure of education and training which had withstood the test of time. This had two elements: first, a level-related education programme; and second, a needs-related programme. The former meant that for each stage up through the grading system there was a specific education and training package. Moreover, there were tests which had to be passed in each case. The needs-related programmes were designed to cope with rapid change in the business environment. There were five main types as follows.

- New Entrants' Training   In the first 12 months new entrants are given a structured programme of classroom education and shop-floor experience, the main aim being to transmit information about the company and its culture. It is given an elevated status. The first part is held at head office and comprises an 'entrance ceremony' followed by three full days of orientation. Second, there is factory experience including a spell in a hands-on position with experience of overtime work and night shifts. During this period the new entrants live in the company dormitory near the works, an experience intended to foster some camaraderie among the cohort. Then follows a temporary assignment period of a longer duration – approximately six months. During this time further training courses are made available. This is followed by a further gathering at head office of four days' duration. Top management share their visions for the future, the history of the company and its philosophy.

- Sub-Managerial Grades   This period (the *senmonshoku* grading period) relies heavily on self-development aided by personal coaching and a systematic OJT programme organized by the *kacho*. In the final year the OJT takes on a more formal management by objectives (MBO) character. The *kacho* sets clear targets and the candidate is expected to make monthly progress reports to him. Notably at the intermediate and final stage (that is, six months and 12 months of this MBO phase) the candidates have to make presentations to the *bucho*; not only the candidate but, by extension, the *kacho* is judged by the degree of progress and success. All candidates must pass this and other assessments in order to progress to the next grade. The assessment includes a performance report and an interview based on this 'essay'. The material is judged by a panel of adjudicators and candidates are ranked in order of merit. From here a proportion of the *senmonshoku* are selected to attend a one-year 'management study committee' programme.

- New Management Grade Staff   A course is given to all staff who have reached *shusa*, the first of the management grades. The content covers lectures on company policies and strategies and company expectations of its managers; discussions are held and papers are written by the *shusa* on their reactions to this information. These courses are of three days' duration and they are held in groups of 20 at Sumitomo's mountain lodge. Then a further three-day course is held at the lodge which brings the level of analysis down to basic management skills.

- Central Management Study Group (*chuo keiei Kenkyukai*)   Significantly, those *kachos* who have been selected (a privilege in itself) to lead the local groups of *senmonshoku* discussed above also meet regularly among themselves (once a month) . The meetings are held over a couple of days at the company's recreational establishment. Notably, both the president and vice-president make a point of attending at least one of these meetings per year in order to explain company policies and to meet the managers who are in effect their front-line trainers. The regular monthly meetings are built around the format of topic preparation, presentation and discussion.

- Middle and Senior Management Training and Development   Meetings are also held, approximately twice a year, for *buchos* and *kachos* along with a few top executives. These meetings are designed for both communication and development.

Managers' Responses to this Training Provision   How were training programmes regarded by our sample of Sumitomo managers? First, middle and senior managers were rather neglected by the existing provision. Some of these managers were very much in favour of introducing regular courses for senior managers. Second, there was also some concern that the system tended to produce managers who were perhaps rather too similar in their attitudes and responses. A third area of concern was that albeit systematic, the training was heavily reliant on internally accumulated expertise. There was a danger of parochialism and insularity; a felt need was expressed for some fresh ideas from outside the company. Thus, a departmental manager pointed out that there was no training course above the level of *shusa* provided within the company. When he was appointed to factory manager (a post he held prior to his present appointment in another division) he had received no preparatory training to equip him to take on the challenges of the post. He reported that he therefore needed to embark on some months of hard self-study to allow him to undertake the factory manager's job effectively. He, along with many others, said that they felt gaps in the areas of 'leadership' training as well in areas such as international planning, labour law, health and safety law and cost management. In sum, it would seem that, despite long and fairly elaborate training and development programmes, there remained significant perceived gaps in provision – particularly in a range of immediate practical areas of operational importance. It was, understandably, in these areas that the devices such the *ronbu* (essay) system and the local and central management study groups failed to satisfy the felt needs of managers suddenly posted to responsible positions.

In general, however, most Sumitomo managers were rather contented with the training and development which they received. Awareness of the various components of the system was high (this in itself was in marked contrast with a number of our British sample) and most judged the system to be effective. The assiduity with which individual supervisors and managers operated OJT did of course vary and not all parts of the formal training courses were seen as helpful. Nonetheless, the main finding was that the overwhelming majority of our sample of managers had themselves been through the parts of the system described by the 'architects' as in place, and moreover, tended to endorse it as effective.

In our final meeting with Mr Tanaka, the managing director, we asked him how the company had arrived at this happy state of affairs where training and development had become so imbued that it seemed to require no periodic relaunches or major new policy initiatives. He replied:

> There are perhaps two main reasons: first, we have been doing it a long time, and it is now part of the corporate culture, and second, the lifetime employment policy means the transmission of values is essential and easier. I myself have now worked for the company for 40 years and during that long career I have been heavily socialized into the ways of the company and I continue to pass on that tradition to those who come after me.

To flesh out these and other points we now use illustrative examples from some specific interviews. First, consider a *bucho*, aged 44, a production head of electronic appliances. He became a manager at 36 years and had been with the company 22 years having joined as an engineering graduate from Tokyo University. He confirmed that his induction and new entrant training broadly reflected the system as described by those responsible for management training and education. Indeed given that he went through the system some two decades ago the first most notable feature was the sheer stability of the system. The new entrant classroom sessions, the talks from board members, the initial OJT placement, the close supervision and coaching from a *kacho*, the dormitory, essays and tasks as described above were all in place in this man's personal experience. He did report, however, that apart from the MBO sub-management stage, no other formal OJT system existed though a certain amount of OJT occurs at management level in a more informal sense. For example, he instanced his factory general manager who had, to date, no capital investment experience. His *bucho* said he intended giving him this task next time the opportunity arose and he would help and advise him personally on the project. (This echoes the key experiences plan being mooted at Lucas Aerospace as reported below.)

In his evaluation of Sumitomo's management education provision he argued that the training is systematic but basic and was heavily geared to newly appointed managers. He said that more was needed over the longer term for established managers.

A *shocho* (director) of a chemicals research laboratory helped us to understand another facet of the way the system operated from a senior management perspective. He was responsible for some 80 staff (40 specialists and 40 technicians). The largest part of his career had been spent in R&D but he had also spent three years as a GM of a small manufacturing plant. He told us that the GM experience had been very rewarding and that as a long-term goal he would like to repeat the experience on a larger scale – especially if it was related to the kind of advanced technologies he was now dealing with. Interestingly, he did see a path towards this dream: this was through the *ringisho* procedure. By this method he would submit a *ringi* proposal outlining a new product idea to the board. He reported that this device is used quite frequently in SEI; new products result from it and also sometimes new subsidiaries. The significance of this kind of opportunity is that it helps maintain motivation and a path for aspirations among senior members of the organization who might otherwise be fearing, or reconciling themselves to, a plateauing in their career.

Mr Tanaka, managing director and main board member for personnel, made a further point. He is now in his 60s and looks back over a lifetime spent within this one company. He recalled an event some decades ago when he was helping to organize a course for newly appointed managers at a hotel using both internal and external lecturers. At the end of the course one of the external lecturers observed that the calibre of the participants was extremely high, which helped confirm the company's reputation for management development, but they all seemed homogeneous and their responses to problems and questions were uniform. Mr Tanaka said he felt rather hurt by this remark and retorted that it had taken a great deal of effort to imbue the corporate culture and to develop this degree of commonality! Whatever the merits or otherwise of this, the striking thing from our point of view was the sheer continuity of practice over such a long period of time. Managers in their 60s were able to report on their early experiences with the company referring to training and development methods which were in large measure still in place today. This continuity seemed to reflect not complacency but commitment. In the words of the MD:

> It would be difficult to claim that Sumitomo's management development approach had a distinctiveness which set it apart from other large Japanese companies. Most large enterprises in Japan have similar training methods: our exchange of information on such matters with other companies is pretty good and so I can say this with some confidence. What we could claim however is that Sumitomo is one of the firms whose commitment to management development at the very highest levels has enjoyed a long history and as a result there has been a well-established and systematic development programme operating now for many years.

The information from our cross-section of informants suggests that this claim can be broadly borne out. The case illustrates how training was taken for granted. As to managers' evaluations discussed earlier, Sumitomo illustrates the general picture in Japan: managers could enter specific comments on where training could be improved, and this may explain the apparent lack of enthusiasm. In the British cases, almost any initiative was welcomed.

Lucas

Lucas illustrates a much more patchy and less stable situation than that in Sumitomo. Up to the 1960s, the firm had enjoyed an enviable reputation for its training – including apprenticeship training and a graduate training scheme. With the struggle for commercial survival in the 1970s and 1980s these schemes went into decline. A general manager of one of the businesses told us he had joined Lucas 32 years previously as a graduate mainly because of its superb training scheme, 'the likes of which there has never been since'. This involved experience in various departments plus training and development in a particular specialism.

It is important not to imagine a 'golden age' of training at all levels. Managers with long experience in the company reported that in mid-career they had gone for many years without any formal training whatsoever. Nonetheless, there had been a far more elaborate training provision which had begun to be eroded by decentralization in the early 1980s.

A major (arguably the major) management training and development measure in the past few years at Lucas had been a major 'audit' of managers across the three sectors. This audit, which included ability and psychometric tests, as well as one-to-one interviews with trained assessors, was first conducted across all the top 300 managers in the group and was then cascaded through the various layers and sectors. In Aerospace, for example, it covered the top 100 UK managers and the top 100 in the USA. This population of 200 embraced all the general managers of all the businesses plus their senior teams. The audit covered strengths and weaknesses, both as individuals and as team players. It included some coverage also of career aspirations. Some use had been made of the resulting data in making appointments and job moves. The company was, however, still looking at what further use it could make of the data.

This corporate initiative had been supplemented in the Aerospace Division using self-assessment, peer assessment, appraisals and tests to cover a wider population. As a result the company had an informative profile of its managers including qualifications attained and strengths and weaknesses. Some 10 per cent had been identified as of 'high potential' (that is, could make GM level in the future). In general the population was seen to be technically well qualified and operationally committed but they lacked assertiveness and business acumen and were not entrepreneurial. Action plans were to target recruitment so that shortfalls could be filled and to follow up the high-flyers and influence their career paths. One interesting aspect was that, while psychometric testing was used in the UK, it was not used for the American managers who were perceived as more litigious.

Lucas was in the process of designing some 'core programmes' in management training which reflected the three main transition stages in a manager's career: entry into junior, middle and executive (strategic) management. The idea was that in future every Lucas manager, irrespective of which division they were in, would go through these. The strategic one was already in place.

Also already in existence was a graduate entry programme of one week. In 1989 Lucas was recruiting 160 graduate trainees and they went on the induction programme in groups of 20. Following induction the new model was for graduates to receive an 18-month structured experience and development programme (including general business education and personal skills training). But within two years of completing this structured programme and the central training payroll, approximately 50 per cent would leave the company altogether. One reason was that once away from this special attention group they were on their own and bereft of career guidance. The real problem lay with the 'gap' between graduating from the initial training programme and the first management appointment, usually some four years later (that is, the 'danger' age was between 24 and 28). Graduates could expect to have two or three positions at pre-management grade during these years, for example as 'cell leader', 'industrial engineer', 'buyer' and 'manufacturing systems engineer'. Some functions such as manufacturing have a more structured set of steps than others. The idea was to extend the structured approach to other areas and functions. At the other end of the spectrum a 'strategic leadership programme' had been introduced. It was located largely at the international management college at INSEAD. This was regarded as an excellent investment; it had changed attitudes and perspectives.

Within particular segments of Lucas it was possible to find special provision. For example, in CAV, the diesel business, a more fully developed management training structure had been installed. At its apex a development programme for the top executive team had been arranged in conjunction with a British university management school; at the next level down a reduced version of this had been devised; and at the next level below that some 300 had been exposed to a management development programme.

Lucas Aerospace had mapped out a list of 'key experiences' such as, 'Have I handled a budget?', 'Have I been involved in devising a business strategy?' Depending upon the responses and the particular career route, 'we would try to offer these experiences and dovetail them with training courses'. Moreover, Aerospace was working on a three-part framework – with functional directors being responsible for specialist training, the division holding responsibility for the provision of core general management courses, and the individual holding responsibility for continuing education and training. This last included personal development plans (PDPs) as used in BT. An Aerospace senior manager said about 70 per cent of all this was already in place.

In short, significant new developments were taking place but, as we will see further in Chapter 6, these had yet to be firmly implemented. In the light of a past lack of interest in training, Lucas managers' welcome to the new efforts is readily understood.

Telecommunications

The two telecommunications firms illustrate the disturbances to established training systems brought about by change, in this case the effects of privatization. The industry also points to some parallels between the two countries, for here, and in the banks, British firms traditionally had developed internal labour markets of a 'Japanese' kind. Change seemed particularly acute at BT, with much training being reduced to the firm's TQM initiative: although there was a great deal of attention to the initiative, wider aspects of training and development became lost.

NTT

The key issue at NTT was how the forms of development which had been revised since privatization would work. The context was a sharp cut in the number of recruits, from around 10,000 a year to 2,700 in 1989. This was accompanied by a shift in recruitment methods.

Before privatization each of the main 13 grades was known as a 'qualification grade' and each was tied to a particular set of posts; hence a move in one necessitated a move in the other. Salary was also tied into this same stacking of posts and grades. Following the McKinsey-inspired reorganization (described in Chapter 3) one of the personnel changes was to base personnel assessment on *shokuno shikaku-seido* (that is, capability qualification). This meant a departure from the previous grade/post/salary structure to a more flexible arrangement based on an assessment of performance, ability and attitude to work. Hence, grading and salary were now attached rather more to individuals than to particular posts. Now, an individual may remain in his post yet still be upgraded; or he can remain in the same grade yet be posted to a new post in a different locality. In adapting this new system NTT was bringing itself into line with the majority of large Japanese firms in the private sector.

Provision for training appeared limited. The training budget as a percentage of turnover was very small. It was estimated as 0.002 per cent of turnover, and the aim was to reduce direct training expenditure. However, as a senior personnel manager explained, cash may not be the best measure:

> The chart showing the education and training system may look impressive but in fact it tells you very little. It tells you nothing about where we place the main emphasis; it cannot reflect the importance of OJT, it shows nothing of the importance of self-development.

As is the case with most large firms in Japan, it is difficult to identify 'management development' in NTT as a discrete set of interventions directed at occupants of managerial posts. There is rather something resembling a seamless web of socializing, training and motivating which commences from the first day of entry into the organization. However, under the revised personnel and organizational system of recent years certain changes can be seen to have occurred. A key factor has been the desire to foster a very different kind of manager in NTT. This was seen to necessitate a rethink of the whole previous education policy. Soon after privatization a committee was established to examine the future of the company's in-house education system. One outcome was the new career development programme which at the time of our study was in place in some parts of the organization. Another was the focus on the development of experts. An Expert College has been launched to help meet this need. A far more tightly organized new entrants' training system has also been introduced. The previous distinction between head office and regional recruits has been abandoned and the total intake is now regarded as a large pool of potential. With over 2,000 graduates entering this larger pool each year compared with about 400 entrants into the old central catchment, the system for education and training has also to be significantly altered. For example, their education has become the responsibility of regional head-quarters though there is a national common curriculum.

The most surprising finding concerning training in NTT to emerge from the interview programme was the virtual absence of systematic OJT until very recently. Under the previous bureaucracy it was generally assumed that learning would take place by virtue of being in post; systematic coaching and planned OJT was rare.

Since privatization, planned OJT has come to be regarded as a high priority. Even so, we found that for most *kachos* currently in post, the systematic practice of on-the-job training of their subordinates was still not apparent. Nonetheless, it is significant that a formal OJT infrastructure had been planned and approved. The programme for all new *kachos* lists the acquisition of techniques for educating their subordinates through systematic OJT. This priority on the development of subordinates has been a post-privatization phenomenon. It has been added to the list of items subject to evaluation in the annual *jinji koka*. In total, the drive to launch systematic OJT in this company has proceeded along a number of reinforcing fronts: a declared senior management commitment to it; the drawing up of a skills inventory detailing how to do it from a super-ordinate's viewpoint; an OJT checklist manual; and, as mentioned, the entering of successful accomplishment of the practice in each line manager's evaluation list of headings.

Another important change in the training and development system at NTT since privatization has been the attention paid to what, in certain Western companies, is known as individual contributors (ICs). In NTT the new term is 'experts' and, as mentioned, to develop these they launched an Expert College in 1988. Its graduates are regarded as people of high distinction and potential. The college was running 16 courses. And six project groups were looking at different aspects of its operation during the period of our study. Although the terms were difficult to translate it seemed that the term 'expert' was intended to convey rather more than the traditional term 'specialist', with its connotations of narrowness. The 'expert' and managerial careers were regarded as parallel in status and there was opportunity and indeed encouragement for interchange between the two routes. Note also the management training centre. Courses on financial control, financial analysis and marketing had become more popular since privatization.

Under the previous 'careerist' system, recruits underwent a three-year training programme similar in broad outlines to that of Sumitomo. Since privatization, the division between career and non-career managers has been dropped and a less bureaucratic approach has been developed. Selection instruments known as human assessment (developed initially by AT&T in the USA) are used to measure strengths and weaknesses; factors assessed include leadership, resistance to stress, and face-to-face effectiveness. This approach is seen as most relevant to a private business, so that the emphasis is increasingly on giving individuals responsibility and monitoring their performance, and less on progression through an established structure.

British Telecom

Privatization and New Training Initiatives   BT, in some ways like NTT but perhaps in more extreme form, was marked by the number of phases through which management development had appeared to move. Provision had moved from elaborate structured programmes to a slimmed-down situation where colleges were closed and the number of centrally provided courses was drastically reduced. Yet debate was moving on to discussions about expanding training once again and even the opening of a new senior 'staff college'.

At the time of our research there was a widespread view at all levels that management training had been virtually dismembered. To this extent the perceived 'trend' was the exact opposite of that in Tesco. Part of the reason was that corporate training along with other functions had fallen victim to the radical cuts and reviews which had followed privatization. This was due in part to cost reduction but also to the change agents' intentions to revise radically all the old structures.

The 'official' version was that training had undergone a 'revamp'. The old, expensive and expansive provision of training courses staffed by large numbers of trainers had been 'rationalized' and what remained was a much reduced rump which had refocused training onto a modular approach based around a clearer definition of 'core skills'. The new 'core management programme' was described as 'a product that meets our present needs'. It was delivered both nationally and locally; for the latter it was operated on a 'franchise' basis, that is, the standard product was delivered by locally licensed trainers.

In explanation of this depleted provision, a corporate divisional chief observed:

> I think it is now like this simply as a result of the priorities certain people have, they haven't seen the benefit of development. Of course there are also the difficulties stemming from the vast size of this organization – the complex number of levels and layers. If you had a small company of 100 people you could design a training and development system in the morning and operate it in the afternoon. But here the dissemination of information is appalling, and too many people get their hands on an idea, it gets changed beyond recognition . . . it's all very frustrating.

Managerial competency lists were being constructed at the time of our research. The company was still trying to define which competencies it wanted to encourage. An 'expert' competencies 'template' had been produced and was seen by some managers as particularly useful in the high-flyer workshops. There seemed a strong possibility that the competency lists would in due course find a wider application and would, for example, be used eventually in appraisal documents. There was, however, a residual worry. As one senior manager observed: 'How will the competency lists fit with our aim to emphasize the goals approach?'

For senior managers in BT (level 5 and above) there had been a series of senior management group (SMG) meetings which had the dual purpose of strategic planning and review, and management development. During the previous two years there had been five such events, each of which had improved 'business awareness' but not skills development in any specific sense. Senior managers reported a general lack of training for senior managers. The SMG programme itself was to be phased out. Notably, the initiative had in any case come from outside the training and personnel function.

One fairly senior BT manager working in a corporate engineering function said he had joined the organization immediately from school as an apprentice. He worked for a switching centre for television signals: 'that was the only time in my career with the company that I felt important'. Then he recalled how he was ambitious and he applied for jobs in London. He went through 'the civil service interviews we had in those days' and was appointed to a post with no training: 'someone just sat with me for an hour and I had to pick it up as I went along'.

> *Q*: So the good old days we have heard about weren't necessarily entirely good then?
> *A*: No, they were often dreadful; it was unbelievably bad. And I was one of the lucky ones.

We then turned to how one could advance and develop in such a situation. He replied: 'In a company like this you must be in a high-profile job to get noticed: if you are not, it doesn't matter how good you are, nobody will recognize the fact and you will just fester.'

He echoed the point made by many other British managers in our case companies – not only in BT but in Lucas also – that it was purely a matter of 'good luck' and 'chance' that certain individuals found themselves in positions which gave them the opportunity to shine and then make headway.

In contrast, the impact of some courses is evidently extremely shallow. For example consider the following exchange with a level 5 BT manager:

> *Q*: Apart from the senior management group programme, what other training courses have you attended in the past two years?
> *A*: Well, there was another one about a year or so ago. It was in Portsmouth, I think, I can't remember anything about it, I think there might have been a bit of financial stuff plus one or two other things.

In order to progress beyond the mere provision of training courses, a number of the key directorates in BT had prioritized management development as a facilitated process. An important part of this was the creation of a facilitator/developer post in each sub-unit. We discovered, however, that many of these posts remained vacant. Sub-unit heads told us that they found it difficult to persuade their talented and credible staff to occupy these positions. We therefore went to talk to a divisional head who had succeeded in making just such an appointment. 'What's the secret?' we asked. 'That's precisely the question I myself asked about the staff development guy we have,' he replied. 'Unfortunately it's not something I can usefully pass on to other divisions: he just enjoys that kind of work.'

In discussing training in BT the place of TQM can hardly be over-exaggerated. The centrality of TQM is emphasized not only at head office but also in the districts. Indeed it was commonly said at senior levels in the district we studied that TQM was 'the very core of what we are doing with our managers'. It is inextricably linked with training: many managers' training experience over the past two years had been exclusively on TQM. As the district personnel manager (DPM) said, 'TQM *is* the management development initiative of the moment.'

Asked about his own recent experience of training, the divisional chief said, 'I have been on a large number of TQM courses as both student and lecturer; apart from that, nothing. Oh, apart from meetings of the SMG group.'

> *Q*: So for you personally, and perhaps for other managers in the company, training equals TQM?
> *A*: Yes.
> *Q*: What do you make then of the high-profile announcement from the company that it is subscribing to a policy of 10 days' training per manager per year?
> *A*: You are trying to wind me up, aren't you? There should have been much more clarity about the thing before that statement was put out. Naturally everyone assumed it meant the equivalent of 10 days' external training. The cost was not sustainable in our budgets, so they had second thoughts. 'What we meant,' they then said, 'was training on the job.'

He then went on to say that in the past he had been on external courses such as one at Cranfield Management Centre: 'I have loved that sort of stuff. I don't know whether it has made any difference, however; I do a great deal of human management, I don't know whether you can learn that from courses.' The underlying ambiguity then about management training is very evident.

We then returned to TQM training. The interviewee had already said he had 'strong views' on this subject. He began:

> I am a passionate believer in TQM as a concept but the application for us has been a disaster. When I speak on these courses I always say, 'look guys, this is a very big company, so don't expect things to change by Monday morning'. Of course I mean change for the better. In reality lots of things have changed but for

the worse! We raise their expectations of providing a better service but the gap has already widened by Monday because there will have been further budget cuts, no promotions, job cuts, blanket bans on this and that . . . now you can see what I really think about TQM training.

The issue was raised also when he talked about trying to fill the vacant post of TQM coordinator. The kind of people he wanted for the role would not apply. The result was:

I didn't appoint . . . in my view it is crucial that we only use credible and talented people in this role. It would be easy to find someone who isn't performing well as an engineer but the signal then would be disastrous, it's a problem we have experienced with TQM.

This illustrates sharply the problem with which our British Telecom managers were struggling: training and development in the British context have traditionally suffered from such a low regard that it has become difficult to find talented and credible staff to take on the developmental role. The company therefore becomes locked in a vicious circle.

Local-Level Experience   So far we have looked at training and development from a corporate-level perspective, but how does the situation appear from the district level? The district we studied in some depth had 6,000 employees, 620 managers and a district board of 12 members. A district general manager (DGM) headed the whole organization. Half of the 620 managers were engineering line managers; others such as computer specialists would be on the managerial and professional grade structure although perhaps not having any direct reports.

Training at district level is rather *ad hoc*. In theory there was a sequential structure: a basic 'transition into management' course for new managers or those about to be upgraded; a range of top-up courses for existing managers; and then some senior management training. In practice, very little of this was taking place. About half of the level 2 managers we interviewed, for example, had not been on any introduction to management course. Similarly, the top-up courses for experienced managers were not well publicized and even the more senior managers who acted as appraisers were in the main unaware of what was available. By far the largest amount of the training occurring in the districts was that associated with TQM and customer service courses.

Perhaps even more remarkable was the fact that very few plans were in place at district level to correct this situation in the future. There was a general expectation that the corporate training function was planning to decentralize training (which in a way was the case) and that the situation therefore would come right very shortly.

Not only training, but management development provision also, was found to be fragmentary at district level. District personnel tended to pin their hopes on the appraisal interview as the key to any action. As a result of strengths and weaknesses identified here, plans for special projects, secondments or job change were supposed to be drawn up. In practice, given the absence of monitoring, very little of this was occurring. There was no fast-track system in the districts. The only mentoring activity was that associated with the new graduate recruits.

Notably, even 'getting people on courses' was reported as a problem in BT – unlike the situation we found in Tesco. One upshot was a reduction in the amount on offer. As a level 1 (acting level 2) manager reported, 'since TQM there has been a lot more training but, apart from this, I am not aware of any other training provision.' With all the district and head office managers we interviewed, we probed about their awareness of the various programmes that had been launched, but very few had even heard of them. For example, a level 3 district manager observed, 'as far as I am aware, none of my level 1s have had any formal management training.' And a level 2 manager reported:

> In the past some of the older ones received a standard training programme for new managers but there isn't any now. There used to be a week's training course either in Edinburgh or on the south coast but they are both closed now.

Was he aware of any suite of courses for managers already in post? 'There is no manual of training courses for managers,' he said. 'There is a district training function but they are purely organizers, it's virtually impossible nowadays to get any training for my level 1s.' There was in fact a 'core management programme' specifically designed for junior managers but in the main only managers in the various head office locations in London appeared to have participated in or even to have heard of this.

Some managers were aware of courses. A level 2 manager in the Network Strategy Division in London reported experience of a number of short courses. In general, however, provision was scarce and unplanned. Another level 2, also in a national network division, for example, was totally unaware of the core management programme: 'I have heard there are certain training initiatives being launched but I think management training in this company really amounts to "sort yourself out".' The 'accidental' nature of some management development experience is well illustrated by the district manager who reported:

> I got involved with rugby in quite a big way and, as a result, mixed with people of a higher social status and I gained a lot of respect through the game. I was often called upon to give after-dinner speeches and as things moved on I wanted to put my job on a similar standing with that status.

At BT, then, the changing environment had upset previous approaches more than was the case at NTT. The firm illustrates the way in which the British context can impinge on in-company developments: from being relatively insulated from market forces, BT had been rapidly exposed to them, and in the process the purpose of training had become confused.

Banking

As with telecommunications, the banks in both countries had a long tradition of established, and highly centralized, training systems. In both cases, too, senior managers were in the process of changing these systems in the light of perceived external pressures. In Mitsui, there were efforts to stress self-development and to strengthen international awareness. In NatWest, the changes were of an altogether different magnitude. There was a similar desire to put the emphasis on self-development. More fundamentally, however, NatWest was attempting to undertake nothing less than a culture change – from what might be described as a 'lender/control' culture to a 'marketing/initiative' culture. Relatedly, it was also trying to grapple with the demands of increasing specialization largely brought about by the growth in the range of activities in which the company was involved. Inevitably, training, though not seen as the complete answer, was expected to play its part.

Mitsui Trust and Banking

In Mitsui, for those currently in a managerial post, the amount of training activity was very small. Senior managers were, however, far from complacent about the current level of provision. In the case of new entrants, the bank has increasingly focused on recruiting good graduates. The *ippanshoku* (management stream) is now in fact an all-graduate path. In April 1989, there were 164 recruits to this grade, of whom only four were women.

The bank took a decision to give closer attention to the training requirements of this group. The newly constituted capability development office (CDO) saw this as its priority. The linchpin was a 21-month training and internship period. Self-development programmes are used – especially for the study in preparation for the professional banking qualifications. Induction begins with a two-week collective event including a ceremony addressed by the president of the bank. As at Sumitomo, the programme not only imparts information about the bank but also makes a clear attempt to change attitudes and lifestyles and to socialize new entrants as 'company men'. Events are organized to engender a sense of identity as a cohort.

After this period trainees are assigned to branches where planned OJT begins. This includes moves around all jobs in the branch for six months, supervised in each section by an OJT leader; reviews every month or so; review periods every three months which involve interviews with middle managers; and sending copies of papers from a learning log to the capability development office. The contents of OJT are twofold: technical knowledge and behaviour. At the end of six months, trainees are recalled to head office in Tokyo for a week's review course. The remainder of the period is spent working with customers, initially working alongside a more senior *ippanshoku*. During this period four further interviews take place with senior managers and one of the board members.

Self-development runs in parallel. It includes correspondence courses on banking law with an essay every month which has a pass mark of 80 per cent. There are other courses in various aspects of practical banking; a total of five examinations must be passed by all the trainees. Additionally ambitious entrants can take higher-level professional qualifications.

Formal training provision for existing managers in the bank is less substantial. The CDO says it encourages all employees to take at least one correspondence course a year. The CDO list contains 79 different subjects for study. There is in-house education for the group known as *chuken shain* (the 'solid middle': managers in their late 20s or early 30s). There are several off-JT courses available in-house, plus some sponsored studentships including two-year MBAs in the US – annually attended by five middle managers. Then there is the tenth-year review course in which managers in their tenth year come together for three days to take stock of their progress. There are regular off-JT courses for those at *kacho* and *jicho* level. For *kachos*, two courses cover the role and function of middle management, the operation of the personnel rating system and the theory and practice of personnel management. At the level of deputy departmental manager two courses exist on strategic planning, together with a three-month study course in the USA.

Despite this formal provision, it is self-development which is particularly stressed at these senior levels. The CDO holds a competition to discover which section has taken the most correspondence courses and publishes a league table of banking examination passes. Considerable effort has also been put into English language skills as part of the bank's efforts at internationalization. A large number of language courses were available through the bank. Particularly notable were the 'voluntary' study meetings held on Saturday mornings. These had been implemented following the official move to a five-day week. The CDO takes the view that managers should engage in some profitable study, and since branch general managers often take an interest in these activities it is hard for any one individual to opt out.

Managers' Reactions Let us use as our first example a fairly senior manager at *bucho* level. He was a 48 year old and was recruited as a graduate entrant along with a cohort of 80 others. He came with an economics degree from Tokyo University. He was able to confirm that he personally went through the usual 21-month induction process. As a head office posting he said he was one of the 20 per cent who did not do the early banking exams (he said he was too busy), but this has not impacted adversely on his career progression. Similarly, he attended none of the off-JT courses. He did say, however, that he had personal experience of formal OJT, albeit over a fairly short duration during the first part of his career: in an informal way OJT had been a more or less continuous part of his experience. He reported self-development activity – especially in the form of reading numerous books to help him deal with various problems of new postings as they arose. He still read a lot, and was currently doing a two-year correspondence course on conveyancing which would allow him legally to draw up and sign contracts for sale of land and property. He saw himself as a specialist first and a generalist second and felt that a board appointment in due course was possible.

A second example is a deputy manager of a central Tokyo branch, 42 years old, who was responsible for 40 employees. Again he confirmed his own involvement in induction, together with no formal off-JT for the next 12 years. But he had recently been on a course for newly appointed *jichos*. This involved three days at head office with 20 others, covering areas of responsibility, how to deal with customers, and personnel management. There was no formal OJT at his present level of appointment but an informal type occurred as he worked closely with the branch manager. As *jicho* he was responsible for development of the five *kachos* who worked for him, and through them, he saw himself as responsible for developing all staff and new recruits. His self-development at present was a correspondence course on real estate offered by an external educational institution. His specialism so far has been in corporate pension fund management. He attends meetings with colleagues from a range of industries to help him overcome the parochialism of internal colleagues.

NatWest Bank

NatWest had extensive training provision and estimated that it spent about £55 million per annum on training in the year of the interviews. A *Guide to Group Training* directory was sent to all line managers and a copy was available in each branch. A periodic presentation to the board took place every two or three years to explain training philosophy and provision.

In recent years basic courses had been supplemented by extensive provision for open learning. Interactive VDU technology, using 1,000 machines across the regions and branches, was also being increasingly used to teach equal opportunities, languages and commercial practice, as well as to respond to questions about training. In the past, explained the head of training, the company had just distributed booklets with no way of knowing if anyone read them. A keynote of the new approach was value for money: the bank was trying to get away from costly one-to-one training.

The head of training told us that the proportion of the total training budget that went to management training had moved from 10 per cent to 35 per cent in recent years. Historically, as well as courses for supervisors and on the 'role of the manager', which tended to 'come and go', the main thrust of management training had taken place on two so-called 'management conference' programmes. There had been a general feeling, however, forcibly expressed by the chief executive, that these programmes were not good enough or fast enough for the bank's changing needs. Following a major review, the management conference programmes had therefore been replaced by what was billed as an advanced management training programme entitled 'essential management skills' (EMS). This was a two-week residential foundation programme held at Heythrop, NatWest's central management college, and at other centres around the country. The focus of the programme was on the core competencies of management; the syllabus covered such matters as teamwork, leadership, cutting costs and delivering better quality service.

The head of training explained that 'what it was all about was essentially a catch-up process really'. It reflected the view that the goals the company had set itself could not be achieved simply by the action of top managers and that they had to be met locally. The programmes were designed, in effect, to enable managers to catch up with the thinking of the top executives.

The target populations for the EMS programme was the so-called 'appointed officers' grades. In effect, these were 'junior managers' aged between 26 and 36 years. The programme had begun in 1988 and something like 3,500 people had been put through it in the year in which the interview was carried out. Eventually, it was hoped that as many as 15,000 managers would be covered.

The head of training went on to explain that he and his senior colleagues thought that it was important to put the basics in from the ground up. There was nothing yet of significance in place for middle managers and a sequel to the essential management skills programme was seen as a priority for the future. Training provision for middle and senior managers, he explained, was 'bitty': there were, for example, individuals within these ranks with no recent management training, despite the increased emphasis being given to management development activity, which is described in more detail in Chapter 6 . He referred, for example, to courses at Ashridge and at INSEAD for the high-flyers.

Other things being tackled included training for regional executive directors and their deputies. A major objective here was to make the new regional structure work. Their successors would come on stream in dribs and drabs.

For top managers there was support to go on courses at prestige business schools in the USA including Wharton, Carnegie-Mellon and Harvard. He reckoned the number came to about 70 a year.

As the next chapter argues in more detail, despite the attempt to encourage self-development, training as 'something that was done to managers' was still very much part of the scene outside the very top flight. Asked whether there was much voluntary demand for training, the head of training admitted that 'rarely do any middle-level managers say they want to go on a course – well frankly it just doesn't happen at all'. In answer to a separate line of questioning, he agreed that management training as a form of 'reward' did happen: 'If you want to give someone a fillip from time to time, send them on say the Cambridge Institute of Bankers' seminar or some technical training in lending: it all broadens the mind in some way.'

One problem the organization was having to face up to was the balance between general and specialist training for its middle and senior managers. Inevitably, there was a growing need for specialisms in functions such as treasury, capital markets, corporate and institutional finance and so on. This problem in turn reflected the more fundamental issue of whether middle and senior managers were to be seen as a group or operating company resource. The chief executive's view was that preparation of managers able to work across the whole group was still a priority objective. This view was, however, the precise opposite of that held by the group management development manager.

There had also been significant changes in the delivery as well as the content of the management training. For example, at the central residential management training college the traditional pattern had been for many of its training staff to come from the main bank businesses and spend a couple of years as trainers on secondment. This situation had changed dramatically in recent years. It was not just that programmes such as the EMS had been designed by external consultants (not 'glorified bank clerks', in the words of the head of training). Much of the training itself was undertaken by what were regarded as 'high-powered' professional trainers, of whom some were permanent and some were on one-year contracts. Altogether, taking into account the central management college and the activities of the regions, NatWest employed over 300 trainers. Each of the 22 regions had approximately a dozen trainers. They were under day-to-day control of the regional managers though broad policy came from the centre. Another indication of the more 'commercial' approach being adopted by NatWest was the funding arrangements for training. An increasing trend has been to regard the training function as a cost/profit centre, which must sell its services both inside and outside the organization. There was even some concern about the very survival of the training function.

Conclusions

The complexity of practice found across sectors and countries defies easy generalizations. Yet some significant patterns do seem to be discernible. While it was not the case that the Japanese companies were spending more on training, they did, nonetheless, have in place integrated and step-by-step programmes which took new entrants through to mid-career in a transparent, well-known and readily understood way. The programmes themselves were a mix of formal training, coaching, planned job moves and self-development.

The 'generalist versus specialist' issue is worth commenting upon because it has been identified by previous analysts (see especially Trevor et al.,

1986) as of central importance. We found that during the first 10 years (the *senmonshoken* grades) in Japan all graduate recruits are seen to be growing in certain specialist skills although job moves took them to different divisions of the company and even in and out of subsidiaries. The job rotation was of such importance that the specialism seemed to become a subsidiary issue.

Aside from the comparisons and contrasts in actual provision there was also the question of how the recipients would respond and what evaluations they would make of the training they were offered. Given the great deal of energy spent by the Japanese corporations to instil a common culture and pride in the enterprise one would not expect ready criticism from the Japanese sample. In the main, this expectation was met during the interview programme: the interviewees were invariably courteous, genial and positive. When using the written self-completion questionnaires they were, nonetheless, often quite critical of the training they had received and of the development opportunities open to them. While it was difficult in the interview situation to encourage them to be very expansive in these areas, our interviewees did clarify the sources of such dissatisfaction. For example, as observed by the Sumitomo *bucho* whom we quoted, the paucity of in-house management courses for persons already in management posts meant that individuals had themselves to exercise some initiative and go out in search of self-help. As a number of Japanese interviewees made clear, this was not an unusual occurrence. Hence we found many Japanese managers continuing with the training and development needs by attending or even setting up local cross-company study groups.

In the British companies – even ones of the calibre included in our sample – training was very variable. In the main, however, the problem was not access to training if people requested it; rather it was the ambiguity surrounding its real value and how it fitted in (if at all) with career progression. Relatedly, there was uncertainty about whether it was worth evaluating the results of training: many in Tesco seemed to deny the point of even attempting to measure such things, but a number of Lucas managers sought to get would-be course attendees to establish what they would be able to do as a result and how that would help the business.

Our detailed investigation of company training provision helps to explain the opening puzzle of managers in Britain reporting more training, and valuing it more highly, than their Japanese counterparts. First, much Japanese activity involved self-development and not formal training, as our illustrations from the companies show. Second, training structures were so well embedded in firms such as Jusco and Sumitomo that managers took their provision as a fact of life. They entered comments, not so much as criticisms but as suggestions that new initiatives were needed. In the British case, training remained sufficiently rare for anyone taking a high-level course to take this as a mark of special favour.

These generic contrasts between the two countries notwithstanding, we found some pressures in the Japanese system, in particular the efforts of

NTT to come to terms with the new demands of privatization. The implication is that the success of the Japanese training system rests on its embeddedness in an accepted structure, as Sumitomo and Jusco illustrate. It was possible to create an environment in which expectations were clear and the values of training well understood. As we discuss in the concluding chapter, training was part of a career development system which depended on and also helped to reinforce a stable corporate environment. We have underlined links between training and both wider manpower planning and business strategy. The contrast with Britain was evident. It was not that training courses in Britain were poor but that their purpose and connection with the wider managerial role were not well established. The issue in the future for Japanese firms is to sustain this degree of integration. In particular, we have seen that there were concerns at Sumitomo about the production of identikit managers and about inflexibility, while NTT was shaken by privatization. Arguably, such shocks can be resisted, but it is plain that the Japanese management development system is neither uniform nor unchanging.

6

Management Development: Processes and Systems

In this chapter we move on from a review of formal educational and training provision to consider the range of rather more *informal developmental processes* such as mentoring, coaching, and other ways of learning on or alongside the job. Additionally, we assess the respective roles played by management development specialists (and others) in the 'making' of British and Japanese managers. The chapter also continues our analysis of the views of the individuals on the receiving end of management development activity in its various forms.

By repute, the Japanese have been seen as especially noteworthy for their use of systematic on-the-job training (OJT), mentoring, centrally planned job rotation, and promotion from within the company. Japanese managers, it has been said, are developed over a long period, using subtle methods, and the apparent result is a broad band of generalists (Hinohara, 1990; Okazaki-Ward, 1993; Shimazu, 1992; Trevor et al., 1986; Whitehill, 1991). These features of the Japanese management development system are well established and have come to constitute the conventional wisdom. What is less well known – indeed, it can be said, is not really known at all – is how these processes work in practical detail and how the participants in the processes themselves read the situations which face them. The purpose of this chapter is to fill these gaps. There are important questions to be answered: not least because the fundamentals of mentoring, on-the-job training and the rest could be said to exist in some form or other in Britain also, but the results have hardly been transformative. Thus, it can be suggested that what matters is not so much that these mechanisms exist in Japan but the ways in which they actually work.

The slow, methodical development of the Japanese is seen to be a rational choice under the circumstances of lifetime employment. In contrast, in Britain, the external labour market is felt to create a more competitive, specialist, financially motivated and employability-conscious manager. There have been few empirically grounded studies of these stereotypes. Trevor et al. (1986) produced one of the more notable reports but their work is based on the Japanese working in Europe. And while the generalist versus specialist divide is used as the central ordering concept in their book, the authors conclude that 'In contrast to the stereotypical patterns of Japanese generalists and European (or American) specialists the reality is more complex and more changeable' (1986: 257). It is a depiction containing, they say, 'only a grain of truth' (1986: 256).

The pattern of development may be complex but its significance in the realization of the Japanese corporate system has been claimed as 'the source of the might of the Japanese economy' (Matsumoto, 1991: vii). (Matsumoto was an official of the MITI.) Thus, the subject is very important but there are a number of puzzles about how it actually operates in practice. The seniority system, based on lengthy and widespread development for whole cohorts of graduates, has been said to be well suited to an economy which is growing (Sasaki, 1990), but how well can it cope with stagnation and higher unit labour costs? The system of lifetime employment and seniority-based promotion and rewards was 'founded and institutionalized in the 1930s' (Yui and Nakagawa, 1989: xv). It has been refined in the intervening period, but how well does it fit the very different demands of a modern economy? And what are the Japanese doing to enable that fit? Equally, to what extent have British managers utilized these sorts of development methods and with what results? There are then many questions but in our view there are four in particular which deserve central attention and which will also serve to embrace most of the subsidiary questions:

1 What are the *mechanisms* used by the eight case companies in the making and replenishment of their management resource?
2 In what ways and to what degree does *organizational structure* impact upon management development behaviour?
3 How do the *recipients* of these various mechanisms respond? What 'status' or standing do the various management development mechanisms and activities enjoy?
4 What importance does *culture* have in shaping management development? We consider in particular here the practice of self-development, as an illustration of the way in which cultural expectation, rather than prescribed training activity, could promote managerial learning.

These four main questions are considered in turn and we use them as the basis for structuring this chapter. In addressing them, we will illustrate the argument by drawing upon the most pertinent examples from the data which we collected.

Mechanisms

In relation to mechanisms of development, it is useful to focus initially on two contrasting British cases, BT and Tesco, before turning to two of the Japanese companies, Jusco and Sumitomo. The former pair illustrate some of the tensions within and constraints on management development, while the latter pair will be used to indicate how these can be overcome.

British Telecom

In British Telecom training was largely separate from management development. There was a head of management development for BT United Kingdom Communications (UKC) which embraced 90 per cent of the BT business. Since privatization BT had acquired a number of other businesses, but the policy was to keep these as separate and distinct as possible. There was certainly no attempt to extend any of the BT operating procedures to them and their managers were not regarded as part of a common corporate resource. Where, on the other hand, BT had grown organically and spun off new small enterprises, there was some difficulty in finding people within the core to run businesses of £50 million or similar.

Following privatization, significant changes were made which affected management development. As indicated in Chapter 5, under the old Post Office regime there had been a seniority-based system of career progression, and career paths were relatively transparent. Following privatization this was altered: many of the functions were changed, new people came in, and restructuring and downsizing were taking place, all of which meant that managers were now left without a view of career paths. Along with the disappearance of career paths went the management development processes which used to accompany them.

In their place was a much slimmer provision supposedly based around individuals – using, for example, an 'appraisal counselling' approach, and allowing for fast-track development. The central management development function had been trying to devolve to the various functions (such as marketing and accounting) the responsibility for the development of their own staff. For example, the head office senior marketing or engineering managers would be expected to have a view on the appropriate training and development for junior managers in the districts as well as in the head office. In general, cross-functional development was not being catered for. UKC had developed a high-flyer programme with appropriate development workshops and centres. Apart from these there was no corporate-wide approach to management development as such.

In the field (the 'districts') up to management level 3, development was a purely parochial affair. For promotion to level 4 and above some geographical mobility was normally required. Traditionally, vacancies were advertised in the *Gazette* – an internal company newspaper. Head office involvement in district appointments occurred only at district board level – that is, heads of functions within districts – but even here, unless the appointment was at district general manager level, head office involvement would be fairly minimal in most instances.

One key initiative at head office level was the Top 300 programme. This was to meet the needs of the many senior managers who had been recruited since privatization and who needed to learn about the strategy and to meet each other. It started as a three-day session on strategy in BT and how the business was seen by the City and by shareholders. There were three key aims: (1) the creation of a cadre of people who could relate cross-functionally; (2) education in the sense of learning about the business; (3) a wider involvement in the strategy. It was a high-prestige programme with considerable expenditure on top speakers from around the world. As one corporate manager told us: 'We went for the best regardless of cost and had speakers from Harvard and so on.' The Top 300 met in small groups of 15 to 20 for two to three day events run back-to-back so that two sessions a week could be scheduled. There was a board member in attendance at each event, and, for many, the managing director himself. As time went on, the priority message which came across moved on from the necessity to reduce headcount to a concern with quality of service. One side benefit is that the emerging strategy is reviewed by some 20 sets of workshops and there is some feedback from these events to the main board.

This Top 300 programme was one of the central planks of head office management development but even here, when pressed, the management development manager observed: 'If I'm honest I have to say it started out as a strategy group initiative; they started it, not us.'

Another activity was known as the 'goals initiative'. Goal setting was established as central to the appraisal process. A link with pay was also emerging. The union, the Society for Telecom Executives (STE), had resisted the individualizing of goals but was persuaded to try it at a unit or departmental level. The corporate aim was to put in place a system suited to a 'performance-oriented' company. Hence, there was a presumed link between performance targets, the goals each unit and individual needed to adopt in order to achieve those targets, and the evaluation process to judge how far the goals had been met. The language here was seen as very important. Objectives which merely required a manager to 'do' some activity, such as 'review' and 'report', were to be replaced with a results-oriented terminology which would stipulate *achievements* associated with agreed *goals*. The success of the pay-phone targets (which set clear targets such as 90 per cent of public phone boxes being fully operable by a set date) was widely cited in the company as an example of what could be achieved if 'goals' replaced mere 'activity'.

The 'goals' initiative was also about clarifying everyone's priorities and stipulating the key results areas (KRAs). The process had started with the managing director: what goals did he 'own'? He was, we were told, 'able to list a hell of a lot', but many of them should have been the goals of people lower down the chain. The initiative was being rolled out across districts and headquarters. But even after just one year, there was a need for a relaunch in some divisions. The aim of the project group responsible for it was 'to get it to stick, to establish it as part of the culture'. There was, however, some uncertainty about whether future appraisals should focus on 'competencies' or 'results'. In practice, some mix of the two seemed likely.

A very British form of 'management development' occurred at the apex of British Telecom. Here there was the post of corporate management resourcing adviser, a person who reported directly to the head of personnel. The main role was to help fill the top-level appointments in the company – the top 600–700 jobs. The senior management grade (SMG) posts covered by this process extended down to the top couple of positions in each district – that is, DGM and deputy DGM. This senior management group were on personal contracts and were beyond the management and professional structure. The adviser collected job specifications from the various divisions for the posts they needed to fill or would soon need to fill. He then acted as an 'internal head-hunter', matching the vacancies with the informal database he maintained about the top cadre. The key aim, he said, was 'to ensure that when appointments are made, full account is taken of the breadth of talent which is available'. A related part of the role involved advice on 'contract packaging' for SMG posts – including salary, car, free telephones and so on. An attempt was made to achieve and maintain a 'coherent structure' to avoid glaring discrepancies and anomalies. Hence, the individual contracts were not 'negotiated' as such but rather 'individually designed'.

The way in which he maintained the top people's 'database' was interesting. He was almost scornful of the capabilities of computer databases for this kind of function: he much preferred to 'get to know' personally as many of the population as possible. A PC containing 2,000 names with career details was used to generate the initial 'long list'. He sought to understand each individual's personality, management style and likely relations with the people they would be working with: 'that's the interesting stuff' he said with enthusiasm. Notably, while compatibility and 'fit' were key objectives, 'the team building concept and its associated paraphernalia of profiles' were regarded as 'far too elaborate for what we do'. Moreover, in reality, each appointment was treated more or less as an isolated event, 'unlikely to involve sophisticated succession planning and the like'. The process was two-way. A queue of senior people wanted to meet him to 'informally flag their concerns and aspirations', and he wanted to meet them in order to make some initial personal judgements. In total, then, the top 'expensive' appointments were made 'on an intuitive basis, as a matter of "feel"'.

At BT, then, there was developmental activity but much of it was new and untried. The development of senior managers turned on internal head-hunting and the creation of individualized packages, not the structured nurturing of talent.

Tesco

Management development in Tesco, by contrast, had progressed past three main landmarks: the creation of a more comprehensive and specialized management structure which opened up opportunities and increased the number of management positions significantly; the introduction of the Hay-MSL job evaluation system which, by measuring every job, allowed a clearer organization and ordering of the management stock; and the installation of a high-pay/high-performance regime. These three elements (aspects of organizational management which would not ordinarily be regarded as part of 'management development' *per se*) were, when taken together, crucial components of Tesco's management development progress.

In Tesco, there was evidence of fast-tracking for exceptional individuals. Several informants cited, for example, the case of one person who had risen rapidly through the ranks to become a regional managing director at the age of just 32. The issue of fast-track development merges with that of career progression practices more generally. Some interviewees made the point that it was unclear how one got promoted in some of the functions and departments. Functional heads had felt some pressure to try to specify 'the different routes people can take', to quote one central departmental head.

In a number of the companies, but perhaps most noticeably in Tesco, the problem of being seen to respond to people's aspirations was quite marked. As the company's reputation as a good training and development organization improved, there was a two-edged result. On the one hand this greatly helped in the recruitment of more talented and ambitious staff. On the other, these staff also became attractive targets for other companies from a wide range of sectors including, for example, building societies, who valued the experience which these people had gained. One major defence was the high level of rewards which managers in the company now enjoyed. They were expensive to poach. Nonetheless, the vital importance of staff development was well recognized. One functional chief from a technical department made this point:

> For the sake of business we really have to get people working together. I went on a trip to Japan with members of the Tesco board and I was struck at Panasonic that the most senior manager on site was the personnel manager. That could never happen here, but nonetheless we have got to get 'people management' as our top priority somehow.

The general culture of high expectations might itself be interpreted as a feature of management development in Tesco. Most members of the board were literally from the shop-floor – that is, the company was run ultimately by grocers not technical specialists. But more than this there was the prevailing view that the company 'expected a hell of a lot'. To quote one new operating board (Tesco Stores board) member:

> The company is tremendously successful and the demands are very high. For the time being at least this is all working positively: people here seem to enjoy the hype, they like being wound up. If there is a downside it is that the company is so

activity-oriented (everything has to be done by yesterday) that the company is not doing enough to get managers to focus on strategic issues. The old adage still prevails: 'Retail is detail'.

Where a company like Tesco maintained a practice of treating people as technical specialists for very long periods of time, then preparations for general, strategic management would always be something of a problem.

Top management at Tesco were agreed that ultimately this problem had to be a corporate-level responsibility. The personnel department was the 'custodian' but basically it was (or ought to be), they said, the responsibility of all senior managers.

In the relative absence of a formal function, heads of department tended to feel some sense of responsibility for initiating various activities which might indicate they were taking development seriously. For example, the director of financial accounts talked at length about how he was trying to break down the barriers between the management accountants and the financial accountants in his department of 100 staff. In addition, he was trying to develop a more 'commercial mind-set' among both groups. This included arranging mini-secondments into the retail and commercial sections of the business.

Departmental heads in general talked of how they spent time counselling key members of their staff. Some of the more sophisticated versions amounted to virtual three-year personal development plans, part of the rationale for which was to make the jobs more attractive and to aid retention. Essentially, it could be inferred, the company was looking to a small number of senior managers who could be held up as role models in the way they developed their own managerial staff through coaching, mentoring, counselling and other methods. When we isolated some of these leaders for interview their view tended to be that once the training function had done its bit with the essential skills training for junior managers, much of the rest had to be added by experienced seniors who needed to adopt a coaching and mentoring posture.

One of the problems to which respondents continually referred was the way in which the managerial career pyramid becomes very narrow at the top. One consequence was a considerable degree of outflow from the company by people in search of more challenging posts. For example, one informant who was a couple of rungs from the top and who had been in Tesco for five years (having been recruited from another company) reported his own conclusions from 'watching' his colleagues at this sort of level: just three had progressed to become functional directors (the top of the specialist tree) whilst during that same period approximately 20 people had left the organization. In consequence, he was preparing himself for a possible company move in due course.

The other key feature was that management development provision was very patchy. Some departments evidently took it seriously; others were doing little or none. In other words, there were very big differences between departments and between divisions; a great deal simply depended upon the style of the manager who happened to be in charge. Notably, however, even in those departments where development was absent, there was remarkable consistency in the observation that the availability of places on training courses was totally unproblematic.

Jusco

How did management development in the Japanese retailer, Jusco, compare and contrast with Tesco's? As we saw in Chapter 5, the training provision is systematic and well structured. Training and development are necessary in order to progress through the management grades; an examination at each grade transition point sees to that.

There are three main stages for the graduate recruit. Stage one is tied to the inculcation of merchandise knowledge and practice in sales competency. OJT and self-study are both used. This training is open to entrants with different levels of qualification and indeed over two thirds on the programme were non-graduates. At stage two, the emphasis shifts to specialization. Entry is by competitive examination. The method of education on the programme is largely by distance learning. The third stage is for management grades, and to gain this upgrading in the first place requires recommendation from the person's superior. Aptitude tests and interviews with senior company executives are also then used. This is the *sanji* candidacy stage – a tough selection point because it is at this stage that the separation between future executives and other middle managers is made.

Jusco was unusual in the extent and sophistication of its assessment techniques in the development process. The critical *sanji* stage involves a three-day 'assessment centre' (Jusco term it 'human assessment'). This is run by a panel of internal and external assessors and they use 15 dimensions to evaluate individuals. The event utilizes the case method and psychometric tests. Also, an assessment is made of the candidate's work over the preceding three to four years. Group discussion, in-basket exercises and presentations are also used.

To what extent had Jusco found a way around the barriers between headquarters functions and the stores which was such a big issue at Tesco? The head of the capability development department said he recognized the problem and that in certain specialisms, such as finance and personnel, people did tend to remain in their area of expertise, though even these people would move between head office, region and stores. In the case of merchandisers and others there was a definite head office policy to move people in both directions using the job rotation system. It was difficult to glean more details from him on this and so we need to look at the details from our interviews with individual managers.

Most Jusco interviews reported previous experience in an average of three functions. These were typically in sales, planning and purchasing, but for some there was also evidence of experience in personnel and administration. The questionnaire asked whether they had worked in headquarters. We scrutinized in particular the current store managers: eight of the 13 store managers in our sample had not worked in head office, the other five had. However, the majority of those currently in regional offices had previously worked in head office. The implication was that the divide between stores and head office which we had found so marked in Tesco was also something of an issue in the Japanese counterpart company but to a lesser extent.

Arguably, even more critical given Tesco's experience would be the information derived from those Jusco managers who were currently in head office posts: how many of these would have had experience of store management? There was no specific question on the self-completion questionnaire which tackled this point, but the information can be derived from questions which asked everyone whether they had worked at other locations and if so how many; the second method is to look at each individual's career history as covered in the interview transcripts. Using the questionnaire first, it became clear that all the head office managers had at some point in their careers worked outside the head office and that the majority had in fact worked in three or more locations. The career history reports in the interview transcripts revealed that Jusco head office managers had extensive in-store experience and the current store managers also had wide developmental experience. Job rotation between stores and/or units occurred on average every 18 months.

Sumitomo

Since job rotation is such an acknowledged feature of Japanese firms, we offer some evidence on this, using Sumitomo as an example. Rotation was regarded as a very important method of development. As a rule each manager could expect to be moved every three to five years. These moves occurred on a specific date each year: one of these dates was in January, the other in July. While we were at the company 500 managers were moved *en masse*. About 70 per cent of the moves were within the same division but even the 30 per cent cross-divisional movement was far higher than the practice in Lucas. Indeed, a central issue at Lucas was a strong divisional orientation, with moves into Aerospace from Automotive being very unusual.

To further the analysis a computer search was conducted by Sumitomo, at our request, on 68 managers who had been recruited into the company as graduates some 20 years previously (the full cohort graduate recruitment in that year, 1969, had been 100). Our sample were now aged between 44 and 46 and were nearing the peak of their careers with the company. Of the 68, some 46 were from engineering courses and they had been placed in the technical stream; the remaining 22 were arts graduates and had been placed in the administrative stream. Of the 46 engineers, 41 had experienced rotation across R&D, production and engineering while five had remained solely in R&D. The administrative stream sample had moved every two to three years and had been placed in marketing, planning, personnel and accounting.

This evidence supports the argument of Chapter 4, that systematic job rotation is a characteristic of Japanese firms, but that this need not be reflected in any quantitatively greater cross-functional experience than is common in Britain. British managers moved around a great deal, generally in early career and often in an unplanned way. In Japan, planned movement continued longer into a career. But in addition to job rotation the mechanisms of development which we encountered also included coaching, mentoring and OJT. In general, the Japanese companies were more practised in operating these processes as part of business as usual. In the UK, company engagement with these practices was more self-conscious and experimental. There were many 'initiatives' to install coaching and mentoring. The results however were somewhat disappointing: coverage was usually patchy, there was a tendency to expect initiatives to fade away eventually, and, above all, the processes were viewed as supplementary to the 'main job'. By way of contrast, these processes in the Japanese companies were more deeply embedded. When talking to us about their roles as managers, the Japanese would more readily (and without being prompted) describe their priorities in terms which placed the development of subordinates among the top items. This was a central component of the way they conceived of what it meant to be in a 'management post'. Relatedly, the mechanisms of developmental support such as regular review meetings, the setting of diffuse objectives, the setting and marking of essays, the expectation (and self-practice) of self-development were enduring parts of the organizational landscape. Our interviewees, when describing their careers and organizational experiences over a 20-year timespan, would readily build accounts of coaching into their narratives. With only one or two exceptions their accounts of what had happened to them aligned closely with the official architecture as described by corporate chiefs – and this not just over a span of months or years but over decades. Finally, the various elements such as six-monthly evaluations (based on demonstrated leadership, conceptual knowledge, completion of essays and of targets), self-development, planned postings to subsidiary companies and steady progress through a structured grade system, were all seen as part of a piece. They were long-standing mechanisms, known about and understood by those on the receiving end as well as by those administering them. We say more about respondents' perceptions later in this chapter.

The main contrasts between training and development in the Japanese and British firms were thus:

1 Training and development systems were sustained over a much longer period in Japan – for at least 20 years, as we have seen from our sample of respondents and their reports of their own career histories with the company.

2 Perhaps partly as a consequence, training and development were imbued as part of business as usual in Japan.
3 The effectiveness with which managers trained and developed their staff was taken seriously as a key part of a manager's job and, further, formed part of their own appraisal.
4 In total, training and development were not Cinderella activities as they too frequently were in the UK.

Within these contexts, there were differences between the British companies. Tesco had seen the evolution of new mechanisms which were clearly linked to business restructuring. At BT, by contrast, there were fewer such linkages.

Organizational Structure and Culture

We now turn to some of the constraints on development stemming from corporate structure and culture. The focus will be on the two British companies experiencing the most difficulties in establishing a 'training culture': BT and Lucas.

British Telecom

There were some 9,500 managers in the London and South East Territory of BT which we studied. Of these, approximately 120 had been identified as 'top management' and the territorial chief of personnel had made it his business to get to know each of these personally. Essentially, this meant knowing something of all district board members plus having some information on their potential successors – hence maintaining files on some 500 or so others. Overall, below the top 120 managers there were 9,000 others in the territory, and they were treated as candidates for short-term (under five years), medium-term (about five years) and long-term (10 years) succession. The district general managers would usually take an interest in short-term succession but not in the remainder.

A great deal of faith within the main operational division at head office was being placed in a new management development initiative centred around a new manager in a small unit. This unit, although starved of resources, at least gave many people the impression that something was being done in management development. This unit's key initiative was the launch of personal development plans (PDPs) for as many managers as possible. Every division would have a staff development manager to assist people with their PDPs and would have, on call, some part-time trainers to help fill any identified needs.

Separate from the central training department (described in Chapter 5), certain head office divisions had their own training and development units. For example, the Network Strategy Division had a unit called the management resource and strategy unit (MSRU). This had two wings: management development and communications. We interviewed the head of this unit and the general manager of the engineering division in which it was located. Both managers claimed that the MSRU initiative placed this division at the forefront of management development in BT. The key initiative was the use of PDPs which were workbooks/logs for each individual manager in the division. At the core of these workbooks was a 'competency-based' analysis. Using an extensive listing of management competencies, the individual manager and their superior would separately assess which competencies had been demonstrated and 'mastered', and which required further attention. Then they would meet to discuss and agree a common log of accomplishments and an agreed list of developmental needs. In particular, for each individual, two prime 'skill areas' or competencies requiring priority attention are identified and an 'action plan' is drawn up to tackle them. Progress against the action plan is periodically reviewed. This was purely a developmental initiative. It was not tied to any career planning or succession planning which were seen as sensitive issues with the STE, the managers' union. However, there were plans to make the link if discussions were successful. It was argued that the PDPs provided a 'mechanism' through which managers could more sensibly key into the core programme of training courses.

The contrast with NTT is striking. Here, the complex organizational structure was used to good effect by management development specialists. There were 4,000 secondees placed in the various subsidiary companies. Naturally, keeping track of them and their re-entry was a major administrative task. In addition there were secondments to external firms and joint venture partners. BT lacked such a structured approach.

Who should be responsible for development? In BT one manager drew the analogy with personal responsibility for health and with medical staff being merely in support: 'in the way a person is responsible primarily for their own health, I think they should be responsible for their own development.' This model does not of course devolve *all* responsibility to the individual. 'We need professional guidance and support. We need to know what courses are available. In our unit we keep a small manual with information about courses people have been on and their comments.'

Not all divisions had, in fact, gone ahead with the appointment of a staff development manager. Some divisional heads were simply waiting in a tactical way to see if expenditure on such a resource was really necessary. Others pointed to another, and rather significant, reason for non-appointment:

> I interviewed four really ace guys who were available because of the demanning programme. But when it became clear I had in mind a staff development manager position they all replied, 'thanks but no thanks, I joined the company to be an engineer and that's what I want to do – practise engineering.' They walked away from this developmental role.

In short, spending time in a developmental role was not seen as a smart move in a BT manager's career path.

Overall, therefore, the intentions of management development were constrained by the organizational structure. Limitations stemmed from the problem of coordinating head office and local initiatives, some uncertainty about who was responsible for development and what it constituted, and BT managers' own reluctance to take on a developmental role. The discussion of managers' responses to these issues, in the following section, takes these points further.

Lucas

We can now make some comparisons with Lucas. Lucas enjoyed a sound reputation as a training company and had undoubtedly produced effective functional heads, but the company was not so good at converting these people into world-class general managers. This was perceived by senior managers as a 'serious strategic weakness'. A much repeated theme in the Lucas interviews was the potential which the small business units (SBUs) within the group offered for developmental experiences in general management. This was particularly the case in the Industrial Systems Division, but even in Aerospace an instance was given of a small business with a turnover of some £8 million. It was a difficult business to operate and a recent strategic analysis has suggested it might well be disposed of; a clinching factor in its retention, however, was that it offered a useful 'proving ground' for Lucas managers.

A persistent issue in multi-divisional and SBU companies such as Lucas is the failure to use managerial talent as a corporate-wide resource. One manifestation of this is the 'hogging' of talent by local managers. Another is the problem which arises if a general manager simply fails to devote any resources to the development of managers and merely 'consumes' the managerial resource.

What were corporate managers doing in Lucas to counteract these tendencies? Essentially, the answer was very little. A senior personnel manager said he would try to engage the chief executive in 'giving pain' to such an individual but also observed that if that support was not forthcoming he would eventually 'back off'.

The main stirrings of a new intent and determination in management development had been felt in the Automotive Division. Here the initiative had come from the divisional managing director and a special management development group had been formed. There were seven sub-divisions within Automotive, each with a degree of autonomy. A key challenge was to get 'ownership' from the seven MDs for any new management development system that might be devised. The need was to get development into the 'bloodstream' so that procedures persisted long after the current 'owners' had departed. Given the politics of the current situation the would-be designers of the new system suggested to us that in order to get things launched there appeared to be a choice between consensus and direction – and as things stood a number were convinced that a degree of direction would be necessary. For this to happen the MD himself had to be fully convinced of the *need* for a revamped system; convinced of the viability of the proposed *solution*; and committed to its full implementation.

Lucas illustrates sharply the problem of coordinating different spheres of activity. These were particularly acute when the wider corporate world was in flux and when, therefore, the nature of 'development' was highly problematic.

Subjects' Responses

From a 'receiving end' perspective two issues stand out. How did our sample of managers view the management development systems to which they were subject? And how did they themselves fit within them, and in particular what factors did they identify as the most important supports for their growth as managers?

Status Accorded to Management Development

We asked the general sample of managers to make judgements about the 'standing' of management development as a function and as a process by giving us a response to five statements each of which was measured on a five-point scale. As can be seen from the questionnaire (see Appendix B, question 42), one of these was a rather general statement about management development as an activity. We focus here on the four questions asking about the situation within the respondent's own organization. Table 6.1 gives the distributions of the two most interesting. The first asked for a general response to the view that 'management development has a high profile in this organization.' The second tried to get at the day-to-day constraints on management development by posing the statement 'There is little incentive for a line manager to give development of subordinates a high priority.' It also proved possible to create an overall index from four of the statements (with appropriate reversal of scoring). This is also given in the table.[1]

Overall, managers felt that management development was treated seriously: 60 per cent agreed or strongly agreed that it had a high profile in their organization. Those in the banks were the most satisfied, while those in British Telecom stood out as being particularly dissatisfied. The latter finding supports the argument developed in Chapter 5 that, while both NTT and BT were suffering the effects of privatization, it was in BT that the disturbance was particularly severe.

This point also comes out strongly from the question on incentives to treat management development seriously. We had expected that managers in all the British organizations might feel that, in practice, there was little encouragement to give real attention to the development of their subordinates. In fact, there was little overall difference from their Japanese counterparts, and only 28 per cent of the whole sample offered any

Table 6.1 *Perceived importance of management development*

	Lucas	Sumitomo	NatWest	Mitsui	Tesco	Jusco	BT	NTT	All
Summary index scores *(1 = favourable; 5 = unfavourable)*									
Mean	3.05	2.35	2.52	2.21	2.45	2.38	3.51	2.61	2.67
Responses to 'management development has a high profile in this organization' (%)									
Strongly agree	9	20	15	17	15	38	3	12	16
Agree	25	33	63	62	61	46	15	52	44
Uncertain	31	40	10	21	4	12	21	12	19
Disagree	31	7	7	0	19	4	45	24	17
Strongly disagree	3	0	5	0	0	0	15	0	3
Responses to 'there is little incentive for a line manager to give development of subordinates a high priority' (%)									
Strongly agree	6	0	5	4	0	4	12	4	4
Agree	31	0	22	13	26	23	55	24	24
Uncertain	13	13	7	4	12	7	6	8	9
Disagree	37	60	54	52	39	50	21	48	45
Strongly disagree	13	27	12	26	23	15	6	16	17

agreement to the statement posed. The proportion in BT, however, was 67 per cent.

Analysis of the overall scores showed that there was a country effect, with the Japanese managers being the more satisfied, but there were also clear sectoral differences, with most satisfaction in the banks and stores. As would be expected from the basic figures, there was also an interaction effect: the scores for Lucas and British Telecom were less favourable than is explicable by country and sector effects alone.[2] This reflects the fact that, in both, management development had only recently been made a priority: there was a widespread feeling that many new initiatives were being made but that these had yet to have a real impact in practice. The other two British organizations had been through much less disruption, and both were giving considerable attention to developing their managers, and these efforts were plainly appreciated.

We paid some special attention to the operation of OJT given its supposed prominence in Japanese management training and development. What would our interviewees say about this process? In the main, the Sumitomo managers confirmed their own experience of it throughout their formative years and, overall, endorsed its importance. For example, a *kacho* aged 42 in marketing reported that throughout his 13 years in the sub-management grades he had broadened his skills steadily through OJT. At the end of each year he had written a report summarizing his developmental experiences and achievements – again he emphasized the point made by many of his colleagues that what mattered most was not the actual achievement *per se* but the 'achieving' of the process which would allow successful outcomes to be reported. In addition to the annual reports there was a more important report submitted to the personnel department at the end of each grade in the pre-management level. Another interviewee, a *kacho* in the planning department at the Tokyo head office, observed that the OJT system was, if anything, even more systematic and closely administered today than it had been when he started with the company 20 years ago. He had certainly experienced OJT (based on an MBO method). Notably, however, he reported that during his five years on a UK posting his boss had been 'too busy' to administer OJT in any formal sense.

The contrast with BT is very sharp. As one level 2 manager commented, 'training is now very haphazard in BT.' Asked whether he was aware of any central coordination of management development, he replied, 'no . . . because of the pressures of the day-to-day job we rush along . . . There is no time to reflect on our careers and nobody to tell us whether we are doing anything wrong.' Another spoke of the need for greater clarity and direction in what was being looked for. A third felt that 'there now appears to be a management development emphasis, but it's still mainly up to the individual. I think there is a need for someone to guide staff, to provide a route map.' This last comment neatly captures a sense of a lack of direction and structure: though development was recognized in the abstract as important, there were few mechanisms to advance it. A district board member said he had not seen any central policy document on training for 'years and years'.

BT may be the extreme case, but our other British organizations did not lack tensions around development. A branch manager at NatWest said the job was basically to keep the customers happy and to lend money at the most advantageous rates. Despite having reached a senior level this manager could see little evidence of any special attention and felt there had not been enough functional moves, for example outside domestic banking. 'How does a person get on in the bank?', we asked. 'By moving into a head office position,' she speculated, though eventually she added, 'to be honest I have no bloody idea!' Likewise, at regional level another top-tiered account executive said he had no mentor and, despite being in his mid 30s, he had not even heard of the central development unit.

Another NatWest manager said that, though he had worked in many functions, he did not think his career had been planned: 'you qualify for promotion after a certain time in a grade and posting, where you go next is happen-chance. I am half-way up the management grades but no one so far has spoken to me about my career aims.' If he wanted specific training in specific skills for mobility purposes it was up to him to find it, and the bank would not provide time off or funds. Graduate high-flyers used to be a source of concern to many of our respondents who had to train them, but the practice was now generally accepted.

Who Is Responsible for Management Development?

Though the banks and stores samples were similar between the countries in how much weight they felt that their organizations gave to management development, there were sharp differences in the way in which the activity was carried out. We listed in the questionnaire seven possible loci of responsibility, such as the personnel department, a special management development department, heads of department, and the individual, and asked managers to say which three were currently responsible for management development and which three should be responsible. As Table 6.2 shows, national patterns differed considerably.

The Japanese gave particular weight to departmental heads and to the individual, followed by the personnel department and each line manager; this applied to both the current and the desired situation. A separate and special development department was given little emphasis. In Britain, it was the individual level which received least emphasis. The two British organizations (Lucas and British Telecom) where individual responsibility was mentioned the most were also the organizations where management development was felt to be the weakest. This would suggest that the job of the individual was seen in terms of being left alone to make the best of the situation rather than any very positive view of individual opportunity. A development department, and in two of the organizations a special executive team, received much more emphasis than was the case in Japan.

Table 6.2 *Views on responsibility for management development* (%)¹

	Lucas		Sumitomo		NatWest		Mitsui		Tesco		Jusco		BT		NTT		All	
	Is	Should	Is	Should	Is	Should	Is	Should	Is	Should	Is	Should	Is	Should	Is	Should	Is	Should
Personnel department	54	35	44	48	79	67	70	67	54	32	44	60	43	35	64	59	57	50
Board	7	21	0	0	0	3	0	4	19	16	0	9	3	28	0	5	4	11
Senior executive team	29	48	7	15	3	10	8	13	23	40	4	9	0	12	4	23	9	21
Management development department	32	31	10	11	72	67	0	4	19	40	11	14	33	63	4	9	26	34
Heads of department	71	76	93	93	33	33	83	79	61	48	67	59	47	38	86	82	65	61
Line managers	29	31	48	37	56	56	50	46	69	64	48	50	77	68	54	64	54	52
Individuals	50	45	90	85	36	41	75	79	35	36	85	59	67	44	73	55	62	55

¹ Percentages saying each function 'is' or 'should' be currently responsible: each manager could cite up to three functions.

The stress on the individual in Japan contrasts with the absence of individual choice in career movement. This suggests a situation in which the company moved managers around but they themselves were responsible for developing their own skills and becoming as versatile as possible. In interviews, several mentioned the 'voluntary' training sessions that were run on Saturdays: going to one of these was an individual developmental responsibility. Sustained attendance, however, would increase a manager's chances of promotion. In the questionnaire we also asked managers about their key training needs. Leadership skills were placed first or second in every Japanese company, and in total 39 per cent of Japanese managers cited such skills, as against only 17 per cent of the British sample.

To assess how far the actual and the desired situations on responsibility for management development were consistent, we compared replies on the two aspects. Anyone saying that a function was and should be responsible was taken to be 'satisfied' with its role. Someone saying that it was responsible, but not mentioning that it should be, we counted as part of the category which thinks the role has too large a say; and someone saying the reverse, we treated as part of the group which thinks the say is too small. We omit those saying nothing about a function's role. The difference between the proportions saying that a function's say is too large and too small indicates the balance of views. Thus, in Lucas, 47 per cent of those mentioning the personnel department at all thought that its role was about right, 41 per cent said it was too high, and 12 per cent said that it was too low. Table 6.3 displays the 'too low' and the 'too high' figure in each case in which there were sufficient numbers to make the comparison meaningful. The results are best discussed for each organization in turn.

In Lucas there was a clear balance of views that the role of the personnel department was too great at present, while that of a special executive team was too limited; there was an interesting difference of opinion on the role of the management development department, with a third of those expressing a view wanting it to do more and a third wanting it to play less of a role. This pattern reflects recent change in the organization: managers knew that initiatives were under way but seem to have wanted more senior commitment, while there was a difference of view as to what the management development department could do. These differences did not, perhaps surprisingly, reflect seniority. It was not that aspiring junior managers wanted more emphatic career support while senior managers wanted to stave off interference. The pattern of responses was more complicated than this. For example, one director and general manager of a business in the Automotive Division argued:

> Management development in this company does not get enough clear direction from the top. We all pay lip service to the idea and we have even agreed a document but nothing has been done to set up the necessary infrastructure. The detailed guidelines really must come from personnel: there must be a recognized system which has to be prescriptive and people in my position should be

Table 6.3 *Balance of views on actual and desired roles in management development* (%)[1]

	Lucas		Sumitomo		NatWest		Mitsui		Tesco		Jusco		BT		NTT		All[2]	
	Lo	Hi	Lo	Hi	Lo	Hi	Lo	Hi	Lo	Hi	Lo	Hi	Lo	Hi	Lo	Hi	Lo	Hi
Personnel department	12	41	19	19	3	19	11	16	12	50	25	19	19	31	0	7	12	25
Board	50	13															69	8
Senior executive team									46	9							57	6
Management development department	31	31			10	16			58	17			55	9			33	16
Heads of department	13	4	7	14	13	13	9	14	0	25	0	28	33	43	10	14	11	19
Line managers	33	25	0	29	8	8	8	15	10	20	19	31	23	27	29	18	16	21
Individuals	12	19	7	18	26	16	10	5	25	25	0	44	13	39	6	24	11	24

[1] Percentage of those expressing a view about a function who felt (Lo) that it should play a role in management development but currently did not do so, and (Hi) that it played a role but should not do so. Blanks indicate that numbers were too small to compute percentages.

[2] The 'All' column includes results not given separately.

compelled to follow through the procedures, otherwise it will simply not get done.

Similarly, another informant, this time a corporate-level director, said:

> The specialists here are planning for evolution when what we need is a revolution. The big push must come from the top, there has to be action not words. At present managers are not evaluated on what they do to develop people, at present the emphasis is very much purely on financial performance.

On the other hand, a general manager of a business in Industrial Systems took a more circumspect stance:

> The centre should be kept very lean. The whole logic of the CAP [the Lucas competitiveness achievement plan] is business autonomy and responsibility. We have already been down the alternative path and it is no longer suited to our needs.

There was yet another view: this elevated management development as a practice but did not envisage the way ahead as led by a central management development function:

> Frankly we have a major problem. The test results we have [from a management audit] are very revealing. What they mean is that I have a very big problem with my people: they think in small business terms, they are making £200,000 profit on businesses with a £2 million pound turnover and they are proud of their performance, it's difficult to get them to see just how pathetic that is. We have to lift their horizons both on turnover and profit, but the way to do that will not be through traditional management development activities. (managing director Europe)

In Sumitomo there was, by contrast, general satisfaction with the current balance, a point which also applies to the two banks. In Tesco, managers sought a reduced role for personnel and more activity by senior managers and the management development department. As with Lucas, this seems to have reflected recent developments, albeit of a different kind. As we saw in Chapter 5, Tesco grew rapidly during the 1980s and also improved its general reputation. Tesco managers reported that they felt satisfied with this growth but they were somewhat uncertain where the company was going. Linked to this was an awareness that they personally had been consequently able to rise rapidly, and several of our sample had reached senior level by their mid 30s. But, with the rate of growth slowing, and with the number of jobs to which they could aspire narrowing, managers were beginning to ask where opportunities or direction for the future could be found.

In Jusco, by contrast, the clear concern was to reduce the role of the individual. This can be linked to the company's emphasis on merit, which appears to have left managers feeling pressurized and seeking a rather more structured approach. Finally, in British Telecom, the wish was for more activity from the management development department, for reasons akin to those applying at Lucas: as noted above, there was a sense that central direction had been lost in the rush to devolution and, as one manager put it, some training institutions that had been scrapped needed to be reintroduced. In NTT there was little clear interest in any change, which again underlines the point made in Chapter 5 that privatization had been less dramatic in its effects here than was the case in BT.

These results suggest that, in general, the Japanese companies used a more devolved approach than their British counterparts, with the role of the individual and the immediate superior being stressed and with specific departmental responsibilities being played down. This point complements the usual picture of Japan, that of strong central direction. We have now seen that such direction was in fact strongly linked to individual responsibility and was not merely a depersonalized head office activity. This probably reflects the country's established history of training and development, which has permitted an understood structure to evolve in which specialist departments are needed only to set the overall shape of the approach. In Britain, there was more reliance on an interventionist and institutionalist approach, which was well established in National Westminster Bank, reasonably successful in Tesco, and only really beginning to be very tentatively re-established in Lucas and British Telecom after a period of decline.

A key implication is that, in the absence of a supporting culture, or at least some measure of consensus about the role of training and development, a 'leap' towards devolved responsibility in Britain could be premature and liable to lead to the neglect of training. Neglect seems to have characterized several British companies. To correct for this a general 'clawing back' of responsibility to the centre was evident; this was certainly the case in three of our four British companies, while in the fourth, the bank, the function was already highly centralized. These results again demonstrate the value of taking account of sectoral variations.

Influences on 'Growing' into the Managerial Role

We asked each respondent about the most influential factors which helped them personally to grow as a manager. They were given a list of 12 factors and invited to identify the ones which they considered to be the main three in a ranked ordering. The results showing the most frequently selected factors are revealed in Table 6.4.

Two factors in particular were most heavily identified as being relevant. These were 'a wide experience of challenging assignments' and 'early exposure to a responsible position'. This finding accords with what is now conventional wisdom on the subject (Margerison and Kakabadse, 1985). The finding held up broadly across both countries and all sectors.

But there were some notable discrepancies. 'Role models' were seen as more important in Japan than in Britain. Hence, 75 per cent of the Mitsui Trust Bank managers cited this as a key developmental factor, compared with just 27 per cent of managers in NatWest. Likewise, mentoring was widely cited by the Japanese managers but far more sparingly by our

Table 6.4 *Factors in growing as a manager (%)*[1]

	Lucas	Sumitomo	NatWest	Mitsui	Tesco	Jusco	BT	NTT	All
Education	38	7	15	8	19	0	42	4	18
Family	9	10	7	8	7	0	12	4	8
Role model	15	70	27	75	19	54	18	44	38
Mentor	3	53	0	50	23	54	6	52	27
Wide experience of life	19	6	24	17	19	4	33	20	19
Challenging assignments	66	70	71	50	46	54	52	48	58
Early responsibility	69	40	44	29	73	54	36	76	52

[1] Percentages mentioning each item; managers could cite up to three.

British sample. For example, 53 per cent of Sumitomo managers said mentoring was one of their top three developmental influences, but only 3 per cent of their counterparts in Lucas said the same. And, whereas mentoring was listed by 50 per cent of Mitsui Bank managers, not one of the NatWest managers was of the same view. It was only in the case of Tesco that the British sample gave any regard to it as a key factor. This partial exception (23 per cent cited mentoring) can be explained by the recent efforts in this company to give each manager a 'guide' or 'adviser' on career development matters.

We can relate this evidence to the question on the value of training, the overall picture of which was presented in Chapter 5. One aspect of training that we identified was 'mentoring/coaching'. Few managers from any company with the exception of Jusco mentioned it at all. Among those who did (a total of 84 out of the whole sample of 239), the British managers were more favourable than their Japanese counterparts, as was the case with other aspects of training. Although the Japanese, therefore, did not seem to value mentoring particularly highly in general terms, they nonetheless readily recognized it as having been one of the more important factors in their own development. This contrast may be due to the ability to identify with a specific mentor or guide whereas the more abstract idea of experience of mentoring was less readily recognized. The fact that few British managers could do likewise suggests that, their general high regard for the concept notwithstanding, it had not yet cut very deep at the level of personal practical experience. This reversal between the two sub-samples was a fascinating finding in its own right.

The fact that the British were more likely to stress 'challenging experiences' than they were to cite role models (while in Japan the reverse was true) highlights the centrality in Britain of a 'school of hard knocks' or a 'sink or swim' approach to management development. In the interviews, several British managers spoke of how they had been thrust into jobs for which they had had little, if any, preparation or even forewarning. Many reported that they had eventually found the challenge to be very useful. For example, a senior BT manager reported:

> I was extremely lucky, I was placed in a demanding job at an early stage in my career. I think it was largely because I happened to have been occupying a previous position that was highly visible.

A Lucas manager made a similar point:

> Looking back, I realise that I was thrown in at the deep end at a very early age. Why me? I think it was mainly that I happened to be in the right place at the right time. If I reflect upon it now the main point that comes to mind is the terrible waste of talent among my contemporaries: they were not given the same break and many of them left the company out of frustration.

A correlation among the range of responses which is noteworthy is the one between the selection of a wide experience of 'challenging assignments' and 'early exposure to responsible position'. In Britain, the managers citing these factors were also more likely to have worked in more functions than those who did not pick these factors out. But in Japan there was no such similar correlation. This suggests that, in Britain, managers often find it necessary to move between functions in a relatively unplanned way. This lack of planning and preparation happens to give rise to a series of 'challenges'. Some individuals rise to these challenges, others fall by the wayside. In Japan, the impression was that managerial resources are used and deployed much more systematically. As Table 6.4 reveals, Japanese managers also frequently cited 'wide experience of challenging assignments' as critical to their growth. But these challenges came along in a far less haphazard way than was often the case for their British counterparts. The Japanese challenges were more genuinely accumulative: each experience led logically on to the next.

An important implication arises. Current thinking in management development circles is that a wide range of 'challenging experiences' and 'early exposure to positions of responsibility' are not only the typically most critical factors for most present business leaders but also to be *recommended as proven ways to develop potential* (Margerison, 1985; Margerison and Kakabadse, 1985). Yet our findings from Japan show that a mentor and a role model were often more important in that setting than either of these two most quoted factors. This suggests the possibility that the Anglo-American 'top two' merely reflect a state of play that arises by default. They may be identified as the most important factors explaining the growth of the current crop of top British managers merely because there has been a failure to provide more appropriate methods.

At Lucas, a common complaint was that the management development which began to appear in the late 1980s was far too 'parochial'. The separate businesses were reluctant to let 'their' best talent go and there was far too little transfer between businesses. If this problem was so well recognized, why had it not been tackled and resolved? There appeared to be two reasons. One was that priority had been given to survival and 'turnaround'. The heroes had been those individuals who could go into a failing business and rescue it. This was, by nature, crisis, short-term management. The other reason, according to a critique mounted by some of the business MDs, was that the top management in Lucas PLC were themselves simply not effective: they were 'administrators' who lacked sufficient 'hands-on' experience. The company, it was said, needed 'hard men' who could implement necessary policies. Whatever the causes of the problem there was certainly a widespread view from managers at all levels in the company that management development was inadequate. The perception was that the training department did not use appraisal reports for the proactive planning of training: if you asked for training you would probably get it, but not otherwise. Similarly, the general perception was that career planning was not occurring. Even graduate trainees were said not to receive sufficient training, mentoring or support and, as a result, there was a problem with graduates leaving the company.

A general manager of a Lucas division put the point from the 'receiving end':

> We have had a lot of management development initiatives which were 'filing cabinet fodder'. But now some useful things are beginning to happen: for example, at Aerospace board level every senior manager has been discussed by name and people have been actioned to do things as a result. In one instance this has meant taking a manager off his line job and employing him as an internal consultant cum trouble-shooter.

In general, however, it was the former situation, of limited impact in practice, rather than the promise of the new initiatives, which was the more common.

Overall, individual responsibility in Japan fitted into a centrally controlled structure. In Britain, there was less direction, and responsibility was much more atomized. Three of the Japanese firms were fairly similar to each other (the odd one out was Jusco), but in Britain Lucas and BT differed from Tesco and NatWest. The implication is that national-level effects need not be uniform; in particular, the competitive environment in Britain had cut more deeply into Lucas and BT than the other two organizations.

Influence of Culture and Role of Self-Development

'Privatization' was one of the forces which impelled an attempt to engineer culture change. The opportunity to study this process was available to us in the cases of BT and NTT. The various attributes of management development – including career planning, systematic training, high-flyer schemes and similar devices – were all seen as part and parcel of BT in 'the old civil service days'. But, with the run-up to privatization in the early 1980s and with privatization itself, most of these formal practices were either severely curtailed or abandoned altogether. As one senior manager put it,

> Jefferson and Bett [chairman and MD of the period] cleared the decks, Pol Pot fashion. The old sausage machine was destroyed.

In consequence, as another commented,

> When I joined BT in 1986, around the same time as Richard Worsley [the personnel director], we both commented that we could find practically no management development activity within this organization.

These comments express much about the prevailing view within BT during the years up to 1990. Management development was almost invariably seen as either absent, deficient or constituted by newly launched initiatives. The initiatives were, however, fragmented and usually seen as partial when compared with the more comprehensive system which had been displaced.

The previous long-standing seniority-based system had been dismantled and the training and development function which had supported it had also been drastically cut. A number of rather disparate initiatives such as the Top 300 programme had taken its place but there was now no comprehensive system; there was ambiguity about the relative responsibilities of head office, districts and functions; and, in all, training and development were seen as a much lower priority than the business objectives of cost reduction and headcount cuts. Those initiatives which were in place were generally regarded as experimental and unlikely to survive over the long term. The size, complexity and multiple levels of responsibility were causing immense confusion not only about what management development processes were operable but even about who was responsible for what.

The general line manager's view of the management development process was summed up by one level 3 manager with 20 years' experience in BT:

> Managers occur as an accident in BT; basically people with innate talent develop themselves *in situ*, they then rise to their level of incompetence . . . The whole system of training and development deteriorated until it just about disappeared completely. But in the last 18 months or so there has been some renewal – mostly as a consequence of TQM. We are now all desperately hoping that TQM was not a one-off and we hope we can really build it into our 'culture'.

While top corporate managers talked about the need for separate components of BT to develop their own processes to meet their particular needs, line managers had the opposite expectation. They wanted a lead from the centre and sense of a total business.

The contrast with NTT is clear. As in other Japanese firms, it is difficult to separate 'management development' from ongoing 'capability development' in NTT. It is a long 'slow-burn' process starting at the day of entry and targeted as much at attitudes and behaviour as at specific skills. However, with privatization there had been an interesting attempt to revise the system in order to produce a new kind of manager. As the head of management development told us, 'since privatization both senior and lower management need to be able to innovate, they can no longer merely follow what was done by their predecessors.' But how had the Japanese telecommunications company developed such an orientation? 'There is no better way,' we were told, 'than to expose staff to the direct stimulus of the market. Yet at the same time you need an enterprise culture which does not punish failure but applauds effort and ideas.'

It did seem that the largest proportion of Japanese managers were imbued with the notion that the development of subordinates is a critical part of what it means to be a manager. Development was not a secondary add-on or a luxury. As the NTT capability development head observed: 'We would expect that each manager will remember being told that one should perform one's work with regard not to how it might appear to your superior but how it appears to your subordinates.' In other words, continuous good examples are expected. Another part of the philosophy was the strong group orientation: 'People grow as part of a team. Achievement very seldom occurs as a result of the effort of a single individual' (*kacho*, technologist).

The old distinction between head office and regional recruits was removed and instead a potential management cadre of 2,000 graduate entrants a year was created (instead of the 400 'careerist' head office entrants under the traditional system). Regions became responsible for graduate training using a common curriculum. Notably, however, the selection and development of management resides with central personnel. Self-development was very important though not universal: ironically it was easier in the regions than at head office because only in the latter was overtime worked and staff therefore had little spare time.

NTT managers tended to confirm the existence of the management development devices described to us by the corporate architects of these systems. Line managers at all levels and all ages had almost invariably personally experienced all the elements of the system including two-month induction and OJT. The uniformity of experience was striking. A widely held view, despite the amount of on-the-job development, was that 'management training' *per se* was relatively slight and that managers had to absorb the craft of management along the way. There was also confirmation that OJT was taken seriously by colleagues – though it was not a matter of a systematic programme but rather a more generalized expectation of responsibility. Also some questioned whether it was forward-looking or merely copied old ways of doing things.

Summarizing the position concerning self-development is rather more difficult: a large part of the sample was engaged in an impressive number of activities while others in head office were so busy with overtime that they hardly had any time for anything else. One manager said that he attended evening classes twice a week between the hours of 5 and 7 p.m. and then returned to the office for a further two hours' work! Another said he had been attending English language classes in the evening for three years and in the first year he attended classes every weekday evening from 6 to 9 p.m. He subsequently moved on to use radio and audio tapes. Regional managers and others were often undertaking a surprising amount of self-development in the form of seminars, study groups and the like. And most were also doing OJT for their subordinates. None of them placed any primacy upon particular management training courses as of special significance – though MBA study in the USA had some cachet. The use of correspondence courses by managers was far higher than in the UK. A typical arrangement would see the firm paying half of the fees.

The careerist recruits had a sense of being chosen as an elite: they felt impelled to live up to this expectation. Self-development can be explained in part in this way: failure to live up to expectation would have been shameful (Ruth Benedict in *The Chrysanthemum and the Sword*, 1946, famously refers to a 'culture of guilt' in Japan).

At corporate level, the management development manager at Lucas was acutely conscious of the 'change management' character of what he was attempting. 'Implementation' was the crucial issue: systems and culture change there had to be, of that he was certain, but just how to proceed was giving cause for concern. The political dimension had somehow to be added to the equation. As suggested above, linkages between culture and management development remained uncertain.

By contrast, capability development in Sumitomo Electric was rooted in a philosophical base. The vice-president, Mr Nakahara, observed: 'We believe in personal fulfilment as well as corporate success.' Management development in Sumitomo, in Mr Nakahara's view, has two dimensions. One of these is to do with the acquisition of knowledge and this can, to a considerable degree, be transmitted by external experts as a universal and independent set of ideas. But the other is the inculcation of what might (somewhat inadequately) be termed 'corporate culture'. This latter cannot be entrusted to external trainers; managers need to be socialized into it over a very long period. But it is through this process that

> the manager must cultivate adaptability to the Sumitomo way – it demands collaboration and cooperation . . . Using this dimension of 'management development' individuals learn goals and values: these they can help to re-create as well as transmit to their subordinates in due course. (vice-president, Sumitomo)

One part of those goals and values is indeed the importance of continued self-development. Hence, one of the most enduringly impressive features of most of the managers we met (at all levels) was their engagement in developmental activities – often at their own instigation. Examples included managers learning in their spare time, attending and indeed organizing seminars associated with their areas of expertise and interest. Notably, much of this effort was underpinned by direct or indirect support.

Another Sumitomo manager, a general manager of a plant, talked of the self-development opportunities arising from the requirement upon him to make presentations about four times a year on the international economy and Sumitomo's place within it. For these presentations he stressed how, in preparation, he drew heavily upon his 'year mates' who are spread across many parts of the business. He also said his loyalty to them was very deep-seated and he would put a request from any one of them right to the top of his priorities.

We were informed by senior management that it is an accepted part of the duties of *kacho* and *bucho* to ensure that their subordinates are motivated enough to undertake self-development. In other words, rather than seeing self-development as a mere optional extra with the responsibility entirely resting with the subordinate to develop themselves, superiors would see it as a failure if appropriate self-development activity was not occurring. We asked for an estimate of the proportion of senior managers who, in practice, had embraced this responsibility. We were told that as many as 90 per cent of middle and senior managers had demonstrated that they had accepted this as a real duty. Mr Okayama, *bucho* in the head office personnel department, reported that some managers had in fact been demoted because of their failure to perform this 'vital function'.

The habit of self-development is apparently inculcated at an early stage. Mr Ariumi (now a *bucho*) recalled how, as a new graduate recruit, he had been assigned to two and a half month's practical experience on the shop-floor of a factory. He had had no previous experience of factory work and so everything he encountered was entirely novel. He began keeping detailed notes on many aspects of economic life at the sharp end – including the values, attitudes and problems of shop-floor workers. His observations were written in the form of a daily report and these he used in order to write a weekly report, a copy of which he sent to personnel.

The form taken by self-development is in the main somewhat similar to OJT. Subordinates are set small projects with a target date for completion. A project report and analysis has to be presented for assessment to the *kacho*, who may indicate aspects that could be investigated further, and some reading associated with the task may be set. The subordinate is also expected to consult with colleagues and then report back to the *kacho*. Even though the procedure can be described in this way, it was suggested to us that self-development should really be regarded as an ideal and 'an attitude of mind', rather than a particular methodology.

In NatWest the main trend was towards an approach which, compared with the past, was more systematic and more scientific while at the same time being based on self-development as opposed to the 'laying-on of hands' or something 'done to you'. A management development professional underlined the former aspect, and its business rationale:

> We are not here to give people sexy career paths: everything we do in management development has to support the business; management development used to be seen as a fruit machine to be played . . . If you were not having fun and an interesting career . . . then blame this function!

Contrary to the image of management development specialists as the kind of people who might be expected to promote career mobility in the face of opposition from line managers who would want to hold on to valued staff, in some cases it was rather the development specialists who were found to be insisting on the centrality of business needs. For example, a young bright manager in a senior post in a West Country branch had been in post for just 12 months. When a job came up in a corporate business centre, he applied and he secured his regional executive director's support, and the move was almost a *fait accompli* when:

> I stepped in. 'Who are you looking after,' I asked, 'what about the customers?' We need to avoid some people getting over-hooked on the promotion culture. (corporate-level management development manager, NatWest)

The career development unit in NatWest employed some 40 staff. They were involved in graduate recruitment and the running of assessment centres. In addition they were the overseers of a fast track of about 500 people. They summarized their responsibilities as: to induct, train, conserve, and maintain contact with the main body of graduate recruits. Graduate recruitment was costing the bank about £1 million a year – that is, 250 graduates per annum at about £4,000 each. All the clearing banks had a fast track but NatWest was considered to have a more centralized and elaborate scheme than the others; it was the undoubted leader in aftercare service and this showed in the reduced wastage rates of graduates under its wing.

There was a major controversy over whether the 'one-bank' concept should be preserved or whether development should encourage the emergence of a series of separate specialisms. Corporate and Institutional Banking (CIB) had three main parts: corporate banking (looking after the banking needs of large corporations); group treasury; and capital markets. Corporate banking was seen as the 'glamour' side of the business. CIB managers and staff were part of the same corporate arrangements for recruitment, pay, and development and appraisal as other domestic parts of the bank. But, senior managers in CIB argued their distinctiveness in terms of higher levels of expertise than the average banker. A manager in CIB, it was argued, 'must be able to stare into the whites of the eyes of finance directors of some of the world's major multinational corporations and know their business'. In this situation it was expected that managers here would be highly trained as specialists and become aware of state-of-the-art developments. In consequence, it was argued by CIB that there was a need to alter employment arrangements to allow for distinct terms, conditions and development arrangements to emerge more clearly.

NatWest was in the middle of a shift from a lending/control culture to a sales/marketing culture. It was said that 'overnight half of our management stream could be unsuitable!' Under such circumstances people complained, '"it's not what I joined the bank to do" – you can hear this complaint every day'. And it was thought not to be a problem entirely amenable to a training solution. As one manager put it, 'we need chaps who are prepared to ring up the MD of companies on the local trading estates and in effect say, "you don't bank with us at the moment but there are some good reasons why you ought to, I would like to come and see you."'

Additionally, there is increasing specialization including relationship banking, IT, campaigns and mail drops, audit, planning and strategy, lawyers, accountants. There is also a move to develop experts in specific industries:

> In the future we will need to facilitate these specialisms rather than going for the all-rounder. The models have switched: the old one was like a pyramid with a wide common base, but the bank is now moving towards something that might look more like an umbrella – that is an early common spine but then a branching out into separate spokes. We no longer say that you have to learn all the jobs in the way that we did 10 years ago. (senior executive, CIB)

A branch development manager, who had his wife and two sons working for the organization, illustrates the changing culture. He said that during his own first 10 years with NatWest he had stagnated: he had not stood out in any way, or even bothered to take professional examinations (like 50 per cent of others). He then worked with a series of people who had a critical effect on him: 'I have learned as much in 14 months as I had done in the previous 14 years.' This led him to view it as 'all about creating and taking your own opportunities'. The implication here, of course, is that even under the 'old system' there was no guarantee that individuals would take advantage of the training opportunities – in contrast to Mitsui, where there was no such option. As for the current situation, this manager was critical of way the bank screened at too early an age, citing his sons who had not got on the management development programme because they answered questions wrongly and, he suggested, not aggressively enough. Yet he was still willing to subscribe to the social Darwinist view that cream rises to the top in due course. We have seen, however, that such optimism may be misplaced and that the talents being sought were changing rapidly as NatWest changes its commercial culture.

Overall, therefore, we have argued that changing expectations were, in organizations like BT and NatWest in particular, altering the whole context and meaning of management development. It is no wonder that the recipients of management development devices expressed such uncertainty.

Discussion and Conclusions

The strengths of the development process in Japan are brought out in this chapter. But this should not be taken to mean that the Japanese organizations had no problems in this regard. Two key ones deserve emphasis here. First, there are some indicators of dissatisfaction in Japan. As we saw both in this chapter and in Chapter 5, there was a concern that the management development system was just too formalized and standardized, with the result that its products lacked independence and entrepreneurial skills. Our findings here thus add empirical weight to widespread general arguments on this point (for example, Whitehill, 1991). It also has to be said, however, that our results do not support those who see the system as being in deep crisis. There were tensions and new challenges, but the overwhelming impression is of a system that remained valued and admired and that worked because it was deeply embedded in the workings of the Japanese corporation. A related set of issues concerned the pressures faced by managers themselves, notably the expectation that they would devote time at weekends to self-development. As is often noted, the Japanese system is an extremely demanding one, and at least some of our respondents were recognizing this as a problem. Again, however, the tensions remained implicit, and it was only a minority who even identified them at all. And then there were also the external pressures on the system. At NTT, privatization was challenging existing assumptions, while at Jusco the move towards an approach with more emphasis on merit, and with the acceptance of recruitment by means other than the internal labour market, was leading to adaptation of the 'Japanese system'. The system had strong resemblances in all four firms, but it was not identical.

Second, giving individuals more say in their career development and personal development may be an issue with which Japanese organizations will soon have to grapple. To some extent the trend is already in that direction. Japanese managers in our sample were being encouraged to make more effective use of the information coming forward from the 'self-reporting' system. Another move in recognition of this need is the increasing practice of advertising vacancies internally – though at the moment such instances are still unusual and are mainly confined to special project assignments.

The whole issue of encouraging rather more 'individuality' to counter the famed 'groupism' in Japan is recognized as an especially difficult problem. But steps are being taken to address it. For example, there is an increasing tendency to introduce merit pay into the hitherto seniority-based payment system. The stage at which merit will play a part in determining the pace of promotion is also tending to be brought forward in people's careers. Such steps are designed to encourage a rather different type of managerial leader to come forward to help face the rapid pace of change.

The last five years in particular have witnessed the whole system of capability development in Japan. Interestingly, what is most notable amidst the range of changes is that the function of in-company education (note that management development is just one part of this totality of commitment and provision for education, training and development of the human resource) has acquired an even higher profile during this period. In each of the four Japanese firms which we researched, this fact was very evident. That is, firms were looking to strengthen their systems of capability development. The contrast with Britain was striking, for here, and most notably at BT and NatWest, the move was away from structured internal labour markets towards individual activity and concepts such as employability. 'Development' had become the property of the individual manager – with a vengeance.

This point comes out very clearly from the views of 'recipients'. In Japan, self-development was emphasized, but in a context strongly defined by the corporate centre. In our British organizations, there was much less certainty about 'ownership' and a very varied view of the actual and desired role of management development professionals. In Lucas and BT, for example, individual responsibility was stressed even though central systems were relatively weak. We noted above the specific implication of such findings: that prescriptions as to the benefit of early experience of managerial challenges may work only in an Anglo-American context and may then only serve a small minority of managers with the talent, or luck, to use the opportunity.

A wider implication concerns the 'British system'. We have seen that Japanese management development (in large companies, which are not of course representative of the whole economy) was relatively homogeneous. In Britain there was more variety, as the contrast between Tesco and the other firms shows, and also more sensitivity to the external environment:

the shock of privatization was felt more deeply at BT than at NTT. Here we have a good example of the nature of 'national systems' of organizational management (Hickson and Pugh, 1995). Distinct Japanese and British contexts have been identified above. Both exerted influences on in-company developments. But the British environment was more permissive in the sense that individual firms could swim more easily against the tide.

Finally, to address adequately the bigger picture of how managers are made, it is necessary to go beyond the consciously designed mechanisms of recruitment and selection, career planning, training and management development. Our research suggests there are other processes which are influential in shaping managerial capability and behaviour patterns and these include the ways in which managers are set goals and targets, the way they are evaluated, the mechanisms used to control managerial work and the system of rewards. We turn to these issues in the next chapter.

Notes

1 A reliability analysis showed that a 1–5 scoring had additivity problems. We therefore created a new index in which the scores were transformed to run from 1.00 to 1.71. This index had an acceptable reliability coefficient (alpha = 0.71) and the additivity problem was removed. For the sake of simplicity, the table reports the scores based on a 1–5 scale, but for the analysis of variations in the index we used the transformed measure.

2 The analysis of variance results were as follows:

	Sum of squares	*Sig. of F*
Sector	9.34	0.00
Country	2.38	0.01
Interaction	4.58	0.01
Explained	16.00	
Residual	81.85	

7

The Evaluation, Reward
and Control of Managers

Studies of management development, like many other parts of the management literature, have often assumed a fundamental identity of interest between managers and their employers. The organization is taken to want to maximize the potential of its managers, who share the interest in being trained and developed. Yet in the complex and uncertain world of business it is not always possible to reconcile individual and collective needs. Promotion opportunities may not match the demand, managers may be allocated posts that they do not want, and during the 1980s the phenomenon of managerial redundancy raised in stark form the issue of the expendability of managers. More fundamentally, managers are employees, and they are likely to have interests which diverge from those of the shareholders. A growing literature has addressed what is termed the agency problem: managers act as the agents of their employers, and the problem is to find mechanisms to ensure that they act in ways consistent with the employers' interests (Armstrong, 1987; 1989). One mechanism is to build up a relationship of trust and a sense of obligation. Other, more overt, levers include the 'carrots' of reward and the 'sticks' of systems to monitor performance and to put pressure on managers to fulfil their obligations.

It is with these matters that this chapter is concerned. We thus broaden the perspective from the specifics of career planning to a consideration of the constraints and conflicts of the managerial role, a key component of the overall 'making' of managers.

Previous studies contain surprisingly little information on these topics. A volume on *Managers as Employees* (Roomkin, 1989), based on research in several countries, contains material on the demographic profiles of managers and career patterns but very little on how managers are motivated and controlled. Kotter's (1982) well-known study of 15 very senior general managers in the United States says nothing about their agency position or about how they were monitored. A few studies are beginning to address this issue. Smith (1990) conducted an interesting analysis of middle managers in a Californian bank. She found that wide-ranging restructuring, involving a shift from a bureaucratic and predictable environment to a more uncertain and market-driven situation, was having a profound effect. Managers came under two sorts of pressure: first, to control their subordinates more forcibly, so that they were expected to 'manage out' the least productive, the bank's formal commitment to a no-layoff policy notwithstanding; and, second, to take on more responsibility and be more 'entrepreneurial'. Managers were required to use their own discretion while also being under closer control from above, a situation which Smith describes as one of 'coercive autonomy'. As we will see, there were similar tendencies in some of our organizations, and we return to the implications of Smith's study in the conclusion to this chapter.

Some British studies have also suggested that control may be becoming tighter and more overt. Dopson and Stewart (1990) studied 11 firms and noted that pressures for change were increasing the responsibilities of middle managers and that computerized information systems made their performance more visible to their superiors. Scase and Goffee's (1989) survey of 374 managers from six organizations contains several pointers: managers stated that their working week had increased; there was a sense of being overworked and under-utilized; and pay compensated for these dissatisfactions to only a limited extent. Scase and Goffee present no information on appraisal or on monitoring systems, but their attitudinal data can be set against the results of the present study. We certainly found strong demands on managers. But the situations in our four British companies differed considerably, and a universal picture would be inapplicable. Moreover, the managerial response was more nuanced than it was in Scase and Goffee's study, for reasons which we explore in the conclusions to the chapter.

Other British work has explored the tensions of control and autonomy. Keen (1995: 93), in a study of middle managers in a county council, finds that budgetary devolution had increased their control over the deployment of financial resources. However, autonomy was constrained by 'the increasingly detailed and prescriptive nature' of financial control systems. Monitoring and control were increasing features of managers' lives.

While the Anglo-American literature stresses work pressure and the measurement of individual performance, the picture of Japan is one of more diffuse modes of control. According to Ouchi (1981: 40), control is achieved not through specific targets but through an approach or philosophy, with objectives being much more loosely defined than they are in American firms. Rohlen's (1974) detailed study of a bank confirmed the group-based nature of decision-making and of authority as being based on involvement and not impersonal bureaucratic rules. But it also underlined the pressures of the system such as ten-hour days, six hours of work on Saturdays, and the practice of staying at work beyond even these hours, a practice which was formally voluntary but which in fact stemmed from group expectations. How, though, are Japanese managers appraised and rewarded, and what do they think of these systems? We hoped to be able to throw some light on such questions.

Our material is not as detailed as it might be. The study focused on management development and not on control systems as such. When we were designing the study, moreover, issues of the control of managers were less firmly on the agenda than they became by the mid 1990s. Nonetheless, the questionnaire part of the study sought managers' perceptions of how closely they were evaluated, of the fairness of the evaluation system, of the reward system, and of the factors which motivated them. In some but by no means all of the interviews we explored in more detail managers' feelings about the reporting system and any pressures or constraints that they felt they were under. Within the design of the project as a whole, we feel that we have at least been able to address some issues that have rarely been studied at all.

We begin by considering the clarity of the objectives set for managers and how they were evaluated against these objectives. We then turn to systems of reward before looking at motivation and work pressures. Finally, we draw out the implications of the results in the light of previous studies.

Objectives and Evaluation

Objectives

A theme running through the interviews in every company was commercialism: managers were expected to view their duties in the light of the market needs of the company, and not in a narrowly technical way. This was most evident in the two telecommunications companies, where privatization had brought market pressures sharply into focus. As a senior NTT manager put it, before privatization initiative was discouraged and following established procedures was rewarded, but now those who could relate to customers and be entrepreneurial were favoured. But similar processes were at work in the other sectors. Banks were traditionally very bureaucratic organizations, but competition during the 1980s, with other financial institutions as much as with other banks, changed this situation. As a NatWest manager saw it, in the past bank managers had been evaluated against technical criteria such as care in lending but now there was more emphasis on being 'close to the customer' and being able to market new products.

The impact of such expectations on managerial jobs was, however, far from automatic. The more apocalyptic American studies of the new corporation, with titles such as *Thriving on Chaos* (Peters, 1987) and *When Giants Learn to Dance* (Kanter, 1989), imply that a whole new flexible approach has swept through the business world. Yet our firms were all large organizations with formal grading structures, to say nothing of legacies of history, and the bureaucratic manager does not turn into an entrepreneur overnight. Neither would firms necessarily desire this, for they would hardly want to have to discipline an army of frustrated *entrepreneurs manqués*. Market needs impacted in more complex ways. The timing of our study was fortuitous in enabling us to tap into these factors.

The stores offer one set of examples. Some Jusco managers suggested that the autonomy of store managers was declining as more of the key decisions were made centrally. More detailed information on Tesco pointed to a similar process. Store managers operated within tight limits defined centrally. Not only was purchasing done centrally but so was the layout of stores. Moreover, a central organization and methods (O&M) department established baseline figures for staffing, setting a further set of parameters within which managers had to work. The objectives for managers were not entrepreneurial but involved working within clearly established systems.

Lucas offers a different example of similar processes: since stores and banks offer a nationwide service of a standard product, it is to be expected that they will have strong central direction, but Lucas included a wide variety of businesses. Yet here, too, managers were not left to tackle the market as they saw fit. The key instrument of objective setting was the competitiveness achievement plan (CAP), which was a detailed assessment of the state of an operating unit and a statement of its aims over the short and the medium terms. The CAP was negotiated between the manager of a unit and his or her superior: it was not imposed, but it was subject to close scrutiny before it was agreed. After its agreement, progress was monitored carefully. Managers who were not themselves responsible for a business were not directly subject to CAPs, but the senior management team would be involved in preparing a CAP, and all managers had their goals shaped by the aims established under the plan.

It might be expected that such moves towards central direction would produce specific objectives for managers; alternatively, entrepreneurial expectations could generate only general guides to action and a degree of uncertainty. The former tendency predominated. We asked our questionnaire sample whether key objectives were clearly specified in writing, were not written but still clear, were written but formed only a broad guide, or were not written and were subject to some uncertainty. As Table 7.1 shows, the overall pattern was for the former to predominate: 45 per cent of the sample felt that objectives were clearly specified in writing, with only 5 per cent expressing some uncertainty. There were, however, differences between sectors and countries. Both banks were marked by very clear objectives, as would be expected from the fairly precise criteria against which bank employees can be assessed. Uncertainty was strongest in telecommunications, particularly BT. This probably reflects the difficulties surrounding the process of privatization, in which case we can conclude that the process threw up more uncertainties for BT managers than for their NTT counterparts. Given the highly charged atmosphere surrounding the BT privatization, this would seem to have been likely.

In the stores, the tendency was for objectives to be written, no doubt for reasons similar to those applying to the banks, but there was also a 'country effect' in that the tendency was stronger in Jusco. In engineering, there was the reverse pattern. However, the main difference was whether or not objectives were written down, with Sumitomo having a uniquely low tendency in this direction. Taking the two 'clear' categories together, however, there was no difference. Our interview material developed the

Table 7.1 *Clarity of objectives* (%)

	Lucas	Sumitomo	NatWest	Mitsui	Tesco	Jusco	BT	NTT	All
Clearly written	41	7	66	72	50	74	28	20	45
Unwritten but clear	41	73	15	20	19	22	25	56	33
Written, broad guide	16	20	15	8	15	4	28	16	15
Some uncertainty	3	0	2	0	8	0	16	8	5
Other	0	0	2	0	8	0	3	0	2

implications of this. Sumitomo managers were no less certain than their counterparts elsewhere of the objectives that they were set. But the company tended to prefer relatively informal ways of setting goals. As we saw in Chapter 4, it used interviews in preference to more formal recruitment techniques, and stressed the importance of finding people with appropriate attitudes. And we describe below several ways in which cultural expectations were established. The result was that written objectives were less necessary than they were in Lucas.

It appears, then, that there were some clear sectoral differences and that there was a tendency for objectives to be more clearly specified in the Japanese companies. This would go against any idea that Japanese managers are organized only through a diffuse loyalty to the group: this may have been important, but our Japanese firms also used more overt methods of establishing objectives.

We have some information on how our questionnaire sample felt about the targets that they were set, though this is far from comprehensive. In Tesco in particular, several managers commented on the tightness of their objectives. One argued that work pressures had increased through a more rapid pace of work and tighter schedules. Others, while making similar points, also stressed that they accepted the need for close control. As a trading director put it, he was assessed against weekly sales targets, but he had no problems with this, having entered the job with his eyes open; he also felt that he was highly paid, and expected to have to show that he was earning his salary. Only one Tesco manager explicitly raised the issue of whether tight targets led to an unduly short-term approach. In his view it was not a problem: he had absolutely clear objectives, central direction was essential for success in the retail sector, and he was comfortable with the direction which the company was taking. These comments captured the general atmosphere of the company: there was a strong awareness of the developments of the past decade, there was a sense of direction from the top, and hence the tight targets within which individual managers were expected to work seemed to fit into an overall purpose.

Similar forces were at work in NatWest, where several managers spoke of their targets being tighter and more explicit. But this did not necessarily produce discontent. One branch manager explained this at some length. He was set sales targets which were in principle negotiable with regional management, but since the region was operating within targets established at a higher level there was in practice little room for manoeuvre. Targets were constantly being refined and tightened, as illustrated by the fact that each region had a sales manager with whom branch managers had to work closely. This long-serving branch manager might have been expected to complain about such close controls, but in fact he welcomed them, for two reasons. First, they established discipline and a sense of purpose, though there was a need to refine some of the targets to fit the circumstances of each branch. Second, they encouraged a close working relationship with the region, in place of the former bureaucratic reporting system.

In these two organizations, short-term targets seemed to fit with longer-term goals, which is perhaps not surprising given that they were both in the retail business and did not need to invest large sums in complex and risky new projects. Lucas, by contrast, has increasingly defined itself as competing in the world market for aerospace and automotive parts. It is thus a particularly suitable case to consider the argument that British firms are driven by short-term financial considerations and are therefore unable to take the longer view. The debate about short-termism is often unduly simplified. As several Lucas managers pointed out, a stark contrast between the short and the long term is inappropriate, since without short-term profits there can be no long term. We see Lucas, not as an example of a company which had or had not evaded short-termism, but as a particular example of how the dual pressures of the short term and the long term are handled.

The CAP was the key instrument in this process, and several managers described their experience with it. At one extreme a couple of managers in Aerospace complained of short-termism: the CAP was dominated by profit targets for the coming year, and there was no room to develop proper long-term plans. They felt that stiff annual targets interfered with other aims of growing the business, particularly when the complex technologies that they handled could need a five-year planning horizon. One gave the example of the year's profit target, which had been increased without warning, a practice which jeopardized longer-term thinking. The company could also make demands without providing the means by which the demands could be met. An illustration of these themes comes from a general manager:

> The CAP system is very good as a goal but in practice the company is still dominated by short-termism which results from trying above all to keep the City happy. The annual forecast is extremely detailed with stiff targets on return on capital and the like. We are also set aims of growing the business. Last year it took me four attempts to get my plan accepted and that was frustrating. (general manager of a Lucas business)

This quotation encapsulates the themes of external pressure and short-termism, negotiation of targets (rather than simply following instructions), and strong centrally determined parameters of business unit performance.

Yet such concerns were less evident in other parts of the business. Managers in Industrial Systems, for example, tended to say that they had a reasonable and often informal relationship with their superiors and that the CAP system was creating a strategy within which different businesses fitted. Emphases certainly varied. One managing director of an operating unit described in detail how the CAP worked and did not see it as constraining long-term plans. Indeed, in the past each unit had been virtually free-standing and simply a source of profits for the company as a whole, but now there was a longer-term view as to how they fitted together. Others were less sanguine. One, for example, noted that a stress on profit could lead to a neglect of business growth.

These differences were probably due to the different natures of the activities of Aerospace and Industrial Systems. The former was a long-standing part of the 'core' of Lucas, and it involved long-term relationships with the major aeroplane manufacturers. A long-term vision was particularly important. The latter was composed of a mix of businesses which had in some cases been run in the past as free-standing units, so that short-termism had been a way of life and moves away from it were welcome. Lucas as a whole was endeavouring to handle a range of pressures. We are not in a position to judge how successfully it was managing them. We did not, for example, set out to assess its overall business strategy. What we can say is that the company exemplified the tensions of an organization attempting to give profit responsibility to its operating units at the same time as exercising central strategic control. These tensions had not produced anything approaching a crisis of confidence among middle managers. Even the two Aerospace managers accepted much of the logic of the business. And there was no evident solution to the tensions, for they were an inherent aspect of the position of the company. They arose in sharper form than they did in NatWest or Tesco because of the different character of the companies, and they required recognition and active management if they were not to provoke real difficulties in the future.

In BT, targets as such did not appear to be such an issue. As noted above, BT managers were much the least likely to feel that targets were clear. Their criticisms tended to focus around other aspects of the control system, such as evaluation, to which we now turn.

Evaluation Systems

All our organizations operated formal systems for appraising their managers. We did not set out to look at the schemes in their own right but concentrated on the methods which our questionnaire sample felt were used to assess them, their views of the evaluation system, and how closely they felt that they were evaluated.

Operation of Evaluation Systems   The methods of appraisal showed striking differences between the two countries. As Table 7.2 shows, appraisal at least once a year was (perhaps not surprisingly) virtually universal. But it was rare for British managers to be appraised more often than annually, whereas in Japan this was very common. Jusco reviewed managers every six months to determine the size of the bonus to be paid; the bonus depended in part on overall company performance but was also related to each manager's personal rating. There was, in addition, an annual assessment of broader managerial capabilities such as leadership and the development of subordinates. In both appraisals, the initial evaluation was conducted by the immediate superior, but the resulting grades were then checked by the next highest level in an attempt to ensure consistency and fairness. Mitsui employed a similar system, except that three levels were

Table 7.2 *Methods of evaluating performance (% mentioning each item)*

	Lucas	Sumitomo	NatWest	Mitsui	Tesco	Jusco	BT	NTT	All
Annual appraisal	58	56	100	12	77	100	100	60	64
Appraisal more than once p.a.	19	52	7	84	31	81	6	48	37
Unit results	52	7	83	12	65	4	39	12	42
Own performance	29	11	68	4	31	4	30	24	31

involved in the assessment of a manager. NTT also had a six-monthly system of three stages, in this case with first marking by the immediate superior, second marking by the next level, and final adjustment by the personnel department. The particular feature of the system was the way in which it had changed with privatization. Under the old system, points had been deducted for errors, which encouraged a cautious, rule-bound approach, but now points were added for new initiatives in an effort to stimulate innovation. Sumitomo practised six-monthly appraisal of managers at more junior levels (up to and including the status level of *shusa*, which a manager might attain after 13 years with the firm), and annual appraisal for the higher levels of *kacho* and above.

To British eyes, at least as remarkable as the frequency of evaluation was the detail of the process. Mitsui's annual reporting form, for example, required information not only on expertise and qualifications but also on managers' domestic situations and the state of health of themselves and of their family. The biannual performance evaluation form listed achievements and efforts made, commented on the manager's diligence, and evaluated performance into five bands. The two bands of 'excellent' and 'average' were further sub-divided into three levels, so that there was a nine-point scale of performance. British organizations certainly employ detailed appraisal forms (Long, 1986). But the combination of the frequency of assessment, the way in which the process was built into the operation of the business, and the careful checking of appraisals by higher levels pointed to a more systematic evaluation of performance in Japan.

A final distinctive feature of the Japanese system was the lack of feedback to the individual. As Endo (1994: 73) explains in an important analysis of the personal assessment system in Japan, superiors evaluate performance but the appraisee is 'not informed of the final score'. As an executive director of Sumitomo put it to us:

> In America appraisal takes place at the time of the evaluation and the manager and subordinate enter into a dialogue. In this company, evaluation takes place without consultation [and] there is no feedback to the individual.

The contrast with the Anglo-Saxon model of feedback and personal target setting is very clear. But the manager just quoted also made the significant point that 'a *kacho*'s contact with his subordinates is frequent and intimate – it does not require a special meeting at the time of the reporting of the evaluation.' As we saw in Chapters 5 and 6, in important respects Japanese managers do own their own careers, and expectations as to conduct are developed through frequent informal interaction with superiors. The system balances closed, formal and apparently rigid reporting with dense informal relationships.

In view of this, it is at first sight surprising to find our Japanese managers reporting only rarely that their own performance was evaluated. Mitsui, in particular, had a particularly extensive procedure, including in the annual report a list of 15 traits such as attention to detail and initiative against which the appraisee was required to judge themselves and which the appraiser then confirmed. Yet only one of the Mitsui respondents cited 'own performance'. The explanation is probably that appraisal systems in Japan are rooted in a group or collective approach. As is well known, decision-making is a group process and individuals are locked into a corporate culture. Though they were evaluated in terms of their own competence and skills, our Japanese managers did not think that this meant that their own personal performance was measured; arguably, they would not be able to make a distinction between their own performance and that of their group.

The small numbers of Japanese managers citing 'unit results' would fit in with this interpretation: evaluation meant assessing the talents and activities of each manager in terms of what they were contributing to the organization, not looking at a balance sheet of results. The system was not atomized as it commonly is in Britain. Of our British firms, unit results and the manager's own performance were particularly important in NatWest and Tesco, which is consistent with the above argument that in these organizations the establishment of clear targets, and the measurement of managers against them, was more feasible than it was in the less structured environments of Lucas and BT.

In terms of the overall concerns of this study – to see how far various structures and practices vary between our two countries and how far within a particular industrial sector there are common forces at work – this suggests an important conclusion. That systems differed so much between the banks and the stores in the two countries suggests that the 'country effect' was dominant here. At the same time, the use of close measures of performance in the British bank and store suggests that, where the national situation is conducive, the product market circumstances of such sectors promote a strong focus on individual achievement.

Managerial Responses to Evaluation How did managers react to these systems? We asked them to rate the system used to evaluate their performance on six criteria such as efficient/inefficient and fair/unfair. Each was measured on a five-point scale. We found that replies on these criteria were correlated, so that we could add them together to produce one measure of attitudes.[1] As Figure 7.1 shows, the overall response was generally favourable. A score of 3 represents the mid-point of the scale, and in seven of the eight companies replies fell on the 'favourable' side; in the eighth, Jusco, they were exactly on this point. But favourableness was far from total. The overall mean score of 2.7 was not far from the mid-point, and the lowest mean was 2.41. Moreover, as the results show, very few managers (one from BT and one from NTT) gave replies indicating complete satisfaction.

Though scores were similar between companies, there was a complex pattern of differences. There were no significant differences between the average scores of the two countries, which is interesting enough in suggesting that the Japanese are not always more 'successful' than the

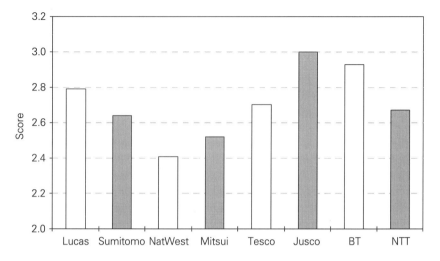

Figure 7.1 *Views of evaluation system (scores: 1 favourable, 5 unfavourable)*

British. There were sectoral differences, with the banks having the most favourable attitudes and the stores the least favourable. There were no differences between each pair of companies within a sector, which strengthens the view that there were some sector-specific forces at work. When we looked within countries, we found that NatWest scored significantly 'better' than the other British firms, and that Mitsui did likewise in Japan. The 'poor' score in Jusco was significantly different from the average of the other three Japanese companies. This was not the result of a few outlying observations, for replies in Jusco clustered close to the mean, indicating a widely shared set of responses to the evaluation system.

The appraisal scores can be taken as a continuous variable, for which an analysis of variance (see Appendix A) is appropriate. No statistical interaction was discerned: although Jusco had a particularly high score, this could be attributed to a sectoral effect. The reason for a lack of statistical interaction is not hard to see: Jusco had the highest scores of the Japanese firms whereas Tesco had the second lowest scores among the British firms; but BT had the highest British scores while NTT did not do similarly 'badly'. There were some particular idiosyncrasies in the results but these did not fall into a clear pattern of statistical interaction. What is clear is that the banks in the two countries recorded favourable scores, that BT and Jusco did rather badly, and that there was no overall tendency for Japanese managers to be any more satisfied than their British counterparts.

Our interview data help to explain part of this picture. In Jusco, to begin with the case of most dissatisfaction, one manager argued that the bonuses attached to the appraisal system were not large enough to compensate for the generally low salary level of the retail sector; this connected with his wider feelings that the reward structure was not very motivational. There was an interesting contrast here with Tesco, where managers generally stressed the high level of rewards that they enjoyed. A second Jusco manager felt that six months was too short a period for a serious measurement of performance, while a third saw the process as too narrow: the focus was too heavily on immediate results, with the developmental aspects being neglected. Similar themes emerged from some of the Tesco interviews. One manager felt that the system worked reasonably well on its own terms but that it was not a motivational tool: whatever he did, he would probably receive a 'fully competent' rating and nothing higher, but this had not interfered with being promoted, and he was motivated by more general needs and responsibilities than a score in an appraisal. Another saw the system as unduly subjective and prone to the establishment of 'woolly' objectives which he should not, in retrospect, have accepted. But the system was in its early stages and would settle down in time. Others spoke of the subjectivity of the process; as one put it, a manager given a rating of 3 on the five-point scale that was used would find it hard to give a higher rating to his subordinates however much they deserved it. The implication of such comments is that managers, while far from enthusiastic about appraisal schemes, were not deeply discontented. As one Tesco manager put it, it was helpful to discuss where he was going, and the system helped to clarify what he was doing, but there were problems of subjectivity and his ambitions were wider than the system could embrace: he was saying, in effect, that the system was useful as far as it went, that it had its limitations, and that it was not something to be very excited about.

In BT, the other organization with a relatively high level of dissatisfaction, the situation was rather different. Here, views on appraisal inevitably became connected with those on the performance-related pay system that was being introduced even though the two systems were supposedly kept separate. Three broad responses could be distinguished. At one extreme, one manager said that he found the system totally demotivating because of its vague criteria and the uncertain way in which they were applied. At the other were those who thought that appraisal was broadly satisfactory and indeed inevitable. But perhaps the commonest response was one of uncertainty. As one manager put it, he could be given goals but did not have control of the resources to achieve them, leaving him unsure of how he would thus be evaluated. Another saw the criteria for appraisal as shifting and unclear, while a third saw them as unduly complex. Performance-related pay, together with the many other changes that BT was undergoing, arguably created an environment in which familiar landmarks had disappeared but no new markers had become established.

In our other organizations, similar criticisms to those quoted above appeared from time to time. The subjectivity of appraisal was perhaps the most common theme. But this seemed to be taken more or less as an inevitable part of managerial life. In NatWest, for example, there were few criticisms of the appraisal system as such. As one branch manager explained, the process was very formal, everything was written down, and there were no real problems. There was, however, one concern which emerged in the Japanese companies, particularly Sumitomo. This was the lack of feedback of the results of the appraisal. Sumitomo managers explained that the rules of their system forbade the reporting of the results of an appraisal to the appraisee, and several commented on the secrecy and unfairness that this engendered. In other companies, there was apparently little discussion of the results of appraisal, though the ban on communicating the outcome was less rigid than it was in Sumitomo.

Two conclusions thus emerge. In general, managers were not enthusiastic about appraisal. Academic analysts of the subject have highlighted several potential difficulties, but the experience of managers themselves has less often been charted. For our managers, it was the vagueness of aims and the subjectivity with which the achievement of these aims was assessed that provoked most concern. The fact that British and Japanese managers shared these concerns indicates that, in this respect at least, the Japanese system of managerial organization was not in advance of Britain's. Moreover, the nature of the appraisal system means that the system, unlike, say, a distinct mode of training, is dependent on specific aspects of the Japanese business environment. A lack of openness in the criteria used and in the communication of the result would go against all expectations of appraisal in an Anglo-Saxon context. This closure was also provoking some adverse comment even in Japan. It is one part of an issue, which has already arisen in the discussion of career planning in Chapter 4 and of training and education in Chapter 6, facing Japanese firms: namely, how far they treat managers as pawns within a system and how far they give them choice in careers and a say in systems of appraisal.

Second, reasons for differences between companies can be suggested. Thus the uncertainties of BT managers fit in with our other information on this company, and the worries about subjectivity in Tesco can be related to the novelty of the system. Quite why Jusco managers were so discontented is less apparent, though it may be related to two features of the organization. First, as noted above, their overall pay levels and their status as compared with that of managers in the more prestigious financial and manufacturing sectors were perceived to be low. Second, as seen in Chapter 3, the company was unusual in Japan for the extent to which it relied on merit, and not seniority, to promote its managers. The result may have been that appraisal was more fateful for Jusco managers than it was for their counterparts elsewhere, and hence that they were critical of the system.

Influences on Attitudes to Appraisal   Of possible correlates of views of appraisal, the most interesting is the extent of written objectives. It is possible that formal, written aims will promote discontent. In fact, we found the reverse to be the case. Even controlling for sector, there was a clear tendency for appraisal scores to be more favourable the more formal the setting of objectives. Where objectives were clear and written the mean score was 2.58, as against 2.97 where objectives were only broad guides or unclear.[2] The important implication is that managers did not resent detailed objectives; on the contrary, they welcomed the sense of certainty and mission which they implied.

The third aspect of evaluation was how closely managers felt that they were assessed. This is plainly a subjective measure, and it does not tell us about how actual practice differed between our companies. But we thought that it would be useful to tap managers' perceptions of how closely they were controlled. As Table 7.3 shows, there was a very clear pattern of sectoral differences: evaluation was felt to be very close in the banks, less so in the stores, relatively broad in telecommunications, and least close in engineering.

As with views on the appraisal system, we examined how far the variations that we observed were due to differences between sectors, to differences between the countries, or to the interaction of sector and country 'effects'. The appraisal scores form a continuous variable, and hence an analysis of variance was appropriate. In the present case, we have a cross-tabulation of closeness of evaluation by sector by country. We therefore used loglinear analysis. The results showed that closeness of evaluation was indeed strongly influenced by sector but that there was no country effect.[3] We can thus conclude that closeness of evaluation stemmed from features of the organization of work in each sector and that these features were common between the two countries.

This is consistent with the data on targets, with banking being the environment in which clear-cut targets could most readily be identified. There was in fact a strong relationship between the closeness of evaluation and the formality of objectives: 54 per cent of those saying that objectives were clearly written felt that they were evaluated closely, whereas only 23 per cent of those seeing objectives as broad or uncertain said that they were closely evaluated. Given, however, that there was a strong sectoral pattern in the closeness of evaluation, it may be that this simple relationship in fact shows no more than that written objectives and close evaluation were both particularly common in the banks. Within the banks, there was indeed no relationship between forms of objectives and closeness of evaluation. But there was a link in the other three sectors, strongly in engineering and stores and on the borders of statistical significance in telecommunications. We can conclude, therefore, that the simple link was not the result of sectoral effects and that written aims and close monitoring went together.

We have seen that written aims also went along with satisfaction with the evaluation system. A similar association was observed between the closeness of evaluation and views on the appraisal system. Far from those reporting close control being the most dissatisfied with the way in which they were evaluated, close monitoring was correlated with satisfaction. (The mean score on the satisfaction with appraisal index for those seeing evaluation as close was 2.44, as against 3.14 for those seeing evaluation as

Table 7.3   *Closeness of evaluation (%)*

	Lucas	Sumitomo	NatWest	Mitsui	Tesco	Jusco	BT	NTT	All
Closely	16	17	61	74	46	35	24	32	38
Broadly	59	63	37	26	42	56	67	68	52
Occasionally/not evaluated	25	19	2	0	12	8	9	0	10

occasional or non-existent, a difference that was highly significant even when we controlled for country and for sector).[4] There was a similar relationship between views of appraisal and the presence of written objectives, even when sector was controlled for. This suggests that managers were not reacting against tight evaluation but instead respected it.

Some other associations may be briefly considered. As noted above, the assessment of managers in terms of unit results and their own performance was common in Britain but not Japan. We therefore looked within the British sample at the link between these measures and the closeness of evaluation. Not surprisingly, there was a strong association in both cases. Small numbers make analysis within each company hazardous, but the direction of association was generally repeated. Finally, one might expect some link between the seniority of a manager's position and closeness of monitoring, possibly with the more junior positions being the more closely assessed. In fact, there was no tendency of this sort, suggesting that the general pattern of monitoring is the same throughout the management hierarchy.

Pressures and Demands

Means of setting targets and evaluating performance thus varied between countries and sectors. We have suggested that, despite this variation, managers faced common pressures to meet demands on them. We can pursue this theme by looking at the changes which managers had experienced.

The picture in all our organizations was one of increasing demands, though their nature varied. In BT, as one manager put it, demands came from increasingly vocal customers but also from corporate headquarters. Several others noted the detailed demands in which they had to work. One particular issue was the regulation of overtime, with managers having to keep to tight guidelines as to their expenditure on it. These demands were not necessarily resented: one senior manager suggested that challenging jobs could enable managers to develop to their potential, while another manager said that the broad aim of being customer-oriented was not in question, the real issue being what mechanisms could be put in place to achieve it. And, as noted above, there was some uncertainty about performance appraisal. Thus, reactions differed, but there was little doubt that the structure of jobs was changing as expectations became more specific and performance was measured. At NTT, too, one manager spoke of a decline in discretion and a growth in pressures while another cited in particular expectations to do overtime and to work at weekends.

Such pressures were also evident at Mitsui. Compulsory Saturday working had been eliminated, but there were some suggestions that the objective of reducing total working hours had not been achieved: extra hours were put in during the week. Moreover, there was moral pressure to attend 'voluntary' study activities on Saturdays. As a senior manager explained, the manager of a branch would join a study group, and it was difficult for more junior managers to stay away. A different development in Mitsui concerned the age of retirement. This had recently been raised from 55 to 60, but the effect was to increase, and not reduce, pressures and uncertainty. Only a small number of the very senior posts could be held by the over-55 age group; for the rest, continuing beyond this age would involve a salary cut of 40 per cent. Moreover, growing competition resulting from the deregulation of the financial services sector was increasing the pressure on labour costs. Some managers spoke of the need to prepare for a move away from the bank before becoming 55; this could include, for example, maintaining relationships with customers so as to have contacts to find another job. Though managers accepted the need for the bank to remain competitive, the pressure on the individual was clear.

In NatWest, pressures arose from the nature of targets and their evaluation. One manager cited the extreme detail that branch managers had to prepare in producing their business plans. Another cited growing competition coming not from the other big clearing banks but from the specialist financial services companies as a factor leading to tighter targets. Again, this could promote a degree of concern but not straightforward discontent. The manager just quoted is a good example. He had risen to be a sales manager, having joined the bank with O levels, and had plainly done well in career terms. His concern was not about demanding targets as such, and he claimed to work hard and effectively, averaging 54 hours a week, which he saw as just part of the job. The real problem was the bureaucratic, centralized and proceduralized approach of the bank, which demanded customer orientation but at the same time refused to allow its managers to use their own expertise and initiative. Several people had, he said, left as a result. It was not the pressures but their management that concerned him.

In the stores, as argued above, there were similar pressures arising from the centralization of control. As one Jusco manager put it, the autonomy of the store manager was being reduced as a result. Tesco showed this trend more clearly, as it had moved away from the original model of leaving everything to the individual store manager to emphasizing a corporate image, with strong central buying, store layout and O&M departments. There were evidently pressures in the old system: as one manager explained, this had been a hire-and-fire era with managers surviving on their wits. We would argue that it was a matter not of pressures where there had been none but of the formalization and systematization of demands on managers, together with more systematic means of appraisal.

In Lucas, demands stemmed from a less complete but still evident move towards central direction. As noted elsewhere, after the trauma of the early 1980s, the company set about deciding what business it was in, shedding those units which did not fit and buying others which did. Activities such as the management audit highlighted a central concern with the quality of managers. The result, as several of our respondents noted, was a formalization of the evaluation system and a tighter integration between operating units and the centre. Finally, Sumitomo was similar to the other Japanese firms in the creation of a strong cultural expectation of conformity. As elsewhere, voluntary overtime in the evenings and on Saturdays was common; one manager said that he regularly worked until 8.30 in the evening. There was also a specific tradition of requiring managers to live in company dormitories during their first year with the firm; as one manager explained, this was intended to develop some common identity among each cohort of entrants, who were spread through scattered locations and who would otherwise lack any cohesion.

The Japanese firms thus shared several pressures especially on hours of work. One other common pressure arose from the system of job mobility discussed in Chapter 4: though managers were asked their preferences, in practice company demands took precedence and it was common for managers to be moved to a new location with little notice. This created pressure on the manager himself, as he was prevented from becoming set in his ways and was required to meet new demands. It could also create tensions in his family life since his wife and children might stay in one place in order to maintain continuity in the children's education. The companies were not entirely impersonal. Thus one NTT manager said that he had asked to stay in one location in order to care for his ageing parents (another important family obligation in Japan), and had been allowed to do so. But the general pattern of movement planned by the personnel department, with individual involvement being a concession and not a right, plainly increased the manager's dependence on his employer.

The situations facing managers were thus different. It is, for example, well known that long hours of overtime are built into the fabric of Japanese organizations in a way which has no parallel in Britain. The strong expectation that managers should mould themselves to the demands of the organization is foreign to Anglo-Saxon expectations and helps to explain, for example, why a hierarchical and non-participative appraisal system provoked only limited criticism. Yet there were also similarities across all the firms, with the tendency being for managers to report both growing pressures and a formalization and rationalization of company expectations. These pressures were far from universal, and the trend should not be exaggerated, but the direction of change was evident. This tightening of demands on managers is an important but somewhat neglected theme. Yet managers also enjoyed some compensating benefits, as we now proceed to show.

Reward Systems

All eight companies, being large and complex organizations, had structured payment systems. In the four British firms, posts had certain grades attached to them and each grade had a salary range, with a manager's position in the range being determined by seniority. Appraisal systems did not affect this basic grading but influenced the amount of a pay increase. In the Japanese companies the relationship between posts and grades was different. To take Mitsui as an example, the grading, known as the qualification grading system, came first: managers had to attain a certain point on the grading system before they were eligible for a given level of posts. Places on the grading system were determined by seniority and merit, with the seniority aspect being the more fundamental. There was a minimum period, in Mitsui about four years, during which a manager must remain in one grade before being able to move to the next. The differences should not be exaggerated, for plainly British managers would be appointed to a post only if they were thought capable of it. But the Japanese system was more formal, and in particular the stress on seniority meant, as we discuss in other chapters, that progression through the grading system was much more predictable. For present purposes, we focus on rewards within a given grade and on managers' perceptions of the reward system. We also comment briefly on the significance, or as it turned out the lack of significance, of share ownership.

Pay Structures

We asked our questionnaire sample about the way in which they were remunerated, asking them to indicate whether or not certain features were present. It might be expected that some of the features would be standard across a company, so that there would be no point asking about them: whether or not a firm uses annual pay increases, for example, is a characteristic which would not vary between individual managers. We therefore need to explain the logic of our questioning. We asked about eight features. One of them, whether bonuses were important, was plainly a matter of each manager's own perception of the system. A second, whether the outcome of appraisals affected pay, can also be seen as perceptual, in that the manager is being asked how far, in his or her view, appraisals really were meaningful and, if they were, how far the outcome had a significant effect on pay. Most of the other six might well vary between levels or functions of an organization with, say, some units being profit centres according to whose performance managers might reasonably be rewarded, while others, say a head office department, had managers who were not able to be assessed in this way. We were, then, looking at the range of ways that companies used to reward their managers.

Table 7.4 lists the seven main categories of replies; the eighth, 'individual negotiation', had very few answers and is omitted from the table. As would be expected, some form of annual award was virtually universal. Only in BT were there managers who did not specify some type of annual increase, reflecting the organization's move towards individual contracts and performance-related pay which may well have led managers to feel that they had moved away from a system of straight annual awards.

There were two main differences between Britain and Japan. First, in line with the finding that Japanese managers were rarely evaluated in terms of

Table 7.4 *Factors influencing pay (% mentioning each item)*

	Lucas	Sumitomo	NatWest	Mitsui	Tesco	Jusco	BT	NTT	All
Annual award	75	73	80	76	53	63	45	76	68
Award tied to:									
Company profits	19	20	73	24	50	22	27	16	33
Unit profits	28	0	58	4	27	18	0	4	20
Other performance measure	25	23	65	36	46	25	9	20	33
Company discretion	28	7	12	4	15	4	21	4	13
Appraisal results	56	56	85	64	89	52	69	80	70
Bonuses	56	50	70	44	23	4	30	48	46

unit performance, linking pay awards to unit profitability was rare in Japan, being at all prominent only in Jusco, where the performance of a store could meaningfully be assessed. Such a reward system was also far from common in Britain and was entirely absent in BT. It was widely mentioned in NatWest, but cited by only about a quarter of Lucas or Tesco managers. This suggests that moves to individualize the relationship between managers and their firms have been less advanced than is sometimes thought. Managers were, as shown above, carefully evaluated but this had not reached the stage at which their pay was dependent on the profitability of their own operating units. The second difference was that company discretion featured relatively little in Japan, which is consistent with the picture of formalized payment systems there.

Looking at differences between companies, NatWest stands out for the large number of different ways in which pay was linked to performance. The differences from Mitsui are striking; for example, nearly three-quarters of the NatWest managers reported that their pay awards were tied to company profits, whereas only a quarter of the Mitsui sample gave this reply. As the head of management development at NatWest explained, pay and appraisal were being linked increasingly closely. In the past, even senior managers had found it hard to sanction, let alone dismiss, poorly performing staff. Now, these issues were being tackled. 'The view that appraisal and pay review shouldn't be linked,' he said, 'belongs to the wet liberal end of the spectrum and we certainly don't subscribe to it.'

This difference between the banks contrasts with the similarity in terms of the closeness of appraisal and the use of targets. This suggests that certain features of banking may have helped to shape the ways in which managers were evaluated but that the links between this evaluation and the reward system reflected corporate pay policies which were not determined by the nature of the business. The differences between Tesco and Jusco, though less striking, point in a similar direction.

As might be expected from the above discussion, NatWest and Tesco also scored high on the impact of appraisal on pay. But in every company at least half the managers felt that appraisal had a significant impact on pay. Without similar data from the past it would be dangerous to infer too strong a trend, but it seems likely that these figures are, at least in the case of Britain, higher than might have been expected five or ten years previously. Certainly the tendency in popular discussions is to stress a tighter link between pay and performance. Though direct links with unit profits remained rare, the general dependence of pay on evaluation of performance was striking.

Finally, the importance of bonuses varied widely. The large number of NatWest managers seeing them as important is not surprising. The lower level in Tesco can be related to the fact that managers there were rewarded through performance measures, with additional bonuses being relatively unimportant. The Japanese replies are more surprising in view of the fact that our firms, like most Japanese companies, used annual bonuses as central aspects of their pay systems. The very low weight given to bonuses at Jusco probably reflects the emphasis given to merit in this company, with bonuses being seen as less influential: they may have increased the salary, but do not seem to have been seen as 'important' in the sense of affecting motivation. In the other three companies, merit was given less attention and there was more room for bonuses to play a role, but even here they may well have been taken somewhat for granted. As an NTT manager explained, bonuses were paid twice a year. In the summer they averaged about three times the monthly salary (that is, they added 50 per cent to salary over the six months), while in the winter they added rather less than this. Plainly the sums were large, but to the extent that they were an expected part of remuneration they were not important sources of motivation. Because of a lack of feedback, individuals said that they were unsure what was actually being rewarded through the bonuses. Similarly, in Sumitomo senior company managers made it clear that bonuses were not seen as a direct incentive, and the amount was not much affected by a manager's personnel rating. The interview sample also confirmed that they did not see bonuses as motivational. This confirms the expectation that bonuses are used in Japan, not as direct spurs to performance as they are in the West, but to reward past performance and to underline the general message that rewards are ultimately dependent on the continued success of the company.

Some of the associations between methods of reward and means of evaluation develop this theme. Thus there was a strong link between having the pay award tied to unit profitability and being evaluated against unit targets: 85 per cent of those paid according to profitability were evaluated by comparing unit results with targets, as against 30 per cent who were not so rewarded. There were also differences between countries. We took those saying that they were evaluated against unit results or against indices of their own performance. Of the British sample, 70 per cent were evaluated on one or both of these measures; in Japan the picture was reversed, with 70 per cent being evaluated on neither. And the relationship with the pay system was different. Within the British sample, there was a strong association between being evaluated against performance targets and being paid according to measures of performance. In Japan, there was no such connection: Japanese managers paid according to some performance indicator were no more likely than others to be evaluated against performance criteria. This pattern of associations supports the above argument that criteria of evaluation in Britain tended to be individualized and based on meeting specific targets, whereas in Japan the evaluation process was more generalized and long term in nature with no direct link to pay.

Responses to the Pay System

We asked managers to agree or disagree with four statements about the pay system: that it helped to motivate, was fair, was efficient, and did not need reform. The proportions giving favourable replies are shown in Table 7.5, which also shows how many criticisms of the system were entered. The main area of difference between the countries was on motivation, with managers in all the British firms other than BT being more likely than their Japanese counterparts to say that the system was motivating. This plainly represents a significant vote of confidence in the pay systems that the British firms used. But it does not follow that the Japanese found it demotivating. As argued above, a key measure of success in Japan was speed of promotion through the grading system: it was promotion to a higher grade, and not reward in the present grade, which was the key motivator. As one Mitsui manager explained, actual pay differences between managers at the same level were quite small, but what these differences indicated was one's position in relation to one's peers, and hence the likelihood of gaining promotion. This is not to say that pay was unimportant. Several Mitsui managers pointed to the small size of differentials between grades and said that this reduced the incentive to work hard. But this arguably reflected a view that pay should be a recognition for effort, and not an argument that it was directly a motivator. As one senior manager said, pay differentials did not reflect growing responsibility, and there was also the problem of no longer being paid overtime for extra hours. A high performance rating did help with promotion chances but should also receive a higher monetary reward.

On the other aspects of the pay system, there were no clear differences between the British firms and their Japanese counterparts, except in the case of telecommunications, where BT managers were significantly less satisfied than their Japanese counterparts. This picture is confirmed by the count of the number of criticisms of the pay system, with 39 per cent of BT managers being dissatisfied on at least three of the four aspects. Not only were they more dissatisfied than their NTT counterparts but they were also the most dissatisfied group of all. Lucas and Tesco managers, by contrast, were significantly more satisfied than their Japanese counterparts, with Jusco managers being notably dissatisfied, while there was no difference between the banks.

We scrutinized these relationships more rigorously with loglinear tests. The simplest result was on efficiency, where there was only a country effect: Japanese managers found their pay systems more efficient than did British managers, and there was no variation between sectors. For fairness, both country and sector effects were present: fairness was reported to be highest in Japan and in the engineering sector. For the other two dimensions, and also for the measure of the number of criticisms, only a more complex model of interaction between sector, country, and the dependent variable fitted the data. That is, differences on motivation, for example, between the countries depended on which sector a manager was in. We can conclude that on two aspects of pay Japanese managers were clearly the more satisfied but that on the other aspects satisfaction depended on circumstances within each company.

Table 7.5 *Views of payment system (%)*

	Lucas	Sumitomo	NatWest	Mitsui	Tesco	Jusco	BT	NTT	All
Agree that system:									
Motivates	83	21	79	39	80	35	53	64	58
Is fair	80	100	66	75	74	73	59	86	76
Is efficient	60	100	65	83	74	81	47	91	74
Does not need reform	50	59	40	42	52	20	28	59	43
Number of criticisms of system:									
0	45	21	40	33	46	15	19	52	34
1	19	41	22	9	23	19	21	13	22
2	16	38	15	29	11	37	21	22	23
3 or 4	19	0	23	29	19	30	39	13	22

Some of these circumstances can be readily addressed. As indicated above in relation to appraisal, there was a widespread feeling in BT that the criteria for performance-related pay were unclear, and there was an atmosphere of uncertainty as to what was happening. Though more than half thought the system was broadly fair, only a quarter felt that it did not need reform. The major changes that the organization had been undergoing seem to have generated a sense of insecurity as the known bureaucratic systems of the past were replaced with something new. In the case of Jusco there were complaints at the low level of pay. One manager made a direct contrast with manufacturing firms with similar general reputations as Jusco's: basic wage levels in Jusco were lower, and there were also problems associated with the frequent geographical moves that the company required its managers to make, since the housing which was provided was often of a poor standard. In Tesco, by contrast, there were a few general comments about the subjectivity of the pay system but in general these were seen as minor niggles; several managers noted the high levels of pay that they enjoyed. In other companies, too, there were scattered criticisms of specific features of the pay system. Taken on their own, it would be hard to assess their significance, but in the light of the quantitative material it appears that they were less widespread than they were in BT or Jusco.

These criticisms of the pay system not surprisingly went along with dissatisfaction with the method of evaluation. For example, across the whole sample there was a strong relationship between the score on the measure of evaluation and the number of criticisms of the pay system. This relationship held when sector was controlled for.[5] It was also statistically significant within four of the companies, and in another two the relationship was in the same direction but not significant. There was no relationship in the other two, namely BT and Jusco, which were those with most dissatisfaction with the evaluation system: where managers were strongly dissatisfied, this discontent remained regardless of the number of criticisms of the pay system.

In summary, the majority of managers saw the pay system as fair and efficient, a tendency that was particularly strong in Japan. It was seen as a motivational feature in the three British firms other than BT. But most of the sample felt that some reforms were necessary, the main criticisms being the subjectivity of the process and the difficulty of relating rewards to effort. Unlike the closeness of evaluation, where sector-specific forces were at work, reactions to the pay system reflected the circumstances of individual companies and the reward structures that they had evolved.

Share Ownership

The final aspect of managerial rewards that we considered was ownership of shares in the company, some form of direct stake in the firm being widely seen as a way to promote a sense of commitment. In seven of the eight firms, virtually all our managers said that they owned some shares in their firm. The exception was in Lucas, where only half the sample held shares. Elsewhere the proportion ran from around 80 per cent (NatWest and NTT) to 100 per cent (BT and Sumitomo). The British average of 80 per cent contrasts with the findings of a survey in 1984 (Edwards, 1987). We can compare our results with those relating to the general managers of large manufacturing plants belonging to divisionalized corporations, all our British firms being divisionalized. The figure for this group was 35 per cent (1987: 51). Our figures for Lucas suggest that share owning in manufacturing remains low, but the spread of share ownership, encouraged in a case like BT by the issue of shares to employees at privatization, seems clear.

The implications are less apparent. We asked those of our sample who owned shares how their shareholding affected the way in which they performed. More than half (55 per cent) said 'not at all' and only 3 per cent said 'very much'. Managers in the two stores were the most likely to say that share owning affected their performance (80 per cent in Tesco and 69 per cent in Jusco). By contrast, two-thirds of respondents in each of the other three sectors, including, that is, the privatized telecommunications companies, said that share ownership had no effect on how they performed. Just why managers in the stores differed from the others is hard to determine. It may have something to do with the strength of the financial motive among them. As discussed in the following section, we looked at different factors which motivated our sample. On financial rewards, 46 per cent of the Tesco managers said that they were 'very much' motivated by these, as compared with 20 per cent of the other British managers; the figures for Jusco and the other three Japanese companies were 52 per cent and 31 per cent. Share owning as a means of increasing financial returns would thus seem to have fitted into the wider ambitions of the stores sample.

There were some notable associations between the reported effect of share ownership on performance and other variables. Not surprisingly, managers whom we classified as senior were more likely than middle or junior managers to say that share ownership made a difference: for those doing relatively standardized jobs, share ownership was unlikely to stimulate higher levels of effort, but senior managers have more discretion and share ownership is more likely to make a difference. Those saying that share ownership made a difference were also likely to have a favourable view of how they were evaluated and to make relatively few criticisms of the pay system. But there was no association with the closeness with which they were evaluated.

The overall picture is of share ownership making little difference to managers' behaviour. As several respondents said, they took their jobs seriously, and whether or not they owned shares in the firm made no difference. This, unsurprising, result is consistent with Ramsay's (1990) conclusions from a survey of employees in five British companies using share option schemes: attitudinal differences between participants and non-

Table 7.6　*Sources of motivation (%)*

| | Motivated: | | | |
	Very much	Quite a lot	A little	Not much/ not at all
Prospection of promotion	44	40	10	6
Financial reward	30	48	16	6
Status	27	44	22	7
Sense of achievement	73	24	3	0
Fear of failure	6	17	35	42
Company success	18	55	20	7
Unit success	55	37	6	2
Meeting targets	50	39	10	2
Creating opportunities	33	50	12	5
Respect from colleagues	22	44	23	11

participants in the schemes were almost wholly absent. As our results also suggested, it was only among senior managers that share ownership seemed to have any direct connection with performance.

Motivation

As well as asking specifically about evaluation and reward systems, we asked a general question about factors which motivated managers in their work. We listed 10 factors and asked managers to rate each on a five-point scale from 'very much' to 'not at all'. Two of the factors, financial reward and the prospect of promotion, related to individual material success. Three (status, sense of achievement, fear of failure) covered the less material aspects of success and failure. Two, unit and company success, referred to collective or organizational, as distinct from individual, achievement. Two, meeting targets and creating opportunities, tried to tap a sense of individual achievement in meeting collective goals or advancing organizational interests. Finally, respect from colleagues addressed the fit of the individual into the social group. We had anticipated that we might find different dimensions of motivation, with a high interest in financial reward, for example, being inversely related to respect from colleagues. In fact, we found that scores on the 10 items were correlated with each other and that they could be combined to form one index.[6] Our interpretation of this is that the items were measuring how strongly managers were motivated to work hard, and we therefore considered possible influences on this index. Before setting out our results from this overall measure, it is worth looking at some of its components. One might, for example, expect Japanese managers to be particularly motivated by the prospects of promotion and, if popular stereotypes are believed, by respect from colleagues, with their British counterparts having a more individualized set of attitudes.

Table 7.6 summarizes the findings. Not surprisingly, the managers proved to be a highly motivated group, with most items leading well over half the sample to say that they were motivated by them. Overall, unit success and 'sense of achievement' were the most reported motivators. The differences were considerable. Statistical tests showed, for example, that the mean score on the measure of unit success was significantly greater than that on promotion or company success. Taking our managers as a group, therefore, it was the immediate work unit, and neither the larger company nor purely individual achievement, which was the key focus in providing motivation.

On differences between countries, Japanese managers did not appear to be strongly motivated by respect from their colleagues. This was confirmed when we looked at differences between companies in each sector. As Table 7.7 shows, in two sectors, banks and telecommunications, the British managers proved to be the more highly motivated on this factor. On most items, however, the Japanese were the more highly motivated, and differences were particularly apparent regarding promotion, financial rewards, and status. Unit success, by contrast, seemed to be a universal motivator.

These results are consistent with part of the general image of Japanese firms, the stress on promotion being particularly important. But it was in only two of the four sectors that a difference was apparent. In the case of the banks, for example, it seems plausible that the highly developed internal labour markets which have long characterized British banks contributed to the emphasis on promotion that we found in NatWest. Similarly, lifetime employment in Japan is often seen as promoting an extreme sense of loyalty to the company; and fear of failure, with its concomitant loss of prestige and of opportunities for advancement, is seen as a key source of pressure. Yet we found that company success differentiated between the British and Japanese managers only in the case of the banks, and that fear of failure was actually more intense in one British case, Tesco, and no different in the other three.

Some of the associations between our measures of motivation and managers' reports of the structures within which they worked are of interest. For example, were those who said that they were most motivated by company success particularly likely to be rewarded on the basis of overall company profits, and was the motivation to meet targets related to the use of specific targets to measure performance? There was no tendency for those motivated by company success to report that they were paid in relation to success. Direct financial benefit did not seem to be important in engendering an interest in the success of the company. But the importance attached to share ownership did make a difference: of those saying that company success motivated them very much, 63 per cent also felt that share ownership made a difference to their performance, while only 25 per cent of those giving little or no importance to company success saw ownership as significant. Managers who saw company success as important not surprisingly tended to see owning shares in the company as contributing to their own performance, but the basic structure of pay made no difference.

Table 7.7   *Motivation: differnces between companies (% saying a factor motivates 'very much')*

	Lucas	Sumitomo	NatWest	Mitsui	Tesco	Jusco	BT	NTT	All
Promotion	25	40	60	44	50	59	16	52	44
Financial reward	16	30	32	28	46	51	7	36	30
Status	8	30	23	28	38	41	9	44	25
Sense of achievement	87	73	80	68	84	56	69	56	73
Fear of failure	6	7	7	8	19	0	3	0	6
Comany success	23	27	10	17	23	30	6	12	18
Unit success	67	60	68	44	57	44	41	38	55
Meeting targets	43	59	42	40	65	67	41	48	50
Creating opportunities	32	40	35	40	31	41	13	40	33
Respect from colleagues	31	17	20	24	27	15	33	8	22

Table 7.8   *Relationship between performance targets and*
motivation (%)

	UK[1]		Japan	
	Yes	No	Yes	No
Targets are used	71	29	30	70
of which, meeting targets motivates:				
Very much	51	35	55	54
Quite a lot	37	38	42	39
A little	12	22	3	4
Not much/not at all	0	5	0	3

[1] In the UK sample the differences are significant at the 5 per cent level.

The pay structure was important at the more immediate level of unit success. Of those whose pay was tied to unit profitability, 77 per cent saw unit success as a very important motivator, whereas only 48 per cent whose pay was not so related gave such importance to unit success. There was a similar tendency for those evaluated against unit targets to see unit success as a key motivator. The implication is that linking pay to company profits does not heighten the importance given to company success because the profits of the whole company are determined by macro-level factors over which the individual manager has little influence. The connection between unit success and rewards related to this success is much more direct. But this was also very much a British phenomenon. As shown above, very few Japanese managers were rewarded in relation to unit success, but this did not prevent them from rating such success at least as highly as did their British counterparts. A pay–performance link may work in some circumstances and not in others.

We looked, moreover, at the link between being measured against targets and seeing achieving targets as a motivator. The results are set out in Table 7.8. As noted above, most British managers were evaluated against targets either for the performance of their units or for indices of their own activities, whereas most Japanese managers were not. In Britain there was a tendency for the use of targets to promote seeing achievement of them as important. But there was no link in Japan: meeting targets was important even if there was no specific mechanism of defining set tasks and judging success in performing them. This is consistent with the common argument that Japanese managers are motivated in a relatively diffuse manner and that in Britain, by contrast, managers need or expect specific mechanisms of evaluation.

Turning from particular aspects of motivation to the overall picture, we may consider our summary measure of motivation, on which a low score indicated a high level of motivation. The obvious point, as Table 7.6 has already suggested, is that there was a high level of motivation. The index can run from 10, representing a very high level of motivation on all 10 features, to 29. The mean score was 15.47, with Jusco recording the lowest score, at 14.75, and BT the highest at 17.0. Differences were thus far from large. An analysis of variance by sector and country showed that both effects were at work and that there was no interaction: motivation levels were higher in Japan than in Britain, and were high in the stores and low in telecommunications. But only 7 per cent of the variance in the scores was explained by sector and country effects, confirming that the differences, though plainly present, were far from great.[7]

Those saying that share ownership made a difference to their performance were also most likely to say that they were highly motivated. This is not of course the same as saying that the fact of owning shares made a difference. (There were too few non-shareholders to permit us to investigate this.) It merely says that those who felt that owning shares encouraged them to work hard were most likely to feel that they were highly motivated more generally.

Perhaps the most intriguing finding, however, was the association with the reported closeness of monitoring. We have already seen that close monitoring was associated with satisfaction with the system of evaluation. Similarly, the extent of motivation went along not with loose monitoring but with close control. This association held when we controlled for country and for sectoral effects. It also held in a more complex multivariate analysis. For this we used a regression of the motivation scores on a measure of the importance of share ownership, the closeness of monitoring, variables controlling for sector, and also our index of satisfaction with the evaluation system. We also included several measures of managers' personal characteristics such as their age, seniority, and age on taking up their first managerial appointment. Taking these in turn, it might be that younger managers are the most strongly motivated, that seniority is important, or that those starting early on the managerial route will have the strongest level of motivation. None of these characteristics turned out to be important. Neither did satisfaction with the evaluation system have any effect. But the closeness of monitoring retained its importance even when the influences of the other variables were also included. The only other variable to have any effect was that representing the telecommunications sector, with working here tending to lower levels of motivation.

Motivation was thus strongest in Japan and in the stores, but when these factors were included in multivariate analysis along with the closeness of evaluation it was this last factor which predominated. We have seen that this variable was also strongly associated with views of the evaluation system. We have now seen that these views were not themselves associated with levels of motivation, from which we can conclude that the closeness of evaluation had separate effects. In both cases, being evaluated closely produced a favourable response, even when other possible influences were taken into account. Of the particular factors which motivated managers, the success of the specific work unit was felt to be the most important, with company success, and also such factors as status and financial rewards, being less significant. Managers were motivated most strongly by their responsibilities to their work units, and were most likely to be strongly motivated when they felt that their activities were closely evaluated by their companies.

Conclusions: Pressures, Control and Responses

As noted at the start of this chapter, two important, but rather rarely debated, themes are how tightly managers are controlled and how far systems of control vary between countries and companies. In drawing together our findings, we comment on each in turn before summarizing managers' reactions to the ways in which they were controlled and rewarded.

Extensive control systems were evident in all our organizations: more than three-quarters of the interview sample had clearly specified objectives; there was systematic evaluation of performance, in the case of Japan through frequent appraisal meetings and in Britain through evaluating performance against unit results or indices of individual achievement or both; and only 10 per cent of managers felt that they were evaluated only occasionally or not at all. Interview material pointed to a sense of growing pressures as targets were refined and as central coordination was extended. An NTT manager felt that local discretion was being reduced and that job pressures were growing. A BT manager saw early voluntary retirement as having a control dimension: it was damaging in so far as the organization 'lost the good people as well as the bad' but it also stimulated a change of culture and a change of expectations. Tesco managers felt that the role of the store manager was changing: away from being free to run the store while also being liable to rapid dismissal and towards fitting in more closely with an overall corporate style.

These findings parallel those from Smith's (1990) in-depth analysis. She stresses how restructuring was changing managers' jobs. Branch managers in the bank that she studied were losing such traditional functions as making loans while also coming under increasing pressure to sell products. Some of our NatWest managers reported similar developments. But Smith also notes the ways in which managers shaped their own world: they were not passive dupes. Branch managers, for example, were told to hide from their staff the corporate goal of staffing reductions. But they found that the only way to gain cooperation was to reveal the truth. There were also important variations between different groups. Branch managers were in general losing autonomy whereas managers in the bank's credit card centre had more freedom. The picture from Smith is threefold. First, restructuring was changing the demands on managerial jobs. But, second, there were important variations, and a loss of autonomy was far from universal; and, third, even where autonomy was being reduced managers were to some extent able to handle the process. A variety of reactions, and not a uniform sense of discontent, would thus be expected.

This last feature points to a theme of some importance. We are not arguing that the control of managers has simply been tightened in the sense of imposing new demands on an unresponsive and unwilling group of workers. The nature of relationships between organizations and employers has changed, as the Tesco case shows: management development was being given serious attention, training was carefully considered, and managers were encouraged to look at the wider picture of the business as a whole. Yet there remained a control dimension. Whether or not Tesco managers were controlled more tightly than in the past may be strictly unanswerable, because the whole mode of control has changed. What we can suggest is that control has become more considered, more sophisticated and perhaps more subtle; it has, in short, been rationalized and routinized. The modern manager is not treated as a mere underling. In all our organizations, there was a general awareness of the importance of developing talents and using the skills of the managerial stock. Yet the ways in which these talents were used depended on the overall character and direction of the business. Managers could not be left free to define their own approach, and performance expectations were clearly established. Demands were clearly felt, but they were often internalized rather than being imposed from outside. Kanter captures some of this when, having noted evidence that the average number of hours worked by American executives rose during the 1980s, she writes, 'post-entrepreneurial workplaces increase the lure of work' (1989: 271). Managers want to work hard because they find it rewarding but, our evidence suggests, they are also well aware of the closeness with which their behaviour is monitored.

That close monitoring can go along with satisfaction is suggested by several patterns of association within our data. We found that tight evaluation was linked to a favourable view of the system of evaluation and to a high level of general motivation; these associations were very robust, and remained even when we allowed for the effects of several other variables. Some associations with issues considered in other chapters are consistent with this evidence. It might be expected, for example, that managers who are tightly controlled will be the most likely to consider only measurable aspects of their performance. They would, accordingly, be most prone to say that the development of their subordinates was a low priority. In fact, close monitoring was associated with a tendency to say that a high priority was given to the development of subordinates. Some of this could be due to a company effect whereby a firm that has close monitoring also has managers who are keen on developing their subordinates even though the two variables may have no causal connection. When we looked at the relationship within companies, however, the direction of association remained in all cases except BT, even though small numbers meant that the results were not statistically significant.

An even more suggestive result emerged when we looked at the link between developing subordinates and the use of predetermined targets to assess a manager's performance. In Britain, such targets were linked with a strong emphasis on development, which again suggests that tight control did not lead to a purely individualized pursuit of self-interest. But in Japan the relationship was in the reverse direction, implying that in this country targets, which were as we have seen used rarely, interfered with managers' willingness to look beyond the 'bottom line'.

Finally, when we considered managers' perceptions of the attention that their organizations gave to management development, we found that those saying that it was given a high priority also felt that they were evaluated against tight criteria. This association held in both countries, as did that between a high priority given to management development and the use of clear written objectives. Such associations suggest that some concerns about tight performance evaluation (namely, that it promotes narrowness of vision and can lead to discontent) are not borne out.

It is of course possible that increasing demands will lead to longer-term pressures as managers face longer hours and declining promotion prospects. But such pressures had not so far impacted very heavily on managers in our study, who plainly felt able to live with a regime of tight controls and strong demands. The fact that such controls went along with positive indices of satisfaction does not mean that there was a direct causal link, still less establish the direction of causation. But some causal connections can readily be suggested. Companies with demanding targets may appear to know where they are going and what they want from their managers, thereby promoting a sense of satisfaction. At the very least, the results strongly suggest that tight evaluation does not produce discontent.

Turning to differences between the two countries, some of our results were consistent with the image of British managers being controlled by specific objectives and of a more diffuse process in Japan. Not only were performance targets more common in Britain but they connected with other aspects of managerial behaviour, such as attention to the development of subordinates, in ways which were absent in Japan. And the idea that the reward system could be motivating plainly had greater resonance in Britain than in Japan. But clear objectives and close evaluation were far from foreign to the Japanese firms. In some respects, notably the use of six-monthly appraisals, these firms exercised closer scrutiny than did their British counterparts. It was not the fact of close control which differed between the countries but the context in which it operated. In Japan, control was less oriented to specific targets and it was part of a carefully structured grading and seniority system. As described in other chapters, the qualification grading systems characteristic of Japanese firms created an order which was absent in Britain. Tight controls were not lacking in Japan, but they connected more to the assessment of the manager's role within a broad set of developmental aims than to measurements of specific targets of sales or profits. The stronger emphasis given by Japanese managers to promotion as a source of motivation is one example of this. The social meanings of close evaluation were different in the two countries.

We have also been able to take into account distinct sectoral patterns in methods and degrees of evaluation. Written objectives featured most prominently in the banks and stores, and formal tests on the measure of the closeness of evaluation showed that sector-specific factors were important whereas there was no 'country effect'. This suggests that it was organizational imperatives, and not the culture of a particular country, which was important here. This result plainly contrasts with that for the means used to evaluate performance. We have, in short, been able to differentiate between various aspects of the control of managers and to explain why some are sector-specific while others reflect national differences in organizational character.

The managers subject to these control mechanisms felt comfortable with them, as the positive associations with motivation and with views of the evaluation system testify. There was no generalized resentment to tightening controls. Yet there was also awareness that pressures were indeed growing, as indicated by concerns about hours of work. In Japan there were also concerns that the way in which managers were moved around the firm could conflict with family duties. Again, this was not a generalized source of discontent but it was a further indicator of growing tensions in the relationship between the manager and the company. Managers were, moreover, far from eager about how they were controlled: scores on views of the evaluation system were not far from the mid-point of the range, and two-thirds of the sample entered at least one criticism of the pay system. Also relevant is the fact, discussed in other chapters, that managers, across all companies other than Lucas, felt that promotion opportunities had been declining. If these fears are realized, frustrations may begin to surface. There may also prove to be limits to the 'lure' which work can offer. To the extent that firms cannot offer the material rewards and sense of achievement that have been available in the past, motivating their managers may prove to be more difficult. Though our findings did not point to widespread dissatisfaction, there were indications that the situation could change, and plainly there are limits to how tightly managers can be evaluated before there are depressing effects on motivation and creativity.

Notes

1 A reliability analysis on the six items produced an alpha coefficient of 0.81, and there were no problems with additivity (see Appendix A).

2 An analysis of variance was performed with appraisal scores as the dependent variable and with sector and the formality of objectives (collapsed into a three-point scale of written, clear but unwritten, and all others) as independents. Mean scores were as follows:

	Sector			
Objective	Eng.	Bank	Stores	Telecom.
Written	2.46	2.46	2.79	2.61
Unwritten	2.82	2.43	2.92	2.50
Other	2.72	2.39	3.17	3.29

The tendency to lower scores where there were more formal objectives was clear in three of the four sectors. The analysis of variance results were:

	Sum of squares	Mean square	F	Sig. of F
Objective	3.66	1.83	4.98	0.008
Sector	5.11	1.70	4.64	0.004
Interaction	5.46	0.91	2.48	0.025
Explained	15.37	1.40	3.81	0.000
Residual	75.27	0.37		

Proportion of variance explained is 11 per cent.

3 The details of the technique, together with the results for this particular task, can be found in Appendix A.

4 The analysis of variance with closeness of evaluation (in three categories) displayed a similar pattern to that reported in note 2, except that the tendency for low scores with close monitoring was present in all sectors. There was no interaction effect, and the proportion of variance explained, 15 per cent, was similar.

5 In order to ensure adequate numbers in each cell, the pay criticism variable was dichotomized between those making no criticism or only one, and those making two or more. Scores on the measure of views of the evaluation scheme were 2.51 and 2.91 respectively. Calling the pay criticism dichotomy Paycrit, the results were:

	Sum of squares	Mean square	F	Sig. of F
Paycrit	8.42	8.42	23.1	0.000
Sector	5.51	1.84	5.0	0.002
Interaction	0.37	0.12	0.03	0.992
Explained	14.19	2.03	5.57	0.000
Residual	76.44			

Proportion of variance explained is 16 per cent.

6 In contrast to the creation of the scores of attitudes to the evaluation system described in note 1, it was not possible to add the scores from 1 to 5 on the measures of motivation. A reliability analysis showed that there were problems of additivity, and suggested an appropriate rescoring, namely, raising each observation by the power of 0.67. Thus, in place of scores of 1 to 5, each measure was scored 1, 1.587, 2.08, 2.52, and 2.924. A second test showed that additivity problems had been overcome. What this says is that the original scoring made the distances between each point on the five-point scale too great, particularly where there were high scores. Lest it be thought that our rescoring was arbitrary, it should be noted that a 1 to 5 range is equally arbitrary. Our tests revealed the metric underlying the scores. Far from being arbitrary, as in the social scientist's common resort to assigning scores purely on the basis of convention (with these scores then often being added together with no consideration of whether they in fact form a reliable scale), our index can be shown to be a reasonable reflection of the underlying features of the data.

7 The adjusted scores as discussed in the text (with the raw scores in brackets) are as follows:

Lucas	15.7	(20.4)
NatWest	15.3	(19.8)
Tesco	15.1	(19.4)
BT	17.0	(22.9)
Sumitomo	15.3	(19.6)
Mitsui	15.2	(19.4)
Jusco	14.8	(18.6)
NTT	15.4	(19.7)
Total	15.4	(20.0)

8

Conclusions: Comparative Lessons

This final chapter returns to the main themes outlined in the introduction. It is structured around four tasks. First, we begin by summarizing the main findings about managers and management development in Britain and Japan. Second, we put these findings into theoretical context by returning to Dore's model of organizational versus market orientations which was outlined in Chapter 1. Third, we ask what implications can be drawn about the link between management development and competitive performance. Finally, we suggest a number of lessons for practitioners.

Main Themes and Findings

This book has tried to get beneath the surface appearance of management and the making of managers in Britain and Japan. We have tried to understand how systems work in practice and how they are viewed by their subjects. In reviewing the findings, we begin with national differences before considering sectoral and organizational variations.

The main contrast we found was between the relative robustness and stability of the Japanese management development systems and the relative vulnerability and instability of the British. This central divide had a number of aspects and consequences. The Japanese managers at all levels were able to describe the training and development systems in their companies; this was often simply not the case at all in the British companies. There were dramatic lurches in the British cases: elaborate suites of training courses were designed and refined for one period, only to be totally disbanded the next. Self-development would be the main emphasis at one time and then it would be more or less disregarded at another. As a consequence, line managers were confused and sometimes cynical.

How did this come to be? Arguably, a key source of this crucial contrast can be traced to the 'market-oriented' character of the British scene described by Dore (see Chapter 1, this book). But we believe it is in fact not quite so simple as that. Management development specialists were anxious to stress that their cue was taken almost entirely from 'the business strategy' or 'needs of the business'. When they drew their mental models of the place of management development in diagrammatic form they invariably placed business strategy or business needs at the centre or top of the figure. They tended to make a point of being rather dismissive of 'external' influences emanating from government, the civil service, the MCI and, to some extent, business schools as well as other vested interests whom they perceived as having wrong-headed or political agendas. Now, given this central focus on business need it is rather easier to understand that adaptability was equally prized. Hence, there was little compunction about making a clean sweep of a suite of training programmes or the closure of a management training college. Self-development, mentoring and close attention to individual development needs would be happily stressed for a period of four or five years and then a new chief executive (or sometimes even the same one) would declare a need for a sea-change and so a new era of more systematic, programme-based provision would be launched to 'meet the needs of a new phase in the business'. What was going on here was as a result of a deep-seated conceptualization of management development as necessarily a second-order, downstream, activity. The (turbulent) marketplace and the business strategy(ies) designed to engage with it were seen as unquestioningly paramount. In Japan, by contrast, there was less of a tendency to begin all conversations about the place of management development with a reaffirmation of the primacy of the market. There appeared to be a more securely based belief in the enduring value of *growing managers* in order to *meet* the changing character of market conditions.

As a result of this interpretation of our cross-cultural study, we are highly sceptical of the much publicized declamations of 'the end of the career', the 'end of the job' and similar summations of current 'trends'. Indeed, we very much doubt whether the large corporations will move in the posited direction for any sustained period. Instead, what is being recorded, we suspect, are the kind of fluctuating responses to perceived 'market needs' as noted above. We were fortunate in the timing of our study. We picked up the beginnings of the widespread uncertainty about the viability of the 'traditional' career and management development systems in the face of very significant job cutting among managerial grades. We were privileged to hear the debates about the meanings, significance and implications of this new scale of change. But we were also able to detect that this did not presage a long-term abandonment of one model for another. From our follow-up visits to these and other similar large organizations in mid 1996, we continue to judge that interest in recruiting the best graduates, retaining the very best of them and adding value to them through some kind of 'career development' continues and is likely to do so.

We pick up on this fundamental theme later in the chapter, but we need also to summarize the more subtle patterns of similarities and dissimilarities between the two systems at country level before turning to sectoral and organizational comparisons. In some areas, notably methods of evaluation, systems of reward, and the organization of management development, national differences emerged which, to a large degree, confirmed existing expectations. Take the systematic planning of careers in Japan and the diffuseness of methods of motivation and control. Commitment to goals is attained not through the imposition of specific targets but through a looser definition of duties, and authority is based on a strong identification with a group and not on impersonal rules. These findings reinforce the observations made by Ouchi (1981) and Rohlen (1974). The importance of such confirmation should not be underestimated. We have stressed that much writing on Japan tries to identify a uniform national system and tends to describe companies' procedures without exploring what these procedures mean for those subject to them. The method of detailed comparison of matched organizations has been used to a limited extent in international comparisons of a general sort but very rarely in the management development field. To the extent that this method endorses the assessments of other, often less rigorous methods, arguments about Japan can be more firmly grounded.

Other findings from our study reveal aspects of organizational practice that were less well known. Thus, we have shown, for example, that wide functional experience was not a characteristic of Japanese managers. On the contrary, the British managers displayed this to a far greater extent. The study also produced some surprises, especially concerning the low levels of formal training that we recorded in Japan.

Distinctive conclusions also emerged as a result of talking to the 'subjects' of development. Had we spoken only to 'architects' of systems, we would have learned about policies but would have had an incomplete view of their implementation. This was especially true of Britain, where we found marked criticism and scepticism among the managerial sample. But it was also true of Japan. Four themes illustrate this point.

First, we have shown that the idea of a 'career' may carry a different interpretation in Japan from that in Anglo-Saxon countries, with the personnel department typically moving managers without the individual having any real say in the process. The finding that Japanese managers do not think in terms of 'career paths' is itself interesting and would not necessarily have been expected. What was, of course, well known was the careful planning conducted by Japanese companies, but very little was known about how managers themselves saw the process. We found that they were in fact not particularly satisfied with the way in which this was handled. Apart from the evident implication that the Japanese system is far from perfect, this highlights the nature of the management of managers: they were promised job security, but were expected to move between jobs as they were told.

Second, as against any expectation that Japanese managers will be particularly satisfied with the means used to assess their performance, there were no differences from the British sample. There is certainly some other published material pointing in a similar direction. Thus, it is well established that Japanese employees tend to report lower levels of job satisfaction than do employees in many Western countries. This is usually explained in terms of the high expectations which Japanese may have, together with some tendency to be more self-critical than other peoples.

Our finding is different, however, in that managers were reporting not their own satisfaction but their *assessment of company systems*. The statistical pattern was supported by interview material, which indicated disquiet about the subjectivity of performance evaluation and the lack of any detailed feedback to managers themselves. The typical Japanese company system was more concerned with providing information upwards than with using evaluation to permit the subject of the process to learn from it.

The lack of enthusiasm about evaluation systems links to the third point: the extent to which there was an 'enterprise culture'. Recall that we were interviewing quite senior managers, in some cases people only a couple of steps away from the main boards of their companies. We certainly did not find active discontent, but neither was enthusiasm much in evidence. In our interviews, there was little sense of close identification with firms: managers were often critical of where their firms were going, of a lack of personal direction, and of career uncertainties. Their firms were important to them, but they retained a sense of distance and were not absorbed into an embracing enterprise culture. Pay for performance was one aspect of this. We have seen that pay was generally linked to some measure of performance: majorities in all four British firms said that their pay was affected by the outcome of appraisals, or that bonuses were an important component of their pay, or both. In view of the considerable hype that performance-related pay has received, we might have expected much more keenness about evaluation systems in particular and the operation of the enterprise in general.

Fourth, our approach has enabled us to draw out the pressures and demands of the managerial role. In the Japanese companies these were the familiar pressures of lifetime employment: managers joined as part of a cohort and they constantly compared themselves with their peers in terms of their speed of promotion, and they were able to place themselves within a hierarchy of status. The pressures that this pattern created included expectations that a manager should work 'voluntary' overtime in the week and on Saturdays. A closely related pressure came from the career planning system: managers would know broadly when they were due for a move, but to what role, and to which geographical location, would be unknown and there would be very little chance for the manager to exert any choice. One consequence was tension with family duties, as a manager could be, and often was, relocated with very little notice.

Among the British firms the exact nature of work pressures varied but a common theme was the relationship with the centre. In NatWest and Tesco, as we have seen, the monitoring of performance was closer than in the other two firms. There was also some feeling that demands were becoming tighter so that managers were operating in an increasingly regulated environment. In Lucas and BT there were some trends in the same direction. This trend in the Lucas case was exemplified in the agreement of competitive achievement plans for each business unit. These demands were not necessarily resented. As a BT manager put it, the goal of a customer orientation, backed up with clear individual objectives, was not in question. It was not a matter of some parts of a job being liked and others disliked. It was, rather, one of a set of changes which were seen as inevitable, and even desirable if a firm was to survive, which contained within them demands and pressures. In short, by interconnecting our findings, we have been able to understand something of the pressures and demands of the job instead of simply describing the formal structures of management development. In this approach, we follow writers such as Vicki Smith (1990), who shows how managers in an American bank managed new pressures on their working lives. Our managers, Japanese as much as British, were not corporate ciphers, nor were they wholly disenchanted. They actively managed the world in which they operated.

Our results also throw some light on the pressures which they faced. In particular, the fact that close monitoring and formal objectives went along with satisfaction with the evaluation system suggests that managers responded positively to central direction. They were not looking for entrepreneurial independence. At the same time, the role was demanding. In all the Japanese firms there were the pressures of competing with the peer group for promotion, which often meant working long hours. In Jusco there were the added demands of an even more explicitly drawn merit-based promotion system. In the British firms, managers were competing in a less structured environment in which opportunities could open up or be closed off rather more randomly. One indication of awareness of pressures came in replies to a question about current changes. An area that we highlighted was the opportunity for promotion. Overall, in both countries, 49 per cent felt that opportunities in their organization were decreasing, as against 18 per cent who perceived an increase (see Table 4.6). The largest majorities perceiving a decrease were in NatWest and Sumitomo, and only in Lucas was there a small balance in the opposite direction. If these expectations turn out to be justified, problems of blocked promotion routes may heighten the salience of career progression. There was, moreover, a clear association between perceptions of promotion and attitudes to the evaluation system and to management development: those seeing promotion opportunities as decreasing also tended to be dissatisfied with the evaluation system and to say that their organization gave management development a relatively low profile.

Here we turn to the issue of differences between sectors. In general, there was evidently more uniformity in Japan than there was in Britain, for example in the Japanese firms' recruitment policies and their shared career planning processes. Our findings here support the growing view that systems like the British are more 'permissive' than the more uniform Japanese or German 'models'. We explore below the different ways in which the British firms responded to their national environment. We have shown that some differences between companies were due to the *sector* in which they were located and not to national characteristics. To this extent, the notion of a 'Japanese model' of management is far too simplistic. A 'sectoral imperative' seems to have been at play: far from there being national ways of going about things, many practices stemmed from organizational characteristics. And managers' responses were also strongly shaped by the sector in which they worked. For example, the closeness of evaluation was related to sector, and there was no country effect. There also appeared to be sectoral effects on managerial labour markets, as reflected in the tendency for managers in each of the two stores to have worked in more firms than was characteristic of the other firms in their respective economies. This helps to pin down just what is 'Japanese' and what is not.

The experience of Jusco is instructive, for a move away from the 'Japanese model' towards reliance on merit had produced some clear signs of discontent, notably the strong balance of views that the role of the individual in management development should be reduced. Jusco had replaced the anonymity of seniority with the uncertainties of a meritocratic system which remained heavily centralized. Whether it is possible to square the circle of central direction and individual choice is the dilemma facing this company. In terms of Mumford's (1987a; 1987b) classification of types of management development, the Japanese firms fell between 'type 2' (integrated managerial, which has clear objectives and is owned by managers) and 'type 3' (formal management development, which is also clear and structured but is owned more by developers).

With the exception of NatWest, the British firms were coming at this issue from a tradition of weak central policy. In Lucas and British Telecom there was a strong sense that far more organization of the management development function was required; in Tesco, managers recognized that a good deal had been done but still felt uncertainty about the future. Given the general situation on career planning in Britain, it is not surprising that NatWest managers were, in comparison, relatively satisfied. Nonetheless, the frustrations mentioned above suggest that the organization may have to come to terms with another aspect of the British environment, namely, the image of the active manager as hero and the need to create an environment in which the individual can shape his (and sometimes her) destiny. The Japanese firms were approaching this issue from an even more centralized tradition. With the exception of Jusco they had yet to tackle it directly and it was probably not seen as a central issue of the moment. Yet the fact that managers here did not stand out sharply from their British counterparts in terms of their satisfaction with management development, and were not distinguishable at all on views of the evaluation system, suggests that there may be some issues beneath the surface that will warrant attention.

If there is one lesson to be derived from the Japanese evidence it is that Japan does not have a management development system which is free of tensions or which can be simply emulated. As noted above, the British context is different and a devolved approach may be counter-productive. Japanese firms may also have to consider, in the light of evidence that their managers were not particularly satisfied, the ownership of development activity and the extent to which they can increase individual choice. The case of Jusco illustrates the tensions involved. Like British firms, Japanese companies will have to manage the issue of careers and motivation, and it is the way in which they do so, rather than the exact development techniques that they deploy, which may offer lessons for Britain. We return to this point in the final section.

Organizations and Markets

In terms of Ronald Dore's model described in Table 1.2, all four of our Japanese firms came close to the organizational pole. With the exception of a few technical specialists, all managers were recruited direct from university at the annual hiring in April. Seniority-based pay systems were established in three of the firms. The fourth, Jusco, had made some attempt to move to a more meritocratic system, with results considered below. Career planning was systematic, and job rotation was common. Reward systems were based on diffuse criteria, and managers were assessed against general developmental targets, not specific short-term performance measures.

There was more variation in Britain. We begin by summarizing the position as it was before examining how it was changing. NatWest came closest to an organizational model, with its tradition of a strong internal labour market and careful career progression. Almost 90 per cent of our NatWest sample had worked only for the one employer, and 95 per cent were aware of a system of career planning. More interestingly, a central characteristic of the Japanese firms, namely a tendency to train recruits thoroughly and to give them their first managerial appointments after a lengthy induction process, was shared by NatWest. Only 7 per cent of the sample had taken up their first managerial appointment below the age of 30, in stark contrast to Tesco, where every manager in the sample had done so. BT came next on the scale: three-quarters of the sample had worked only in this one firm, and a quarter had taken up their first managerial posts at the age of 30 or above. Lucas came next, with Tesco being evidently the least 'organization-oriented' firm.

All four British cases departed in important ways from the organizational model, however. This was most evident in relation to reward systems. In this model, motivation is achieved through an emphasis on the group rather than the individual, and rewards are tied to relatively diffuse developmental criteria. As we saw in Chapter 7, however, even in NatWest, 58 per cent of managers reported that their pay was related to the performance of their own units, whereas very few Japanese managers gave this reply. Similarly, few Japanese managers were evaluated against predetermined performance targets, whereas this was common in Britain. Indeed, unit results and the manager's own performance were as important in NatWest as they were in Tesco. Moreover, in Britain there was a clear association between being evaluated against performance targets and being paid according to measures of performance, whereas in Japan there was no such connection. In short, all British managers were evaluated and rewarded in a more individualistic way than was the case in Japan, and NatWest was one of the most, and not the least, likely to follow this practice.

Yet none of the British firms was wholly market-oriented. In a pure market model, career planning and management development would play little role, with the firm relying on the external labour market for skilled staff. Such a model plainly does not fit even the most market-driven of our four British firms, Tesco. Indeed, attention to developing managerial resources was, if anything, greater in Tesco than in the other British firms, as indicated by the perceived clarity of career paths, the weight given by managers to mentoring as a factor in personal development, and the overall level of attention paid to management development recorded by the Tesco sample.

Turning to trends, there was little evidence that the British firms were becoming more organization-oriented. On the contrary, the tendency was in the reverse direction. As we have seen, the pressure on BT to behave more 'commercially' had significantly disturbed existing assumptions about hierarchies and expectations. BT managers generally denied that there was a system of career planning in place, they were the most critical of the perceived low-level importance attached to management development, and they were the least likely to say that they were set clear objectives. Our interview data add to the picture of uncertainty but also indicate that there was some acceptance of the implications of greater commercialization, for example, as seen in the recognition of the need for more precise means to evaluate performance.

NatWest, too, was shifting from the organization model. This was evident in the perceived need to respond to the increasingly competitive marketplace and the use of the language of products and sales. It was also working through to a market orientation in Dore's more precise sense, namely, the way in which managers were treated. Several spoke of growing pressures to attain targets and of a shift away from an older, more bureaucratic, tradition. Responses to these changes varied. Whereas some managers felt that commercialism had gone too far, others believed that the organization had not sufficiently recognized market pressures and tended to frustrate individual ambition through bureaucratic procedures. Under the influence of the conventional wisdom that came to dominate managerial thinking in the UK in the late 1980s, most also accepted that a stable internal labour market was a thing of the past: the best they could hope to expect were opportunities for training and development which would make them more 'employable' should the organization no longer require their services.

These findings throw some light on two issues. First, there is the question of the choices, sometimes dignified as 'strategic', which firms make in response to external forces (see Purcell and Ahlstrand, 1994). The British firms were amending their approaches in the light of their histories and current policies. At one level, they illustrate efforts to connect human resource issues with business policy. For example, Tesco's move towards the high-value-added end of retailing was reflected in its drive to strengthen its managerial stock. The NatWest case of a move from a rigid internal labour market also reflects the changing competitive situation in banking. Yet it was not a matter of a simple 'fit' with business developments. In all four cases, in particular Lucas and BT, there were uncertainties and tensions in the new models that were emerging: what had gone was clear, but what was replacing it was much less clear. There was certainly an explicable logic in what was being done, and we have developed an account of why each firm acted as it did. Yet there were unresolved issues of the loss of long-term thinking about careers and, perhaps, a relatively passive acceptance of 'market forces'. In some respects, the choices made were far from strategic.

The second issue is 'Japanization'. This concept has been extensively debated in recent years (for example, Oliver and Wilkinson, 1992). It refers to the copying of Japanese methods by host country firms, central examples being just-in-time production systems, cell manufacturing and quality circles. Lucas is among the companies which has been identified with this trend (Turnbull, 1986). Analysts rarely suggest that the totality of Japanese practice is being imported. In particular, lifetime employment is not generally used, either by British 'Japanizers' or by Japanese firms operating in Britain. In early 1992 it was reported that the Rover Group had offered its shop-floor workers employment security in return for acceptance of new working practices, but the whole point of the example was its rarity and its late introduction.

Our evidence on managers supports those who, on the basis of shop-floor studies, question convergence (Elger and Smith, 1994). As we have seen, NatWest and BT in the past had what amounted to the expectation of lifetime employment. Both are now more open to career moves between firms as well as, of course, being more likely to announce managerial redundancies. There were some moves in a 'Japanese' direction, notably a growing central role in management development, but this seems to have stemmed more from the internal logic of the firms' situations than from any direct copying. Lucas was the most extreme example of decentralization in the early 1980s, when business units were left to find their own way. This was followed by a conscious endeavour to give management development a higher profile at the heart of the company. Parallel though less marked shifts were discernible in the other firms, with the exception of NatWest, which had always been centrally driven. There were clear links with business developments. Lucas was seeking integration of its constituent parts to pursue a strategy of world-class manufacturing. At Tesco, store managers in the past were 'barons' but they were now operating within a clearly defined structure, with central planners handling pricing policy, the details of store layout and so on. There was thus a significant centralization of direction, but this was not a response to Japanization.

What do these results tell us about the contrast between organization orientation and market orientation? First, these are only ideal types and in the real world the elements of each may be combined in different ways. In Japan, Jusco deviated from the organizational model while in Britain neither model seemed to apply in its totality: market-oriented firms contained contrasting features from an organizational approach, and vice versa. This might be attributed to an accidental assembly of conflicting approaches; it is, for example, commonly noted that many British firms speak the language of involvement while also tightening up performance standards. This was not, however, the case here. Consider Tesco, for example. As we have explained, its approach to its managerial labour market was closely linked to its business policy. As it moved upmarket, it developed a strong corporate style and restrained the autonomy of the former 'barons'. In this respect, it developed an organizational orientation, part of which involved systematic career development. But the world of retailing is heavily dependent on the market, and managers expected to respond to its demands. They certainly did not perceive any contradiction between career development and short-term targets. Different aspects of market and organizational orientations may be appropriate in different circumstances.

Second, and related to this point, there was little support for Dore's (1989b: 443) conclusion that organization-oriented employment systems can be expected to become more common. This point needs specifying carefully. Dore's argument is that these systems help competitive advantage, in services as well as in manufacturing, and hence that a process of natural selection will favour firms using them. We look at links with competitiveness below. The present focus is whether evolution can be detected. There are in fact two ways in which it could take place. One is Darwinian natural selection, wherein entities with the requisite properties out-compete those lacking them. But the other arises from purposive action: managers learn what these properties are and, unlike biological species, they adapt their organizations to try to make use of them (Cohen, 1978: 288). Our evidence pertains most directly to the latter: to deal with the former would require a study of firms' evolution over time. There certainly seemed to be little evidence of purposive moves towards an organizational orientation. Indeed, if anything, the exact opposite was happening. BT and NatWest in particular were in the process of dismantling many of the structures of their long-standing internal labour markets, notwithstanding the importance their Japanese counterparts attached to them in achieving success.

From Dore's perspective, this might be attributed to error: firms simply fail to realize the benefits. It could be argued that BT and NatWest were guilty of this. But this is to ignore the importance of environmental conditions. As noted in Table 1.2, Dore identifies several important factors which militate towards the choice of a market or organizational orientation. To the structural features which push UK firms to a market model – the dominance of the finance function, the centrality of the threat of takeover and the equation of the firm's interests with those of its shareholders only – must be added the emergent conventional wisdom touched on above. Very conveniently for senior managers under pressure to maintain short-term profitability, this proclaimed an 'end to careers', the dawning of the age of the 'professional' manager and the need for 'a new psychological contract' based on 'employability' (for key influences, see Kanter, 1989; see also Goodswen, 1995).

The great similarity between large Japanese companies needs to be seen in this light. If there were a process of evolution, it would surely be unlikely that so many of them had attained the organizational goal. One would expect, rather, to find companies at different stages of development. The similarity is likely to be connected to the similarity of the environment. The *laissez-faire* environment in Britain by its very nature encourages variation. Some firms, such as Unilever and Shell, have been able to develop long-term programmes of growth and to an extent to escape the constraints of the British environment. Others find this more difficult. Goold and Campbell (1987) identify three different approaches to the management of diversified companies ('strategic planning', 'strategic control' and 'financial control'), each of which is, they argue, appropriate in particular circumstances. Arguably, these three types might need further sub-division. Efforts to categorize approaches to employee relations have certainly found a large number of approaches which often overlap (Purcell and Ahlstrand, 1994). In Japan, by contrast, relations between banks and large firms are much more standardized, and the fact that most companies hold shares in others is also a powerful homogenizing force. Moreover, once a lifetime employment system becomes established, it is very hard for any one firm to break away from it: if everyone else recruits annually, there is little alternative but to follow suit. In Britain, firms may be able to work against the constraints of short-termism, but the reverse does not seem to be true of Japan. The implication is thus that Japanese-type systems have a strong national component. It is not the case that there is a culture-free organizational model challenging less efficient systems. Different environments continue to promote a number of different approaches. In the light of this what can be learnt from the Japanese case and indeed what is the value of comparative research more generally? We address these issues by attending to competitiveness and practical lessons in the next two sections.

Competitiveness

We come to the question which is the easiest to ask and most difficult to answer: what does a system of management development do for company performance? The difficulties are evident. Performance is the outcome of a large number of factors and it may not be possible to isolate the effects of any one. More fundamentally, it may well be that it is the combination of elements which is crucial. In the case of Japan, for example, it is not any one item – be it the linkage between firms and banks, the quality of relations with suppliers or the use of lifetime employment systems – which is crucial, but rather their combination into a functioning system.

The present study did not set out to measure competitiveness or to seek its determinants. But in exploring managerial processes it did focus on what has been seen by many commentators as a critical aspect of competitiveness. As Pettigrew and Whipp (1991: 286) put it, in reporting the management of change in seven British firms, the most satisfactory explanations of performance 'are likely to emerge from examining the three-way relationships between strategic policy decisions, the process of change they entail and the contexts in which they occur'. They looked at change in all its aspects, stressing in particular the interconnections between different aspects of the management process. They were able to conclude that different ways of managing the process were associated with different results, but there was no one key to success or failure. We looked at one element in more detail, but the same need to relate decisions to processes and contexts applies. As Miller (1991: 46) concludes from a consideration of a good deal of research, 'it may not be possible for any one firm to establish the relationship of strategic investment in employee development to the organization's effectiveness.' But, he goes on, this is not the point. There is plenty of evidence of a poor training record in Britain and of poor economic performance, and the links between the two are likely to be more than accidental. Within a firm, there may be some sort of linkage, even if its exact nature cannot be demonstrated statistically.

Management development could be seen as a cause, a consequence or a concomitant of competitive advantage. A *cause* is an independent factor, an exogenous variable in economists' parlance. This view may be rejected at the outset: a system of development is plainly not external to corporate policy. It may then be a *consequence*: successful firms happen to employ certain methods. In its strong form, this argument sees development as an optional extra, in which case it would be irrational to devote time and money to it. A weaker version would see career planning, say, as having only minor benefits: it is better to have a clear system than a chaotic one, but the real action in terms of performance is elsewhere. This goes against what has become conventional wisdom, namely, that the deployment of human resources is crucial to corporate performance. Pettigrew and Whipp (1991) certainly make the management of managers' expectations a central part of their analysis. We doubt whether management development can be relegated to the status of a second-order problem. It could, then, be a *concomitant* of performance: not an independent cause, but a factor which interacts with other processes and which is itself sustained by continued competitive success. Success and certain approaches to development may be mutually reinforcing, and, though it may be impossible conclusively to show that the latter helps to promote the former, a very plausible story about the connections can be told.

We first consider some of the connections within our data. Thus one element of competitiveness is the way in which managers behave: do they resent certain aspects of their firms, with the inference that their own and hence their firms' performance is damaged, or alternatively is satisfaction a route to high performance? We then turn to the wider story of development systems.

One might expect closeness of monitoring and formal objectives to lead to a sense of frustration, which would be reflected in criticism of the evaluation system and a low level of motivation. This might in turn tend to promote poor performance. In fact, as we saw in Chapter 7, satisfaction with evaluation went along with close monitoring and formal objectives, a result which held when the effects of sector and country were controlled for. On motivation, our overall measure of how strongly managers were motivated was associated with close, not loose, monitoring. The results for satisfaction and motivation were independent. It was not the case that closeness of monitoring led to satisfaction which in turn encouraged a high level of motivation. The link between closeness and motivation remained even when the effects of satisfaction on motivation were allowed for. The links were still evident when we took account of other possible influences on satisfaction and motivation, and were thus very robust.

The explanation is that managers, in both countries, preferred clear objectives and the careful monitoring of their own performance to being left to their own devices. As several respondents pointed out, they were looking for central direction and a framework in which they could work, not unlimited freedom. This offers an important perspective on the issue of competitive advantage. One view might be that managers want to be entrepreneurs and that they should be encouraged to do so by reward systems driven by clear individual targets. Management development would then be left to quasi-market forces. In our firms, managers did not think in these terms. An indication of this lay in replies to the question about interest in developing subordinates. 'Market-oriented' managers would be expected to say that, under the pressures of everyday demands, it tended to be neglected. In fact, few of the sample did so (the highest proportions being a quarter, in BT and Jusco); and there were no differences between British and Japanese firms, except between the stores where Tesco managers were more and not less likely to stress developing subordinates than their Jusco counterparts. In short, the way to promote managers' productive activity, in both countries, was to set a clear framework of objectives at corporate level and to monitor results closely.

Comparative research thus points to the far from obvious result that structured management development is seen as important in both countries. The implication is that firms need not be overly cautious about agreeing written objectives or evaluating performance closely; indeed, to do so can promote satisfaction among managers. One caveat here is that we chose British firms that were, or had been, active in management development. This excluded the most market-driven firms, where managers may embrace entrepreneurial values. As we have stressed, there are many different approaches in Britain and not one British model. The point is that some firms, such as those that we studied, can avoid a pure market approach: the British environment is constraining but not totally determining of outcomes.

Our results need to be interpreted carefully. As we stressed in presenting the data on managers' responses to evaluation systems, these responses were tapping something different from job satisfaction. Satisfaction refers to an individual's feeling of enjoyment in work. Our questions asked not about managers' own contentment but about their views of the company structures under which they worked. In principle a manager could find the structures acceptable while having a low level of job satisfaction owing to, say, boredom with the work. We found that close monitoring was linked to a high rating of the evaluation system. We interpret this as suggesting links with managers' behaviour: close monitoring is likely to create the conditions in which managers perform effectively. Other things being equal, this is also likely to contribute to the performance of the company as a whole. Whether or not managers are satisfied is another matter.

There is a large body of research showing that satisfaction is not in fact correlated with productivity or other performance measures (Guest, 1990; Staw, 1986). In the case of comparisons between Japan and the West, most studies find, as noted above, that the Japanese do not display high levels of job satisfaction. The competitive success of their firms stems not from workers' satisfaction, but from their commitment to the enterprise, in either the psychic or the structural sense. It is not satisfaction but commitment which seems to be the mechanism at the level of the individual worker which connects the inputs of management development to the outputs of performance. These points align closely with our own findings.

Turning, then, from demonstrated links within our data to broader consideration of what management development might contribute to competitive performance, it is not hard to see what the connections might be in Japan. Careful career planning led to managers' knowing how their work was structured, lifetime employment is likely to have made them willing to make the investment of time to learn new skills, and so on. One particular element is the system of job rotation. This ensures that managers learn new tasks, and are also exposed to different parts of the organization so that narrow sectional interests are broken down. The outcome is a virtuous circle in which growth of the firm allows new opportunities, managers move between them, broad-based careers develop, and further growth is permitted.

In their Japan–US comparative study, Lincoln and Kalleberg (1990) show that high commitment levels, in both America and Japan, are promoted by certain organizational structures, notably a combination of formal centralization and informal decentralization. This combination involves a strong hierarchy and central direction together with the involvement of lower participants in decision-making. Our results are consistent with this picture. Thus the devolution of responsibility for management development to the individual managers fits the model: there was strong centralization of systems of planning, but within them managers were expected to develop their own skills. As we have seen, they did not even see this as 'training' in the sense of a separate, company-led activity. This devolution of responsibility within a strongly defined corporate system helped to establish a set of structures in which managers behaved in ways congruent with company goals.

These findings are consistent with much existing work on Japan. They do not conclusively demonstrate that the approach to the managerial labour market helped competitive success, but it would be hard to think of a 'Japanese system' without such an approach.

The connections in Britain may be considered in relation to certain generic features of the British approach to training and development and how these operated in the distinct market environments that our firms faced. We have highlighted the generic features throughout this study. They include the early exposure to responsibility, a 'sink or swim' approach to development in contrast to carefully planned learning, and tight targets for individuals' performance. They had rather different implications in the varying circumstances of our firms.

NatWest was marked in the past by stable market conditions and by a very narrow competitive environment in which the four main clearing banks dealt with a restricted range of financial services and did not aggressively fight for business. This environment promoted stability in the processes of recruiting and developing managers. We found that career planning was seen as reasonably integrated. It had proved possible to moderate some aspects of the British environment, notably by building a strong internal labour market that did not call for early responsibility or require a sink or swim regime, though tight targets were an important feature. There probably were linkages with competitive performance in that the internal labour market was compatible with the bank's business identity: managers learned the bank's culture and expectations, and as they progressed through the system they were able to work in ways which contributed to the achievement of goals.

As we have stressed, at the time of our study the situation was changing rapidly and fundamentally in the light of massive alterations in the market for financial services. The challenge was to move towards a more market-driven approach and tighter performance standards without losing the benefits of a long-established system. The implication is that the development system may not have been as tightly geared into business behaviour as it had been in the past. In some ways NatWest had the most satisfactory scores among our British firms on our measures of the extent of career planning, managers' perceptions of the attention devoted to management development, and so on. But change was evident in the views of some older managers that performance targets were growing tighter and the desire of some of their younger colleagues to have a less bureaucratic structure.

Arguably, therefore, the contribution of the development system was less certain than it had been in the past.

Turning to Tesco, retailing is one sector in which British firms are generally held to be among the world leaders. Supermarket food retailing is a relatively uniform business (hence our finding that formal objectives and close monitoring were particularly developed, in both countries) and one without serious global competition.

In this environment, early exposure to managerial positions combined with tight financial disciplines may be made to work, and to contribute to competitiveness. We found that systems of development fitted the goal of going upmarket, and there was some coherence between different activities. This contrasts with the situation at the start of the 1980s, when the firm was less integrated and when the 'pile it high, sell it cheap' philosophy was still evident. It is thus likely that development methods came to contribute to competitive advantage as a concomitant of the firm's repositioning in the market. The case of Jusco may also be indicative here, for this firm was moving away from the 'pure' Japanese system towards one in which merit was stressed. In a sector like retail, strands of a market orientation may prove to be advantageous even in Japan.

There was no suggestion that the links between development and business location were coming adrift, but two challenges were evident. The first was internal: as the firm moved from sustained growth to a more steady-state situation, career opportunities were likely to be less available and, perhaps more profoundly, the sense of being part of a firm meeting new demands may have begun to erode. The external threat was intensified competition, including that from American and European chains which have begun to establish massive warehouse-like stores selling a limited range of basic products at low prices. This threat has yet to be very significant, but it could pose new challenges.

In Lucas and BT the market environment had been more turbulent than was the case in banks or stores. This reflected, respectively, the shake-out of manufacturing during the 1980s and the pressures of privatization. Both firms had also been undergoing fundamental changes in the organization of production associated with new technology and new manufacturing systems. These were heightened in the case of Lucas by a significant repositioning in the market, as some long-established British businesses were sold and a strategy of expansion overseas was pursued. In this firm, systems of management development had come under severe strain during the early 1980s; in BT, the 'shock' was more recent. In both cases, the implication is that, until recently, the lack of career planning was a constraint on competitive success. In short, they would be examples of the point that, while development systems cannot ensure competitive success, a lack of them can impede it. Illustrations in the case of Lucas include an inability to fill certain key positions from within the firm and a sense among managers that skills had not been identified and developed adequately.

Lucas is also a prime example of a firm which believed, at the very highest levels, that management development was a crucial element in its new business strategy. At the time of our study, the potential linkages were evident, and their benefits would be expected to emerge in the future, as long as the pressures of short-term demands could be managed. In BT, change has been more recent, and it may take longer for benefits to be identifiable. In both cases, moreover, market conditions are more difficult and the organization of production is more complex than in other sectors, so that the maintenance of links between development and competitive advantage is likely to be particularly challenging here.

The key implications for competitiveness can thus be listed as follows. First, in the case of Japan, there were identifiable links between management systems and performance, the essential feature being that the various elements of the systems were integrated with each other and with the business structure of the organization. This meant that development systems were understood and were part of the bloodstream of the organization. Second, in the case of Britain it would be more difficult to demonstrate a connection because training policies often change: there has not been the time for the linkages between training, development, careers, and managers' expectations to grow up, let alone to feed through to measurable change in performance of the firm.

Third, however, there are ways in which British firms can use management development to affect performance. Part of this is ground clearing: a 'good' development system may not be the centrepiece of competitive performance, but a 'poor' one can impede it by, for example, causing frustration among managers and failure to utilize available talent. More positively, we have suggested that it is not a matter of copying the Japanese: the environment makes that difficult. It is one of balancing corporate goals and individual objectives. We found among managers considerable acceptance of close monitoring of performance, suggesting that they would respond to further attempts to lead from the centre. The way in which a response is sought needs to reflect general and specific features of the environment. The general ones are the expectation that managers 'own' their careers and that they are as committed to their functional specialism as they are to their firm. We have argued that this may imply trying to make appraisal systems match corporate and individual goals by building in clear objectives of developing subordinates and relating success to rewards. Each company also faces its own specific environment.

This leads to the fourth point: the 'British' approach fits some situations better than others. Some elements of it are not to be written off. An organization orientation may be more important where markets are global than where they are domestic, and where the technology of production is evolving rapidly. In an industry like retailing, hard performance targets may be more appropriate than they are elsewhere. The associated systems of management development may contribute to performance. In short, there are circumstances where the British approach can 'work'.

Fifth, our particular sample of British firms were among those taking an above average interest in management development. They exemplify different ways in which the problems of short-termism have been addressed. In many other firms, interest will have been less, and the linkages with performance still less evident. Our firms indicate what can be done in the British environment. But there remains the familiar British problem that a small number of companies achieve global standards, while there is a long 'tail' of firms which do not. The changing economic context is relevant here. We conducted the main part of the study before the 1990–1 recession. Subsequently redundancies have been announced by BT, for example, and there have been several reports of other firms cutting their training and development budgets. The contribution of management development to corporate performance is a long-term one which can easily be disrupted by short-term responses to a recession. Whether British firms can retain a longer-term vision will be crucial to any role which management development might play in their competitive advantage.

This leads to the final point. Many British firms follow fads and fashions, in management development as much as in other areas. Bringing in new systems in a blaze of publicity may make an immediate contribution to a specific problem. But in the longer run, chopping and changing between models is likely to lead to confusion; it may be one of the most damaging of options. Pursuing competitive advantage is a long-term goal, and a new approach to training and development needs to be integrated with other activities over a period of time before any outcomes can properly be expected of it.

The Practical Lessons

We turn, finally, to what organizational managers may learn. A key lesson, which emphasizes the value of cross-national research, is that training is not the same as development. Had we looked only at Britain, one specific issue which might have been expected to have been significant is whether day-to-day job demands interfere with the ability to send managers on training courses. What stands out in the light of the Japanese evidence, however, is development, and not training. Many British managers told us that there was in principle no difficulty with sending people on training courses, and the firms had established some impressive programmes. What tended to be lacking was awareness of where a course might lead and how it would fit in with a manager's career development. The Japanese firms had integrated the idea of development into the whole way in which they operated, whereas in Britain there was more uncertainty and the place of management development was less firmly established. This difference was reflected in the apparently anomalous finding that British managers often reported more training than did their Japanese counterparts. The explanation was that training was much less of a distinct, separate activity in Japan. In short, looking at Britain's training problems as refracted through the lens of Japan suggests that it is not so much lack of training which is the problem but the wider issue of the links between training and development.

A similar point can be made about management education. Whereas our Japanese companies had little interest in business schools, most of the British ones were in the process of expanding their use of MBA programmes. It was not altogether clear, however, what their motives were: whether there was a genuine belief that attendance on such programmes would make a contribution to improved performance within the organization; or whether it was essentially a public relations exercise; or whether it was paying lip-service to the emerging notion of employability, in which the organization offered the opportunity to acquire a publicly recognized qualification as the quid pro quo for loss of career. Certainly our own experience of teaching on executive-type MBA programmes is that there is very rarely any dialogue between the individual and senior colleagues about the role it plays in their development within the organization. In short, the lesson is to focus on the uses of education and its links with development.

In the same vein, the motivation of managers does not depend on 'state-of-the-art' appraisal and reward systems, but on the 'fit' between the various elements of managerial labour markets. The outstanding feature of Japanese arrangements was the way in which the elements reinforced each other: lifetime employment and seniority-based promotion encouraged the careful training of recruits and the planning of careers; this structure led managers to see their own futures as closely tied to those of their firms, which was in turn compatible with the use of diffuse measures of performance and not specific achievement targets.

This connects with our initial interest in exploring how companies themselves use measures of performance. We have been able to show that, although the forms used to assess managers' activities were extremely thorough in the range of information collected, it was not the closeness of evaluation which marked out Japanese firms but the type of performance appraisal that they deployed. In particular, they assessed managers every six months, using very detailed indices which looked not at set performance targets but at how the individual had progressed and what distinctive contribution had been made. This approach to assessment was linked to firms' careful planning of careers. They thus used performance measurement as *part of a package*. In Britain, detailed assessment may have taken place, but there was more of a sense that it did not feed through to the same extent into career planning and hence the deployment of skills to meet corporate goals.

Key among such goals is the development of subordinates. Inevitably, the system of specific targets to which the UK companies adhered runs the risk that managers will focus solely on the targets and will not engage in broader activities like their Japanese counterparts. Japanese firms were able to avoid the problem through the use of many ties binding the individual to the organization. This meant that managers did not see subordinates as a threat and did not have to be set the specific target of developing them. In Britain, the norm is that managers look after their own careers (and, therefore, their own positions) within certain rules of the game. Specific developmental objectives may be included among managers' targets, and the rhetoric is likely to refer increasingly to 'developing', 'facilitating' and 'empowering'. Rarely, however are these developmental objectives related in explicit and meaningful ways to performance-related pay. Some of our Tesco interviewees, for example, had been set the objective of 'delivering' so many qualified managers, and they were evaluated against it. But many managers in the firm were unclear about the importance which the appraisal system placed on this particular item. The implication, in short, is that appraisal, together with the rewards to which it gives rise, needs to be related to the means to persuade managers to behave in the desired manner. Otherwise, the rhetoric of development or quality or other non-quantifiable goals will conflict with the key targets, generally financial ones, against which managers know they are measured.

Our next lesson is implicit in the discussion so far and runs dramatically contrary to recent conventional wisdom. It is that the career and career planning are the linchpins of a system of management development. In Japan each of the companies took for granted that in recruiting young graduates they were making a long-term investment. The bulk of the activity of management development was designed to ensure that the organization recouped as high a return as possible on this investment. In the UK companies there was nothing like the same recognition. There was massive uncertainty about whether it was the organization or the individual who 'owned' the career and, for many managers, almost a sense of embarrassment in talking about the issues involved. As already indicated, faced with the need to justify programmes of job reductions, senior figures in some of our UK companies, notably BT and NatWest, had even become attracted by the notion that the career was a thing of the past and that the best that they could be expected to offer their managers was 'employability' (see, for example Goodswen, 1995). Paradoxical as it may seem, BT and NatWest were the organizations that were in the best possible position to build Japanese-style management development systems.

One result was that our British companies were incapable of integrating their management development activities in the way our Japanese companies were. Another was that many managers did not have a clear idea of what was really important. How much of the Japanese experience could or should be emulated by British companies? Our data suggest the need for considerable caution, which enables us to make a general point. Senior managers concerned for the future of their managerial stock have to think in terms of a contingency approach. There is no universal answer to the problem in this area of human resource management any more than there is in others, despite what the pundits would have us believe. What works in one context may be inappropriate in another. This point is as true within Britain as it is between countries. The bureaucratic approach to career development that used to characterize banks might not fit in retail, and the mechanisms of performance appraisal in a multiple retailer may not work in engineering. Likewise the pay policy appropriate to the retailer seeking to promote a quality image will almost certainly be different from that of the organization which sees lowest cost as its competitive advantage. There really are no short-cuts: senior managers have to sit down and think through the implications of their particular business strategies and are heading for disaster if they simply follow fashion.

Two examples will help to illustrate. The first relates to the pay system. The British environment was one in which early experience of management was taken for granted and in which specific performance targets were expected. In three of the four British firms large majorities of managers said that the current pay system helped to motivate them. A shift towards the more diffuse system of the Japanese companies would go against many long-standing assumptions.

The second example concerns views of how career development takes place and experience in different functions. In Britain, there was a tendency for those who cited 'wide experience of challenging assignments' as important in growing as a manager to have worked in a large number of separate functions. This points to an individualistic switching around between firms and jobs, as part of the 'sink or swim' approach. In Japan, there was no association between functional experience and belief in challenging assignments, suggesting a more planned structure of career movement. Thus, attempting to emulate a Japanese approach could spark off associated problems because it cut across other aspects of managerial behaviour in Britain.

Japanese practice offers a warning as well as a model here. Managers in Jusco were the most dissatisfied with the evaluation system, and they also tended to be unhappy with the role of the individual manager in management development. We compared respondents' judgements about who was currently responsible with who they thought should be responsible. The Jusco managers were unusual in displaying a discrepancy which pointed to a lack of central assumption of responsibility. The reason for this probably lies in the firm's move away from seniority-based pay and promotion towards a system based more on individual merit. Managers complained at the uncertainties that this created and at the subjectivity of the process.

Clearly a major problem for British firms is how far they can insulate themselves from the environment of individualism and short-termism. Tesco had been challenging this by moving upmarket: people now joined the firm for its prospects, and they were a resource that could be developed in a longer-term way. But there was a growing problem of 'poaching' by other firms. Certain elite firms may be able to insulate themselves through their own efforts. But, short of a move to a Japanese or a German type of training system, the majority will have to manage the tension between, on the one hand, internal labour markets and the goal of integrated development systems, and, on the other, reliance on, and constraint by, the external labour market.

Important though the wider context is, our final lesson is independent of it. It is that British firms tend to change their training and development systems far too frequently. Indeed, it is fair to say that some of the senior figures in our British companies did not believe that there could be a programme of corporate reorganization without a change from top to bottom in training and development – and since they were repeatedly reorganizing, this often meant that individual managers were sometimes phases behind in their knowledge of the current development arrangements. Regardless of the merits of the individual schemes themselves, too much change can disrupt expectations. The Jusco case illustrates the same lesson: moving to a new system creates some instability. This may be only temporary, and a necessary cost for longer-term benefits. But the more often there is chopping and changing to meet the dictates of fashion – 'programmitis', as several managers in BT and NatWest referred to it – the greater will be the instability and the longer the time before benefits are discernible. For a system of management development to generate benefits, time is important: it is not a matter of certain techniques having certain inherent advantages but of how they fit within the wider activities of the company and how, over time, connections are made and allowed to grow.

Thus, in Lucas and BT there was a strong feeling that career planning was still weak. On ways to address this situation, Lucas managers felt that the personnel department should play less of a role than it did at present while a special executive team might be more important. In BT, emphasis was placed on the role of the management development department. In Tesco, managers looked for the personnel department to play less of a role and for both a special team and the management development department to be more influential. In NatWest there was no clear-cut felt need for change. Each firm had a distinct context and history, and the need was to relate the aspirations of their managers to this environment.

For those who like their lessons stated as simple imperatives, we can offer five slogans and one warning:

1 *Do not copy unless the total situation is appropriate.* For example, much day-to-day management development in Japan is decentralized to individuals and their line managers. British firms are not in a position to move towards this model. Moreover, and in contrast to argument that there is a process of evolution towards organization-based systems, the environment of the British labour market, with its beliefs in early exposure to responsibility, the absence of tightly constraining internal labour markets, and the stress on individual performance, militates against such a move.

2 *Be patient.* Do not expect benefits from development systems to flow instantly, and be aware that changing arrangements may well disrupt connections that are only just being made.

3 *Integrate, integrate, integrate.* Relate training programmes to career planning and reward systems, and ensure that aims such as a corporate culture are not undermined by a reality in which the effective rule is 'dog eat dog'.

4 *Create appraisal systems which are consistent with the British environment without being a passive reflection of it.* For example, if the goal of persuading managers to give serious attention to the development of their subordinates is important, it will almost certainly be necessary to build in specific performance measures, as Tesco was doing, rather than rely on the diffuse methods which work in Japan.

5 *Build on managers' expectations.* Most managers interviewed in our UK companies were not frustrated 'entrepreneurs' or would-be 'professional' managers who wanted little commitment to their organizations. Many of them sought more, and not less, guidance from the centre, and felt that a central corporate approach to career planning was crucial, not just in their own interests but in those of the company as well.

The warning is to *beware of pundits peddling universal solutions*. In keeping with the overall argument, the lessons to be derived from our study apply to certain types of organizations only: those, like the companies which figured in the case studies, which planned to grow their businesses and which saw integrated management development systems as critical to their long-term success. They also need to be tailored to the specific circumstances of the organization. Evidently, the lessons have little relevance for those organizations – and not just the well-known conglomerates – which made financial engineering into their main business in the late 1980s and early 1990s. Whereas advice on integrated management development systems may do little damage to the latter, it would be disastrous if the prescriptions reflecting their experience, including the 'end of careers', 'professional managers' and 'employability', were adopted by the former as universal panaceas. Though there may just be a Japanese model, there is no one system of management development in Britain.

Concluding Remarks

Japanese systems of career planning and management development are integrated, whereas in Britain approaches differ because of differing contexts and histories. The 'British problem' was not that firms do not monitor managers' performance. Nor was it that management development was neglected. To the extent that there was a generic British approach, it lay in a 'sink or swim' attitude to early career development, a reliance on specific performance targets, and a stress on the 'ownership' of the career by the individual who then had to find a way through the internal and external labour market, drawing where relevant on an organization's resources. This approach had varied implications for competitiveness. In Tesco, it was broadly consistent with business policy, and it seemed to work. At the other extreme, Lucas had abandoned a good deal of central direction during the early 1980s, and it was recognized in the firm that this had deleterious effects and was out of line with the aim of becoming a world-class manufacturer. Seen in its own terms, the 'British' system works in some cases and not others.

Viewed in the light of Japan, the British system is not as weak as it is sometimes portrayed. We have seen that the secret of Japanese success did not lie in managers who were particularly satisfied or strongly motivated in their tasks. It lay in the attention to detail and the integration of different aspects of the employment relationship. The implication for British firms is neither to copy specific techniques, nor to argue that the British context is totally different. It is to find ways of linking corporate and individual goals and of building a system in which the benefits of systematic management development have a chance to work through. As market competition intensifies, and as firms have to rely on making the most of their people, the importance of the topic can only increase.

Appendix A: Sample and Methods

Sample

Our questionnaire and interview survey was directed at 'middle managers'. As is well known, this is a notoriously difficult group to define. Indeed, even the definition of 'manager' and 'management' has provoked lengthy and often inconclusive debate (see Grint, 1995). As noted in an earlier study, there is little point in 'trying to define the undefinable'; it is preferable to identify 'an important role in the social division of labour and [investigate] its occupants' (Edwards, 1987: 7). In the present case, we focused as far as possible on managers responsible for distinct operating units such as a bank branch or a major retail store. We also included managers in head office functions such as planning and purchasing. The rule of thumb was that they should be on grades equivalent to those of managers running operating units. The goal was to obtain a group of experienced and knowledgeable managers who were well above the ranks of junior management and who might be expected to provide the top managers of the future.

The samples were selected in cooperation with each company. We cannot claim, therefore, to have strictly random samples. But we used similar methods in all eight firms, and obtained a sample which covered a range of positions from the very senior to rather lower levels. We categorized managers into three levels, and carried out tests using the main dependent variables of interest. There were no notable differences, which suggests two things. First, we can speak of managers as a group. Second, differences in the structure of the sample between firms do not seem to have vitiated the results.

There is one particular feature of the sampling that must be underlined. In the case of Jusco, the majority of the sample was drawn from managers who were attending or had recently attended a high-level training course. This fact may inflate reported levels of training in this one firm. It may also be thought that this group will be in some way special, perhaps in having a favourable attitude generally towards the company. As our results show, however, in many respects they were more discontented than managers in the other companies, so that we do not think that this particular source of the sample biased the results.

We aimed to include at least 25 managers from each company for the self-completion questionnaire. Because of the strong cooperation with the

Table A.1 *Number of questionnaire returns, by company*

Engineering	Lucas	32	Sumitomo	30	Total	62
Banks	NatWest	41	Mitsui	25	Total	66
Stores	Tesco	26	Jusco	27	Total	53
Utilities	BT	33	NTT	25	Total	58
Total		132		107		239

companies, we had no refusals to participate, which adds considerably to the weight we can place on the replies. The target was achieved or exceeded in all cases, as shown in Table A.1.

The questionnaire itself is reproduced in Appendix B. It was designed in Britain for the Japanese sample, and translated by members of the research team, whose knowledge of the Japanese language and business context ensured that questions were meaningful as well as comparable with those used in Britain. Many of the questions about careers were drawn from previous surveys, or sought factual information, or both. We can thus treat them as reasonably reliable and valid instruments. Our project-specific questions were interrogated in various ways. First, as described below, we used reliability tests when we combined answers to form a scale. Second, we considered the replies in the light of knowledge about the British and Japanese contexts. Third, we used interview material to explore the meaning underlying the replies. As our discussion in the text shows, for example in relation to career planning and training indicates, we did not treat replies at face value and instead explored their underlying significance.

Interviews were carried out with all the 132 British managers and around half their Japanese counterparts. They were structured around questionnaire replies, and were used primarily to explore themes in detail but were also useful in sorting out any ambiguities or uncertainties about the questionnaire itself. Their purpose was to allow managers to enlarge on themes of particular interest, and they were thus loosely structured. Interviews generally lasted at least an hour, and often longer.

Statistical Methods

Where replies, for example on evaluation methods, were combined into one index we use *reliability tests*. These tests measure whether the separate components are correlated with each other and thus whether they form one 'reliable' scale. They also provide a test of additivity, that is, whether the (arbitrary) scoring schemes in fact allow scores to be added together. It may be, for example, that a scale of 1 to 5 does not work. The implication is that the distance between 1 and 2 ('strongly agree' and 'agree') is the same as that between 4 and 5 ('disagree' and 'strongly disagree'). Taking the example of evaluation scores in Chapter 7, the reliability coefficient alpha was 0.81 and no problems of additivity were detected. In one other case, there were problems of additivity, as explained at the relevant points of the text.

Loglinear techniques were used to assess patterns of replies in situations where we wished to explore whether a 'country' or a 'sector' effect was present, or whether there was an interaction between the two. Loglinear models take a familiar contingency table and test how far various models can reproduce the figures in the table. In the present case, we have three variables: a dependent variable, sector (with one category for each of the four sectors) and country (Britain or Japan). The most complex, or 'saturated', model allows for each variable to be associated with each of the others and for an interaction between all three. An interaction effect means that the strength of the relationship between any two variables depends on the level of the third. By definition a saturated model fits the data exactly. The interesting question is whether the data can be represented by simpler models. There are two key criteria in testing for this. First, the goodness of fit is measured by the likelihood ratio, G^2. Its significance is tested by the chi-square statistic. A saturated model has a G^2 of zero and a chi-square statistic of 1.0. Other models can be tested against this benchmark, with a low G^2 and a high chi-square being the criteria; a chi-square of 0.05 is conventionally seen as the lowest acceptable level. Second, the difference between the actual value of an observation and the value expected from the model is assessed. The 'standardized residuals' for each cell should be no larger than 1.96 or smaller than −1.96.

In addition to knowing whether a model is significant, in the sense of coming close to the data in a way that is unlikely to have arisen by chance, it is important to consider its strength; a relationship can be significant but very weak. The strength of a model may be assessed by comparing its G^2 with that of the simplest model. This simplest model is the 'grand mean' model which assumes that all cell frequencies are identical. In the present case, we can write S for sector, C for country and V for substantive variable of interest. Consider the example of closeness of evaluation (see Chapter 7). The interaction of all three in the saturated model is represented as $[V, S, C]$. A model in which V and S were associated but which included only the main effects of C is written $[V, S], C$. A test of no association between any of the variables is V, S, C; and so on. The results in Table A.2 may be noted:

Table A.2 *Loglinear results for closeness of evaluation*

Model	Effects	G^2	Sig.
1	Grand mean	141.0	0.000
2	$[V, S, C]$	0.0	1.000
3	$[V, S] [V, C] [S, C]$	4.86	0.562
4	$[V, S] [V, C]$	7.67	0.568
5	$[V, S] C$	9.65	0.617

Model 5 fits the data very well, with a G^2 barely higher than that of the model including an association between V and C. The worst standardized residual was -1.14. We can therefore conclude that there was a significant relationship between sector and closeness of evaluation; that there was no country effect; and that the relationship was also strong as indicated by the reduction in G^2 as compared with that of the grand mean model.

Analysis of variance may be used where the dependent variable is continuous. As with loglinear methods, it conveniently tests for interactions between variables. We used the technique to examine variations in scores on our measure of attitudes to evaluation. The substantive results are detailed in Chapter 7.

Appendix B: Questionnaire

University of Warwick Management Development Project: Self-completion Questionnaire

Strictly Confidential

Name .... Male/Female   Age: under 30
                                                  30–39
                                                  40–49
                                                  50–59
                                                  60 or over

Company ....
Your work location ....

Present Job

1   Current job title ....

2   Current job responsibilities (main 2)

    ....
    ....

3   How long in present post? (number of years) ....

4   How long with present organization? (number of years) ....

Career

5(a)   At what age was your first managerial appointment? (please tick appropriate answer)

       under 25 years old   26–29   30–35   36–40   over 40

5(b)   At what age did you take up your first full-time job?

       under 18 years old   18–20   21–25   over 25 years old

6   Was it in this organization?

    (1)   yes, but in different division or company
    (2)   yes, and in same division or company
    (3)   no
    (If *yes* go to question 11, if *no* continue.)

7 In how many previous organizations have you worked full-time? (excluding student vacation work)

   1–2   3–5   more than 5

8 In what industries or sectors were these previous organizations? (Tick the relevant ones below.)

   (1) primary
   (2) manufacturing
   (3) construction
   (4) public utilities
   (5) transport & communication
   (6) retail & distribution
   (7) public administration & defence
   (8) finance
   (9) other (please specify) ....

9 In which functions had you worked *before entering* this organization? (Tick the relevant ones below.)

   (1)   finance
   (2)   sales, marketing
   (3)   personnel
   (4)   planning
   (5)   production
   (6)   administration
   (7)   maintenance
   (8)   R&D
   (9)   purchasing
   (10) management trainee
   (11) systems, computing
   (12) quality assurance
   (13) other (please specify) ....

10 Approximately how many previous different *posts* did you hold before entering this organization (i.e. total number of different job positions in previous organizations)?

   (1) 1–3
   (2) 4–9
   (3) 10 or more

11 When you joined this firm did you take up your present post?

   (1) yes   (2) no
   (If *yes* go to question 14, if *no* continue.)

12 In which functions have you worked *in this organization*? (Please tick the relevant ones below.)

    (1) finance
    (2) sales, marketing
    (3) personnel
    (4) planning
    (5) production
    (6) administration
    (7) maintenance
    (8) R&D
    (9) purchasing
  (10) management trainee
  (11) systems, computing
  (12) quality assurance
  (13) other (please specify) ....

13 Approximately how many separate posts have you held in this company?

    (1) 1–3
    (2) 4–6
    (3) 7 or more

14 Have you worked in other divisions?

    (1) yes   (2) no

15 If *yes*, how many?

    (1) 1–2   (2) 3 or more

16 Has your career with this company always been *at this location* or in other parts of the organization as well?

    (1) always here   (2) other locations
    (If *others as well* continue, if *always here* go to question 23.)

17 At how many other locations have you worked?

    (1) 1–2   (2) 3 or more

18 Apart from the take-up of your first appointment have you ever moved house to pursue a job move?

    (1) yes   (2) no

19 If *yes*, how many times have you moved for this reason?

20 If *yes*, in which geographical regions and countries have you been in full-time employment? (Tick as appropriate.)

    (1) North East (including Yorkshire & Humberside)
    (2) North West
    (3) Midlands
    (4) East Anglia
    (5) London & South East
    (6) South & South West
    (7) Wales
    (8) Scotland
    (9) Other country (please specify) ....

21 Have you worked at HQ?

    (1) yes, in past   (2) yes, currently   (3) no
    (If *yes*, continue, if *no* go to question 23.)

22 Did this involve a change of job function?

(1) yes   (2) no

Company Procedures

23 How were you recruited?

    (1) answered advertisement
    (2) joined from school
    (3) graduate milkround
    (4) via a careers office
    (5) direct approach from the company
    (6) indirect approach from the company via executive search
    (7) unsolicited application
    (8) other.......................................

24 What was the method of selection?

    (1) one interview
    (2) two or more interviews
    (3) assessment centre activity
    (4) written tests
    (5) other (please specify) ....

25 Thinking of your present post, how certain are you of the priority objectives set by the organization? (Select from the statements below the one which best approximates your view.)

(1) key objectives are clearly specified in writing
(2) key objectives are usually not written but I have no difficulty in knowing what they are
(3) objectives are written but they form only a broad guide
(4) objectives are not written and there is some uncertainty about key objectives from time to time
(5) other (please specify) ....

26 Would you say that your performance is:

	In a formal way	Informally
(1) closely evaluated		
(2) broadly evaluated		
(3) occasionally evaluated		
(4) not evaluated		
(5) don't know		

27 (*If evaluated to any degree*) How is the evaluation done? (Tick all relevant answers.)

(1) by means of an annual appraisal procedure
(2) by an appraisal procedure more than once a year
(3) by comparing results of my unit with predefined targets
(4) by comparing certain indices of my performance with targets
(5) other (please specify) ....
(6) don't know

28 What is your opinion about the system used to evaluate your performance? (To answer: for each of the concepts *a* to *f* listed below, mark one of the 5 appropriate gradations. For example, if you consider the evaluation system to be marginally more *fair* than *unfair* you would put a tick on the second line under column 2.)

	1	2	3	4	5	
(a) efficient						inefficient
(b) fair						unfair
(c) effective						ineffective
(d) outdated						modern
(e) sophisticated						crude
(f) accurate						inaccurate
(g) other appropriate dimension?						

Reward System

29 Which of the following describes the way in which you are remunerated? (Tick as many as are applicable.)

(1) annual award
(2) annual award tied to profitability of whole company
(3) annual award tied to profitability of my unit
(4) annual award tied to some other performance measure
(5) company discretion
(6) individual negotiation
(7) outcome of appraisal affects pay
(8) bonuses are an important component
(9) other (specify) . . . .

30 What is your opinion about the way managers in this company are remunerated?

(1) helps to motivate   agree/disagree
(2) is unfair   agree/disagree
(3) is inefficient   agree/disagree
(4) needs reform   agree/disagree

31 Do you own shares in the company?

(1) yes   (2) no
(If *yes* continue, if *no* go to question 34.)

32 Have you purchased them under a company scheme offering special terms to employees?

(1) yes   (2) no

33 To what extent do you regard your share holding as a factor affecting the way you perform?

(1) very much
(2) a little
(3) not at all
(4) not sure

34 Which of the following considerations would you say motivates you in your work?

	Very much	Quite a lot	A little	Not very much	Not at all
(1) prospect of promotion					
(2) financial reward					
(3) status					
(4) sense of achievement					

(5) fear of failure
(6) company success
(7) unit success
(8) meeting targets
(9) creating opportunities
(10) respect from colleagues
(11) other. . . . .

Career Paths

35 Are there generally recognizable career paths in this organization?

(1) yes, clearly recognizable
(2) yes, but only broadly recognizable
(3) not really, though intermittent traces exist
(4) no recognizable paths
(5) other. . . . .

36 Is there any system of career planning?

(1) yes
(2) no
(3) don't know

37 If *yes* to above, how well do you think it works?

(1) very well
(2) quite well
(3) not very well
(4) very satisfactorily

Management Training and Development

38 Which of the activities on the following list is currently used in this organization to develop managers? Which have you personally experienced?

	Is used currently	Personally experienced
(1) training courses in-house by internal trainers		
(2) training in-house mainly by external trainers		
(3) off-site training by internal trainers		
(4) off-site training mainly by external trainers		
(5) on-job training		
(6) mentoring/coaching		

(7) special job placement

(8) other (please specify) ....

39 How would you evaluate each of these methods for you personally and for other managers?

	For me (if experienced at question 38)			For others (if used at question 38)		
	very valuable	fairly valuable	not valuable	very valuable	fairly valuable	not valuable
(1) training in-house by internal trainers						
(2) training on-site by external trainers						
(3) off-site training by internal trainers						
(4) off-site by external trainers						
(5) on-job training						
(6) mentoring/coaching						
(7) special job placement						
(8) other.........................						

40 Who do you think is mainly responsible for management development and who do you think should be responsible? (Rank order the main 3.)

	is responsible	*should be responsible*
the personnel department		
the board		
a senior executive team		
a special management development department		
heads of department		
each line manager		
the individual		
no one		
other (please specify)		

41 To what extent, in practice, does the average manager at your level take an active interest in developing the people who report to them?

(1) to a very great extent (is on par with other top priorities)

(2) to a moderate extent

(3) to a small extent

(4) under pressure of everyday reality it tends to be neglected

42 Do you agree or disagree with the following statements?

	Strongly agree	Agree	Uncertain	Disagree	Strongly disagree
management development has a high profile in this organization					
management development has a high profile in my department					
management development is becoming less important					
there is little incentive for a line manager to give development of her/his subordinates a high priority					
the current management development provision is very effective					

43 What do you regard as the most influential factors which helped you personally to grow as a manager? (Rank the main 3 from the list.)

(1)   education
(2)   family influences
(3)   a role model in this organization
(4)   a role model in another organization
(5)   certain training programmes
(6)   private study
(7)   a mentor/coach
(8)   wide experience of life
(9)   wide experience of challenging assignments
(10) self-development techniques
(11) nothing specific, it just happened
(12) early exposure to responsible position
(13) other (please specify) ....

44 Looking at the list again which are the two *least* important factors?

Trends and Changes

45 Against each of the following please say whether you think the tendency in this organization is towards an increase or decrease.

	Increasing	*About same*	*Decreasing*	*N/A D/K*
(1) horizontal job moves for managers				
(2) vertical job moves for managers				
(3) opportunities for promotion				
(4) use of mentors				
(5) better educated and trained managers				
(6) rounded experience among managers				
(7) more specialists				

46 From the list below please indicate your own *two* most important future training needs and then the *two* most generally needed by most other managers in this organization.

	My own	*Others*
(1) familiarity with Information Technology		
(2) foreign language skills		
(3) interpersonal skills		
(4) communication skills		
(5) leadership skills		
(6) marketing skills		
(7) accounting skills		
(8) allround/general manager capabilities		
(9) competence in international business		
(10) planning and scheduling		
(11) statistical and quantitative		
(12) time management		

    (13)   business education similar to **MBA**

    (14)   operational knowledge

    (15)   other (specify) ....

47   Is direct negotiating experience with trade union representatives considered important for managers here?

    (1) very important   (2) quite important   (3) not at all

48   Has an immediate member of your family also occupied a managerial position?

    (1) yes   (2) no

49   How would you locate your father's occupation within the following standard classifications:

professional
managerial
intermediate (supervisory; routine non-manual)
skilled manual
semi-skilled manual
unskilled manual
other ....

50   To what level of academic qualification were you educated?

Below 'O' level
'O' levels
'A' levels
degree
post-graduate
professional
diploma
other ....

51   Do you speak a foreign language?

Yes, fluently
Yes, with difficulty
No

52   If *yes*, tick which of the following languages you speak:

French
German
Spanish
Italian
Other (please state) ....

53 Do you have any direct experience of foreign business?

    (1) yes, have worked overseas for more than 1 month
    (2) yes, make occasional overseas trips on business
    (3) yes, conduct foreign business from UK
    (4) no experience of foreign business

54 How many training days a year do you personally experience? (Use annual average over past 2 years.)

    (1) less than one
    (2) 1–5
    (3) 6–10
    (4) 11–15
    (5) 16 and over

Thank you for taking time to complete this questionnaire. The answers will be treated confidentially. Aggregate scores will be used to trace patterns and to make comparisons with managers in other companies in Britain and Japan. If you have other comments to make please use the space on the back of this form or use an additional sheet.

References

Abegglen, J.C. and Stalk, G. (1985) *Kaisha: the Japanese Corporation*. New York: Basic Books.

Akande, A. (1993) 'The mentor mystique', *Equal Opportunities International*, 12(3): 4–9.

Alban-Metcalfe, B. and Nicholson, N. (1984) *The New Career Development of British Managers*. London: British Institute of Management.

Alexander, G.P. (1987) 'Establishing shared values through management training', *Training and Development Journal*, 41(2).

Annandale, S. (1986) 'The four faces of management development', *Personnel Management*, 18 (10, October).

Antal, A.B. (1993) 'Odysseus' legacy to management development: mentoring', *European Management Journal*, 11(4): 448–54.

Armstrong, P. (1987) 'Engineers, management and trust', *Work, Employment and Society*, 1: 421–40.

Armstrong, P. (1989) 'Management, labour process and agency', *Work, Employment and Society*, 3: 307–22.

Ascher, K. (1983) *Management Training in Large UK Business Organizations: a Survey*. London: Harbridge House.

Ashton, D., Easterby-Smith, M. and Irvine, C. (1975) *Management Development: Theory and Practice*. Bradford: MCB.

Atoh, M. (1995) *Population Dynamics: Its Social and Economic Impact and Policy Responses in Japan*. Japan: Institute of Population Problems, Ministry of Health and Welfare, No. 22.

Barham, K. (1988) *Management for the Future*. Ashridge: Ashridge Management College/ FME.

Barney, B. (1991) 'Firm resources and sustained competitive advantage', *Journal of Management*, 17(1): 99–120.

Barsoux, J.L. and Lawrence, P. (1990) *Management in France*. London: Cassell.

Bean, R. (1994) *Comparative Industrial Relations: an Introduction to Cross-National Perspectives*, 2nd edn. London: Routledge.

Belbin, R.M. (1981) *Management Teams*. London: Heinemann.

Benedict, R. (1946) *The Chrysanthemum and the Sword*. Boston, MA: Houghton Mifflin.

Berggren, C. (1995) 'Japan as No.2', Working Paper, Stockholm: Swedish Institute for Work Life Research.

Boak, G. and Stephenson, M. (1987) 'Management learning contracts', *Journal of European Industrial Training*, 11(6).

Briggs, P. (1991) 'Organisational commitment: the key to Japanese success', in C. Brewster and S. Tyson (eds), *International Comparisons in Human Resource Management*. London: Pitman.

Brown, R.B. (1993) 'Meta competence: a recipe for reframing the competence debate', *Personnel Review*, 22(6): 25–36.

Burgoyne, J. (1988) 'Management development for the individual and the organisation', *Personnel Management*, June.

Burgoyne, J. and Germaine, C. (1984) 'Self development and career planning: an exercise in mutual benefit', *Personnel Management*, April.

Burgoyne, J., Boydell, T. and Pedler, M. (1978) *Self Development: Theory and Applications for Practitioners*. London: ATM.

Burke, R.J. and McKeen, C.A. (1994) 'Training and development activities and career success of managerial and professional women', *Journal of Management Development*, 13(5): 53–63.

Campbell, N., Goold, M. and Kase, K. (1990) 'The role of the centre in managing large diversified companies in Japan', Working Paper, Manchester Business School and Ashridge Strategic Management Centre.

Capowski, G. (1994) 'Anatomy of a leader: where are the leaders of tomorrow?', *Management Review*, 83(3): 10–17.

Chandler, A.D. (1990) *Scale and Scope*. Cambridge, MA: Harvard University Press.

Clark, K. and Fujimoto, T. (1991) *Product Development Performance: Strategy, Organization and Management in the World Auto Industry*. Boston, MA: Harvard Business School.

Clark, R. (1979) *The Japanese Company*. New Haven, CT: Yale University Press.

Clutterbuck, D. (1987) *Everyone Needs a Mentor*. London: Institute of Personnel Management.

Cohen, G.A. (1978) *Karl Marx's Theory of History*. Oxford: Oxford University Press.

Constable, J. and McCormick, R. (1987) *The Making of British Managers: a Report for the BIM and CBI*. Corby: British Institute of Management.

Cosh, A., Hughes, A., Singh, A., Carty, J. and Pender, J. (1990) *Takeovers and Short-Termism in the UK*. London: Institute of Public Policy Research.

Department of Education and Science (1991) *Aspects of Upper Secondary and Higher Education in Japan*. London: HMSO.

Devine, M. (1990) *The Photofit Manager: Building a Picture of Management in the 1990s*. London: Unwin Hyman.

Dopson, S. and Stewart, R. (1990) 'What *is* happening to middle management?', *British Journal of Management*, 1: 3–16.

Dore, R. (1973) *British Factory, Japanese Factory: the Origins of National Diversity in Industrial Relations*. London: Allen and Unwin.

Dore, R. (1987) *Taking Japan Seriously: a Confucian Perspective on Leading Economic Issues*. London: Athlone.

Dore, R. (1989a) *Japan at Work: Markets, Management and Flexibility*. Paris: OECD.

Dore, R. (1989b) *How the Japanese Learn to Work*. London: Routledge.

Dore, R. (1989c) 'Where we are now: musings of an evolutionist', *Work, Employment and Society*, 3: 425–46.

Downham, T.A., Noel, J.L. and Prendergast, A.E. (1992) 'Executive development', *Human Resource Management*, 31(2): 95–107.

Drath, W.H. (1990) 'Managerial strengths and weaknesses as a function of the development of personal meaning', *Journal of Applied Behavioural Science*, 26(4): 483–99.

Dunnell, R. (1987) 'Management development on a tight budget', *Personnel Management*, October.

Edwards, P.K. (1987) *Managing the Factory: a Survey of General Managers*. Oxford: Blackwell.

Edwards, P.K., Hall, M., Hyman, R., Marginson, P., Sisson, K., Waddington, J. and Winchester, D. (1992) 'Great Britain: still muddling through', in R. Hyman and A. Ferner (eds), *Industrial Relations in the New Europe*. Oxford: Blackwell.

Elger, T. and Smith, C. (eds) (1994) *Global Japanization?* London: Routledge.

Endo, K. (1994) '*Satei* (personal assessment) and interworker competition in Japan', *Industrial Relations*, 33: 70–82.

Felstead, A. (1994) *International Study of Vocational Education and Training in the Federal Republic of Germany, France, Japan, Singapore and the United States*. Leicester: Centre for Labour Market Studies.

Field, H.S. and Harris, S.G. (1991) 'Entry level fast-track management development programmes', *Human Resource Planning*, 14(4): 261–73.

Fucini, J.J. and Fucini, S. (1990) *Working for the Japanese*. New York: Free Press.

Fulmer, R. (1986) 'Managing development after the merger', *Journal of Management Development*, 5, 4.

Fulmer, R.M. (1992) 'Nine management development challenges for the 1990s', *Journal of Management Development*, 11(7): 4–9.

Fulmer, R.M. and Graham, K.R. (1993) 'A new era of management education', *Journal of Management Development*, 12(3): 30–8.

Garfield, C.A. (1987) 'Peak performance in business', *Training and Development Journal (USA)*, 41(4): 54 (6 pp.).

Garrahan, P. and Stewart, P. (1992) *The Nissan Enigma: Flexibility at Work in a Local Economy*. London: Mansell.

Gerlach, M. (1992) *Alliance Capitalism: the Social Organization of Japanese Business*. Berkeley, CA: University of California Press.

Gibb, S. and Megginson, D. (1993) 'Inside corporate mentoring systems: a new agenda of concern', *Personnel Review*, 22(1): 40–54.

Goodswen, M. (1995) 'VIP treatment', *Involvement*, May: 10–15.

Goold, M. and Campbell, A. (1987) *Strategies and Styles*. Oxford: Blackwell.

Gow, I. (1988) 'Japan', in C. Handy, C. Gordon, I. Gow and C. Raddlesome (eds), *Making Managers*. London: Pitman.

Grant, R.M. (1991). 'The resource-based theory of competitive advantage: implications for strategy formulation', *California Management Review*, 33(3): 114–35.

Grint, K. (1995) *Management: a Sociological Introduction*. Cambridge: Polity Press.

Guest, D.E. (1990) 'Human resource management and the American dream', *Journal of Management Studies*, 27(4): 378–97.

Hall, R. (1992) 'The strategic analysis of intangible resources', *Strategic Management Journal*, 13: 135–44.

Hamel, G. and Prahalad, C.K. (1994) *Competing for the Future*. Boston, MA: Harvard University Press.

Hamilton, R. (1993) *Mentoring*. London: Industrial Society.

Handy, C. (1987) *The Making of Managers: a Report on Management Education, Training and Development in the USA, West Germany, France, Japan and the UK*. London: National Economic Development Office.

Handy, C. (1994) *The Empty Raincoat*. London: Hutchinson.

Handy, C., Gordon, G., Gow, I. and Raddlesome, C. (1988) *Making Managers*. London: Pitman.

Heckscher, C. (1995) *White Collar Blues: Management Loyalties in an Age of Corporate Restructuring*. New York: Basic Books.

Heisler, W.J. and Bentham, P.O. (1992) 'The challenge of management development in North America in the 1990s', *Journal of Management Development*, 11(2): 16–31.

Henderson, I. (1993) 'Action learning: a missing link in management development?', *Personnel Review*, 22(6): 14–24.

Herriott, P. and Pemberton, C. (1995) *New Deals: the Revolution in Managerial Careers*. London: Wiley.

Hickman, C. (1990) *Mind of a Manager, Soul of a Leader*. New York: Wiley.

Hickson, D. and Pugh, D. (1995) *Management Worldwide: the Impact of Societal Culture on Organizations around the Globe*. London: Penguin.

Hinohara, H. (1990) *Human Resource Development in Japanese Companies*. Tokyo: Asian Productivity Association.

Hirsch, W. (1990) 'Succession planning: current issues and practice'. Report 184, Sussex: Institute for Manpower Studies.

Hirsch, W. and Bevan, S. (1988) 'What makes a manager? In search of a language for management skills'. Report 144, Sussex: Institute for Manpower Studies.

Holmes, L. and Joyce, P. (1993) 'Rescuing the useful concept of managerial competence: from outcomes back to process', *Personnel Review*, 22(6): 37–52.

Horsley, W. and Buckley, R. (1990) *Nippon: New Superpower: Japan since 1945*. London: BBC Books.

Hyman, J. (1992) *Training at Work: a Critical Analysis of Policy and Practice*. London: Routledge.

Iles, P. (1993) 'Achieving strategic coherence in HRD through competency-based management and organization development', *Personnel Review*, 22(6): 63–80.

Institute of Management (1995) *Management Development to the Millennium: the Final Report*. Corby: IM.

Irvine, D. and Wilson, J.P. (1994) 'Outdoor management development: reality or illusion?', *Journal of Management Development*, 13(5): 25–37.

Ishikawa, K. (1992) *Japan and the Challenge of Europe*, London: Pinter.

Itoh, Mahoto (1990) *The World Economic Crisis and Japanese Capitalism*. Basingstoke: Macmillan.

Iwata, R. (1982) *Japanese-style Management: Its Foundations and Prospects*. Tokyo: Asian Productivity Organization.

Jacobs, R. (1989) *Assessing Managerial Competencies: a Report of a Survey of Current Arrangements in the UK for the Assessment of Managerial Competencies*. Ashridge: Ashridge Management Research Group.

Kamata, S. (1983) *Japan in the Passing Lane: an Insider's Account of Life in a Japanese Auto Factory*. London: Allen and Unwin.

Kanter, R.M. (1989) *When Giants Learn to Dance: Mastering the Challenges of Strategy, Management and Careers in the 1990s*. London: Unwin.

Keen, L. (1995) 'Organisational decentralisation and budgetary devolution in local government: a case of middle management autonomy?', *Human Resource Management Journal*, 5(2): 79–98.

Kellner, P. and Lord Crowther-Hunt (1980) *The Civil Servants: an Inquiry into Britain's Ruling Class*. London: MacDonald.

Kenney, M. and Florida, R. (1988) 'Beyond mass production: production and the labor process in Japan', *Politics and Society*, 16(1): 121–58.

Kondo, D.K. (1990) *Crafting Selves: Power, Gender and Discourses of Identity in a Japanese Workplace*. Chicago: University of Chicago Press.

Kotter, J.P. (1982) *The General Managers*. New York: Free Press.

Lawrence, P. (1996) *Management in the USA*. London: Sage.

Lessom, R. (1990) *Development Management*. Oxford: Blackwell.

Lincoln, J.R. and Kalleberg, A.L. (1985) 'Work organization and workforce commitment: a study of plants and employees in the US and Japan', *American Sociological Review*, 50(6): 738–60.

Lincoln, J.R. and Kalleberg, A.L. (1990) *Culture, Control and Commitment: a Study of Work Organization and Work Attitudes in the United States and Japan*. Cambridge: Cambridge University Press.

Lippitt, G. (1982) 'Management development as the key to organisational renewal', *Journal of Management Development*, 1(2): 21–30.

Long, P. (1986) *Performance Appraisal Revisited*. London: Institute of Personnel Management.

Lyddon, D. (1996) 'The myth of mass production and the mass production of myth', *Historical Studies in Industrial Relations*, 1: 77–106.

McClure, L. and Werther, W. (1993) 'Personality variables in management development interventions', *Journal of Management Development*, 12(3): 39–47.

Mahoney, J.T. and Pandian, J.R.C. (1992) 'The resource based view within the conversation of strategic management', *Strategic Management Journal*, 13: 363–80.

Mangham, I. and Silver, M.S. (1986) *Management Training: Context and Practice*. London: Economic and Social Research Council.

Margerison, C. (1985) 'Achieving the capacity and competence to manage', *Journal of Management Development*, 4(3).

Margerison, C. and Kakabadse, A. (1985) 'What management development means for CEOs', *Journal of Management Development*, 4(5): 3–16.

Margerison, C. and McCann, R. (1990) *Team Management: Practical New Approaches*. London: Mercury.

Marsh, N. (1986) 'Management development and strategic management change', *Journal of Management Development*, 5(1): 26–37.

Marshall, G., Newby, H., Rose, D. and Vogler, C. (1988) *Social Class in Modern Britain*. London: Hutchinson.

Masatoshi, N. (ed.) (1994) *The State of Continuing Education in Japan*. Tokyo: Research Institute of Educational Systems.

Matsumoto, K. (1991) *The Rise of the Japanese Corporate System: the Inside View of an MITI Official*. London: Kegan Paul.

Miller, P. (1991) 'A strategic look at management development', *Personnel Management*, August: 45–7.

Ministry of Labour (1992) *Labour Administration: Seeking a More Comfortable Life for Workers*. Tokyo: Ministry of Labour.

Mintzberg, H. (1973) *The Nature of Managerial Work*. London: Harper and Row.

Mole, G., Plant, R. and Salaman, G. (1993) 'Developing executive competencies: learning to confront, confronting to learn', *Journal of European Industrial Training*, 17(2): 3–7.

Mumford, A. (1979) 'Self-development: flavour of the month', *Journal of European Industrial Training*, 3(3).

Mumford, A. (1987a) 'Myths and reality in developing directors', *Personnel Management*, February: 29–33.

Mumford, A. (1987b) *Developing Directors: the Learning Process*. Sheffield: Manpower Services Commission.

Mumford, A. (1989) *Management Development: Strategies for Action*. London: Institute of Personnel Management.

Nagler, B. (1987) 'Cummins' efforts to cut costs', *Managing Automation*, 2(7).

Nixon, B. and Allen, R. (1986) 'Creating a climate for DIY development', *Personnel Management*, August.

Nonaka, I. and Takeuchi, H. (1995) *The Knowledge Creating Company*. Oxford: Oxford University Press.

Notzli, I.M. (1982) *A View of Japanese Management Development: Especially Management Development in Large Business Enterprises*. Zurich: Schuthers Polygraphischer.

Ohlott, P.J., Ruderman, M.N. and McCauley, C.D. (1994) 'Gender differences in managers' developmental job experiences', *Academy of Management Journal*, 37(1): 46–67.

Okazaki-Ward, L. (1993) *Management Education and Training in Japan*. London: Graham and Trotman.

Oliver, N. and Wilkinson, B. (1992) *The Japanization of British Industry: New Developments in the 1990s*. Oxford: Blackwell.

Organization for Economic Co-operation and Development (1995) *Foreign Direct Investment, Trade and Employment*. Paris: OECD.

Ouchi, W.G. (1981) *Theory Z: How American Business Can Meet the Japanese Challenge*. Reading, MA: Addison-Wesley.

Pahl, R.E. and Pahl, J. (1972) *Managers and their Wives*. Harmondsworth: Penguin.

Pascale, R.T. and Athos, A.G. (1981) *The Art of Japanese Management*. London: Allen and Unwin.

Pedler, M. (1986) 'Management self development', *Management, Education and Development*, 17(1).

Pedler, M., Burgoyne, J. and Boydell, T. (1986) *A Manager's Guide to Self Development*. London: McGraw-Hill.

Pedler, M., Burgoyne, J. and Boydell, T. (eds) (1988) *Applying Self Development in Organizations*. Hemel Hempstead: Prentice Hall.

Pedler, M., Burgoyne, J. and Boydell, T. (1991) *The Learning Company*. Maidenhead: McGraw.

Peteraf, M.A. (1993) 'The cornerstones of competitive advantage: a resource-based view', *Strategic Management Journal*, 14: 179–92.

Peters, T.J. (1987) *Thriving on Chaos: Handbook for a Management Revolution*. New York: Knopf.

Pettigrew, A. and Whipp, R. (1991) *Managing Change for Competitive Success.* Oxford: Blackwell.

Porter, M.E. (1985) *Competitive Advantage: Creating and Sustaining Superior Performance.* New York: Free Press.

Preston, D. and Smith, A. (1993) 'APL: current state of play within management education in the UK', *Journal of Management Development,* 12(8): 27–38.

Pucik, V. and Hatvany, N. (1983) 'Management practices in Japan and their impact on business strategy', in R. Lamb (ed.), *Advances in Strategic Management.* Greenwich, CT: JAI Press.

Pucik, V. and Roomkin, M. (1989) 'Japan', in M. Roomkin (ed.), *Managers as Employees: an International Comparison of the Changing Character of Management Employment.* Oxford: Oxford University Press.

Purcell, J. and Ahlstrand, B. (1994) *Human Resource Management in the Multi-Divisional Company.* Oxford: Oxford University Press.

Quinn, J.B. (1992) *Intelligent Enterprise: a Knowledge and Service Based Paradigm for Industry.* New York: Free Press.

Ragins, B.R. and Scandura, T.A. (1994) 'Gender differences in expected outcomes of mentoring relationships', *Academy of Management Journal,* 37(4): 957–71.

Ram, M. (1994) *Managing to Survive: Working Lives in Small Firms.* Oxford: Blackwell.

Ramsay, H. (1990) 'Options for workers: owner or employee?', in G. Jenkins and M. Poole (eds), *New Forms of Ownership.* London: Routledge.

Revans, R. (1971) *Developing Effective Managers.* London: Longman.

Revans, R. (1983) 'Action learning projects', in B. Taylor and G. Lippitt (eds), *Management Development and Training Handbook.* London: McGraw.

Rohlen, T. (1974) *For Harmony and Strength: Japanese White-Collar Organization in Anthropological Perspective.* Berkeley, CA: University of California Press.

Roomkin, M.J. (ed.) (1989) *Managers as Employees: an International Comparison of the Changing Character of Managerial Employment.* New York: Oxford University Press.

Royal Society of Arts (1994) *Tomorrow's Company.* London: RSA.

Sako, M. (1992) *Prices, Quality and Trust: Inter-Firm Relations in Britain and Japan.* Cambridge: Cambridge University Press.

Samuelson, R. (1993) 'Japan as number two', *Newsweek,* 6 December.

Sasaki, N. (1990) *Management and Industrial Structure in Japan.* Oxford: Pergamon Press.

Scase, R. and Goffee, R. (1989) *Reluctant Managers: their Work and Lifestyles.* London: Unwin Hyman.

Schonberger, R.J. (1982) *Japanese Manufacturing Techniques.* New York: Free Press.

Schonberger, R.J. (1986) *World Class Manufacturing: the Lessons of Simplicity Applied.* New York: Free Press.

Schuler, R.S. and Jackson, S. (1987) 'Linking competitive strategies with human resource management practices', *Academy of Management Executive,* 1(3): 209–13.

Shimada, H. (1980) *The Japanese Employment System.* Tokyo: Japan Institute of Labour.

Shimazu, R. (1992) *Company Vitalization by Top Management in Japan.* Tokyo: Keio Tsushin.

Silver, M. (ed.) (1990) *Competent to Manage.* London: Routledge.

Simpson, P., Grisoni, L. and Cox, R. (1994) 'Relative values: qualification programmes or non-assessed development?', *Journal of Management Development,* 13(5): 14–24.

Sisson, K. (1987) *The Management of Collective Bargaining: an International Comparison.* Oxford: Blackwell.

Skapinker, M. (1987) 'Cookson seeks a common management style', *Financial Times,* 22 April.

Skemp, P. (1987) 'Improving management effectiveness', *Management Education and Development,* 18(3).

Smith, B. (1993) 'Building managers from the inside out: competency based action learning', *Journal of Management Development,* 12(1): 43–8.

Smith, D. (1987) 'Culture and management development in building societies', *Personnel Review,* 15(3).

Smith, M.A. (1992) 'The search for executive skills', *Training and Development*, 46(9): 88–95.

Smith, P.E., Barnard, J.M. and Smith, G. (1986) 'Privatisation and culture change', *Journal of Management Development*, 5(2).

Smith, V. (1990) *Managing in the Corporate Interest*. Berkeley, CA: University of California Press.

Sofer, C. (1970) *Men in Mid-Career: a Study of British Managers and Technical Specialists*. London: Cambridge University Press.

Staw, B. (1986) 'Organizational psychology and the pursuit of the happy/productive worker', *California Management Review*, 28(4): 40–53.

Stephens, M.D. (1991) *Japan and Education*. Basingstoke: Macmillan.

Stewart, R. (1967) *Managers and Their Jobs*. London: Pan.

Stewart, R. (1976) *Contrasts in Management*. London: McGraw.

Storey, J. (1989) 'Management development: a literature review and implications for future research. Part I: Conceptualisations and practices', *Personnel Review*, 18(6): 33–57.

Storey, J. (1990) 'Management development: a literature review and implications for future research. Part II: Profiles and contexts', *Personnel Review*, 19(1): 3–11.

Storey, J. (1992) *Developments in the Management of Human Resources*. Oxford: Blackwell.

Storey, J., Okazaki-Ward, L., Gow, I., Edwards, P.K. and Sisson, K. (1991) 'Managerial careers and management development: a comparative analysis of Britain and Japan', *Human Resource Management Journal*, 1(3).

Tack, W.L. (1986) 'Management recycling', *Sloan Management Review*, 27(4).

Thackway, J. (1987) Management development: the Midland Bank experience'. Paper to Warwick/IRS Conference on Developing Effective Managers, University of Warwick, Coventry.

Tharenou, P., Latimer, S. and Conroy, D. (1994) 'How do you make it to the top? An examination of influences on women's and men's managerial advancement', *Academy of Management Journal*, 37(4): 899–931.

Thomson, A., Storey, J., Mabey, C., Gray, C., Henderson, E. and Thomson, R. (1997) *A Portrait of Management Development*. London: Institute of Management.

Tovey, L. (1993) 'A strategic approach to competency assessment', *Journal of European Industrial Training*, 17(10): 2–3.

Trevor, M., Schendel, J. and Wilpert, B. (1986) *The Japanese Management Development System: Generalists and Specialists in Japanese Companies Abroad*. London: Policy Studies Institute/Pinter.

Turnbull, P. (1986) 'The "Japanization" of production and industrial relations at Lucas Electrical', *Industrial Relations Journal*, 17(3): 193–206.

Vicere, A.A., Taylor, M.A. and Freeman, V.A. (1994) 'Executive development in major corporations: a ten year study', *Journal of Management Development*, 13(1): 4–22.

Vogel, E. (1979) *Japan as Number One: Lessons for America*. Cambridge, MA: Harvard University Press.

Wagel, W.H. (1987) 'Leadership training for a new way of managing', *Personnel*, 64(12).

Warner, M. (1992) 'How Japanese managers learn', *Journal of General Management*, 17(3): 56–7.

Watanabe, T. (1988) 'New office technology, labour management and the labour process in contemporary Japanese banking', IRRU Working Paper 21, University of Warwick.

Watson, T. (1994) *In Search of Management*. London: Routledge.

Whitehill, A.M. (1991) *Japanese Management: Tradition and Transition*. London: Routledge.

Whittaker, D.H. (1990) *Managing Innovation: a Study of British and Japanese Factories*. Cambridge: Cambridge University Press.

Wickens, P. (1987) *The Road to Nissan: Flexibility, Quality, Teamwork*. Basingstoke: Macmillan.

Williams, K., Haslam, C., Williams, J. and Cutler, T. (1992) 'Against lean production', *Economy and Society*, 21(3): 321–54.

Womack, J.P., Jones, D.T. and Roos, D. (1990) *The Machine that Changed the World.* New York: Rawson Associates.

Yoshino, M.Y. (1968) *Japan's Managerial System.* Cambridge, MA: MIT Press.

Yui, T. and Nakagawa, K. (eds) (1989) *Japanese Management in Historical Perspective.* Tokyo: University of Tokyo Press.

Zimmerman, J.H. (1993) 'The demand of the future: the complete executive', *Human Resource Management,* 32(2): 385–97.

Index

.